Greatest
Irish Americans
of the
20th Century

Greatest Irish Americans of the 20th Century

Edited by Patricia Harty

Foreword by Senator Edward Kennedy

Oak Tree Press

Dublin

Oak Tree Press
Merrion Building
Lower Merrion Street
Dublin 2, Ireland
http://www.oaktreepress.com

A catalogue record of this book is
available from the British Library.

ISBN 1-86076-206-9 pbk
ISBN 1-86076-207-7 hbk

Designed by Jason Ellams
Printed in the Republic of Ireland by
Colour Books Ltd.

Contents

Contributors

Jimmy Breslin is a Pulitzer Prize-winning journalist who has written several novels. His memoir is entitled *I Want to Thank My Brain for Remembering Me.*

A columnist with the *New York Daily News*, Jim Dwyer won a Pulitzer Prize for commentary in 1995 and shared the same award in 1992 for metropolitan reporting. He has written three books, *Subway Lives*, *Two Seconds Under the World*, and *Actual Innocence.*

Thomas Fleming is the author of *Liberty: The American Revolution* and *Duel: Alexander Hamilton, Aaron Burr, and the Future of America.* His new novel *Dreams of Glory*, set during the American Revolution, has just been published.

Pete Hamill began his writing career as a reporter for the *New York Post* in 1960. He has written for numerous national magazines, including *New York* (where an earlier version of his piece on JFK appeared), has worked as a syndicated columnist and is currently a contributing writer to *The New Yorker.* His books include eight novels, two collections of stories, and *A Drinking Life*, his best-selling memoir of growing up Irish in Brooklyn.

Mary Higgins Clark is the number one best-selling suspense writer in the U.S. Her novels include *Where Are the Children?*, *Loves Music, Loves to Dance* and *Before I Say Goodbye.*

William Kennedy won a Pulitzer Prize for *Ironweed*, one of his six Albany novels. Other novels in his "Albany Cycle" include *Legs* and *Billy Phelan's Greatest Game.*

Irish America columnist Joseph McBride is the author of several books, including *The Book of Movie Lists* and *Steven Spielberg: A Biography.* He is currently working on a biography of the director John Ford, entitled *Searching for John Ford,* which will be published by St. Martin's Press.

After a long career as a schoolteacher, Frank McCourt won the Pulitzer Prize in 1997 for his best-selling memoir *Angela's Ashes.* His next book, *'Tis*, also became a bestseller.

Peter Quinn, the author of *Banished Children of Eve*, a historical novel based on the Famine Irish in New York, is corporate editorial director for Time Warner.

Irish Americans of the Century profiles written by *Irish America* staffers Sarah Buscher, Darina Molloy and Kristen Cotter. Research by Katie Conway. Additional research by Emmett O'Connell.

Acknowledgements

I would like to thank *Irish America* magazine's Assistant Editor Sarah Buscher for her help in bringing this book to press. Thanks also to Darina Molloy, Kristen Cotter, Katie Conway, and Joey Hogue, who worked on the special issue of *Irish America* which was the foundation for this work. And Emmett O'Connell for sharing his invaluable knowledge on the history of the Irish in America.

Some of the finest writers in America also happen to be Irish, and I am most grateful to the following for their contributions to this book: Pete Hamill for his evocative piece on Irish American of the Century, John Fitzgerald Kennedy; Jim Dwyer for his profile of John Steinbeck; Joe McBride who wrote on John Ford; and Frank McCourt for his remembrance of Paddy Clancy. And I am especially thankful to Mary Higgins Clark, Tom Fleming, William Kennedy and Peter Quinn whose personal essays on their family give us a better understanding of those Irish who went before, and to Jimmy Breslin for his thoughtful essay on a painful chapter of our history. I am also very grateful to Senator Edward Kennedy for writing the Foreword.

Jacques Lowe enjoyed the most personal relationship John Fitzgerald Kennedy would ever have with a photographer. Lowe took over 40,000 photos, covering the last five years of Kennedy's life including the White House years. I am most grateful for his permission to use the cover shot of Kennedy taken in Oregon.

Finally, special thanks to David Givens for his unfailing support and the staff at Oak Tree Press for their diligence and attention.

Sources: *The Big Book of American Irish Culture* by Bob Callahan; *The Book of Irish Americans* and *A Portrait of the Irish in America* by William D. Griffin; *The Encyclopedia of the Irish in America*, edited by Michael Glazier; *The Irish 100* by Tom Philbin; *The Irish American Family Album* by Dorothy and Thomas Hoobler; *The Irish Century* by Michael MacCarthy Morrogh; *Erin's Heirs: Irish Bonds of Community* by Denis Clarke; *Textures of Irish America* by Lawrence J. McCaffrey; and *RFK: Collected Speeches*, edited and introduced by Edwin O. Guthman and C. Richard Allen. An earlier version of Pete Hamill's essay on JFK appeared in *New York* magazine.

Foreword

BY SENATOR EDWARD KENNEDY

As this impressive book emphasizes, the ties between America and Ireland run long and deep. It is a privilege to join my sister, Ambassador Jean Kennedy Smith, and others in this celebration of the vast contributions that Irish Americans have made to all aspects of our society.

All of us in the Kennedy family are especially touched by the great honor bestowed upon President Kennedy. He has always been an inspiration to me in everything I do, and he always will be. His ideals still guide our nation, and they inspire countless citizens to serve their community and their country well.

I know that Jack was also deeply inspired by the people of Ireland. As he said in his address to the Irish Parliament in 1963, "It is that quality of the Irish – that remarkable combination of hope, confidence, and imagination – that is needed more than ever today."

By honoring him as Irish American of the Century, this book pays tribute to his life and work, and to the enduring ideals he valued so highly. I know that he would be deeply touched by this profound honor.

During his stay in Ireland, President Kennedy reflected on the close ties between Ireland and America. As he said in Cork, "What pleases me most about coming here is not only this connection which all of us in America feel with Ireland, even though time and generations may have separated us from this island, but also because I find here in Ireland those qualities which I associate with the best not only of my own country but of all that we are trying to do and all that we are trying to be." This book commemorates those ties, and ensures that they will continue long into the future.

The story of the Irish in America is the story of America itself. The enduring spirit of Irish Americans are celebrated on every page in this book. The triumphs of the Irish in literature, music, family life, history, politics, and so many other fields are the triumphs of America too, and all of us are very proud of them.

Island of Destiny

BY PATRICIA HARTY

*"It must have been the Irish who built the pyramids,
'cause no one else would carry all them bricks . . ."*
— from an Irish American song

From the time of St. Brendan, the Irish were drawn to America. Maybe it came from gazing out on the vast Atlantic Ocean and wondering what was on the other side. Brendan made his legendary trip in a skin boat. Later the Irish reached "Inishfail" – that "island of destiny" envisioned by the poets – as migratory fishermen making their way to Newfoundland in the holds of brigs which would make the return journey to Britain laden with timber from the Miramichi.

They came as indentured servants and as prisoners transported for crimes against the Crown. Some made their way up from the West Indies where Cromwell had sent them as slaves. What was merely a trickle in the 17th and 18th centuries became a deluge in the 19th. Fleeing starvation with few or no material possessions, they brought their music and song and tales of home as they spread out across the land until there was not a corner they didn't touch or leave their mark upon.

They gave their names to towns and streets, left their traces in ghost towns, mining museums, and graveyards. A huge Celtic cross on Grosse Ile in Canada marks the spot where thousands of Famine Irish are buried. In San Francisco's Mission Dolores a stone commemorates an Irishman killed by vigilantes. They died in riots precipitated by the anti-Irish, anti-Catholic Native American Party in Philadelphia in 1844, and they started riots such as the 1863 New York Draft Riots that Jimmy Breslin writes about in these pages. In New Orleans they built canals and died in the swamps – their lives deemed of less value than that of a slave. They fought in the Civil War, on both sides, and died in thousands at Bull Run and Gettysburg, Fredericksburg and The Wilderness.

They built the great transcontinental railroad and mined for gold, and kept on keeping on, going right past the "no dogs or Irishmen allowed" signs and emerging from the slums of New York and Boston to prove Orestes Brownson right when he predicted in the *Quarterly Review* (1845), "Out of these narrow lanes, blind courts, dirty streets, damp cellars, and suffocating garrets will come forth some of the noblest sons of our country whom she will delight to own and honor." And indeed, out of the wretchedness of those Famine Irish grew the greatest mobilization of a people in the history of the United States. The schools, hospitals, political clubs, and labor unions that came of their struggle would leave their mark on America forever.

By the 1920s, when those who found themselves on the wrong side of the Civil War in Ireland took the boat, the Irish in America had found a foothold. Al Smith was governor of New York (1919-1929) and the Democratic nominee for President of the United States in 1928. George M. Cohan was reaching the pinnacle of his career with songs like "I'm a Yankee Doodle Dandy" that showed Irish American patriotism, and James Cagney was starting his career in films.

But there was still an anti-Irish, anti-Catholic bias. In the early 1950s the legendary Speaker of the House "Tip" O'Neill led a boycott on a bank in Boston that had no Catholic employees. By the century's end, however, the Irish would go from exclusion to being the most successful of immigrant groups. As Pete Hamill says in writing here on JFK, our Irish American of the Century, "we won all the late rounds". That famous Kennedy helped banish the "No Irish need apply" signs forever and touched the lives of millions of Americans.

He was not alone. Many of those profiled in these pages were so original and unique in their contributions to American life and culture that things would never be the same in their individual fields. The first high-rise, that most American of buildings, was designed by an Irish American, Louis Henri Sullivan, the son of an Irish immigrant from Cork. Another famous son of Cork, Henry Ford, changed the landscape of America forever with his automobile. The history of the labor movement is replete with Irish names, from Mother Jones, the angel of the mining camps, to John Sweeney the head of the most powerful union in America today.

They built grand educational institutions, and joined the military service and were awarded more medals of honor than any other ethnic group. They produced great sporting heroes such as Jack Dempsey and Connie Mack, and became politicians and captains of industry who used their clout to help "the cause" in Ireland – from the early days of John Devoy and Eamon de Valera to the peace process and George Mitchell and Bill Clinton.

They became American, proudly patriotic, yet proud too, as George M. Cohan said, "Of all the Irish blood that's in me". And yet despite their identification with the American way of life, they continue to have an interest in their Irish heritage, and a sometimes poignant emotional connection to the land of their ancestors. You might think of them gazing across the ocean in their mind's eye and wondering about the old country needing help – sending care packages in the old days, peace packages and business investment in recent times.

Today the Irish are celebrated in every aspect of American life, but as we look back over the century we can only wonder at the journey they took, and the American dream that they dreamed and kept alive, as they became one of the most vital forces in a country that for many did turn out to be "Inishfail" – that "island of destiny".

Greatest
Irish Americans
of the
20th Century

Art

Great
Builders

Margaret Bourke-White
Candid Camera

"If you banish fear, nothing terribly bad can happen to you."

Margaret Bourke-White was a woman of many firsts. She was the only foreign photographer in the Soviet Union at the time of the German invasion of Russia, and she was the first woman allowed on Air Force bombing missions in Europe and North Africa.

Corbis / Bettmann – UPI

She was also one of the first photographers for both *Fortune* and *Life* magazines, and her pictures tell of another era: the Great Depression; London during the war years; the liberation of the concentration camps; and what was known as the Trial of the Century long before O.J. Simpson was ever heard from – the trial of Bruno Hauptman, convicted of the kidnapping and murder of the Lindbergh baby. She was a trailblazer – seemingly fearless, and accepting even the toughest assignments.

Born June 14, 1904 in New York's Bronx to Minnie Bourke and Joseph White, Bourke-White grew up in Bound Brook, New Jersey. Her father, an engineer in the printing industry, was of Polish descent, while her mother's father was a successful builder in Dublin.

In her earlier years, Bourke-White was interested in architecture and technology, and she studied engineering and biological sciences at Columbia University, the University of Michigan and Cornell. Her photography career started in 1927 in Cleveland, Ohio.

She subsequently opened a studio in New York City and joined the staff of *Fortune* magazine. Throughout her career, Bourke-White published many books, including *Eyes on Russia, Shooting the Russian War* and *Dear Fatherland*. In collaboration with her second husband, the novelist Erskine Caldwell, she also published *You Have Seen Their Faces* and *North of the Danube*.

Bourke-White's career was cut short when she developed Parkinson's Disease in the 1950s. Her autobiography, *Portrait of Myself*, was published in 1963. She died in Stamford, Connecticut on August 27, 1971. Her photos grace the walls of dozens of museums today.

Alfred Stieglitz

Georgia O'Keeffe
Queen of Arts

"I feel there is something unexplored about women that only a woman can explore."

As one of America's premier artists, Georgia O'Keeffe painted as she pleased, ignoring critics and debates over their interpretations of her work. "I simply paint what I see," she is quoted as saying. Whether massive New York City skyscrapers, large, vibrant botanicals, or bleached bones of the New Mexico desert, her boldly original work reveals an artist ahead of her time.

O'Keeffe knew from the time she was eight years old that she would be an artist. She was born on November 15, 1887 in Sun Prairie, Wisconsin, one of six children. Her mother came from a long line of well-educated women, and her father, the son of a Cork immigrant, encouraged her dream. When he moved the family to Virginia, he allowed her to stay in Wisconsin to attend a convent school well known for its art education.

O'Keeffe's artistic leanings were no surprise given her father's devotion to Irish music and his fiddle-playing ability. Her grandfather, Pierce O'Keeffe, came from a well-off family who owned a woolen business. Pierce and his wife moved to New York via Liverpool in a bid to escape the oppressive tax regime that existed under British rule. Their third son, Francis, married a woman of Hungarian descent, and while their daughter Georgia took after her father in Irish looks, her independent personality more closely resembled that of her mother. She never forgot her Irish roots, and refused to take her husband's name after marriage, due to the belief that her own name was a critical part of her success as an artist.

As an adult, O'Keeffe taught art at various colleges before she arranged to have her drawings shown to Alfred Stieglitz, owner of the famous "291" gallery in New York. He was immediately impressed. Also an accomplished photographer, Stieglitz managed Georgia's work well. Her reputation in New York grew, as did her fondness for Stieglitz. They were married in 1924.

Five years later, O'Keeffe began spending time in New Mexico, and it is a state with which her name has been strongly linked ever since. All of her creative energies came into play when she worked at the Ghost Ranch, which began as a dude ranch in the late 1920s.

After her husband's death in 1946, O'Keeffe moved to New Mexico permanently and remained there for the rest of her life. The landscapes and skyscapes of the desert inspired some of Georgia's greatest work. She died on March 6, 1986.

Library of Congress

Augustus Saint Gaudens
Clay Shaper

"[My mother] had wavy black hair and the typical long, generous, loving Irish face."

Born in Dublin to a French father and a County Longford mother, Augustus Saint Gaudens is widely regarded as one of America's greatest sculptors. His work has graced such public arenas as New York's Madison Square, Boston Common (the Robert Gould Shaw Memorial) and O'Connell Street in Dublin (the Charles Stewart Parnell monument).

Saint Gaudens hoped that this latter memorial, completed shortly before his death in 1907 and erected shortly thereafter, would be considered his finest work, but the cancer which afflicted him during completion of the statue made this goal impossible. Biographer Burke Wilkinson said that Saint Gaudens possessed an openness and desire to please others, traits considered more characteristic of the Irish than the French.

The sculptor brought his Irishness to the fore once again when he used 24-year-old immigrant Mary Cunningham as the face on the Liberty coins he designed at the request of President Theodore Roosevelt. The President commissioned a coinage "worthy of a great civilized nation", and Saint Gaudens' pieces were widely admired. In 30 years of work he produced nearly 150 sculptures.

Six months after his birth, Saint Gaudens moved to the U.S. with his parents and siblings. Apart from a brief apprenticeship in Paris, he was to live in the States for the rest of his life. He and his wife Augusta (née Homer) lived in Cornish, New Hampshire, on an estate named Aspet in honor of his father's birthplace.

After his death the estate attracted visitors from the public and the artistic community. In 1919, his wife and son established the Saint Gaudens Memorial, which described its purpose as being to aid, encourage and assist in the education of young sculptors and to encourage the art and appreciation of sculpture.

The sculptor's home is today officially known as the Saint Gaudens National Historic Site, and visitors can take guided tours of his home, the studios where he worked, and surrounding gardens.

Henry Ford
King of the Road

"Failure is only the opportunity to begin again more intelligently."

He changed the future of this country, and indeed the world, with his revolutionary line of stylish, affordable motor cars. Today the name Ford is synonymous with quality, safety and value for money. He wouldn't have had it any other way.

Born July 30, 1863, Henry Ford was the oldest of Michigan farmers William and Mary Ford's six children. His grandfather was a Famine emigrant from Cork who had almost drowned on the passage over when he was swept overboard.

Ford discovered at an early age that he was more interested in how his family's farm machinery worked than actually using them for chores. At 16, he worked as a machinist's apprentice.

Later, he operated and repaired steam engines, overhauled his father's farm implements, and supported himself and his new wife by running a sawmill.

In 1891, Ford became an engineer and created the Ford Motor Company in 1903. The Model T ushered in a new era of personal transportation with its ease of operation, maintenance, and maneuverability. By 1918, half of all cars in America were Model Ts. Ford's implementation of the assembly line revolutionized automobile

production by significantly reducing assembly time per vehicle, and thus lowering costs – a saving Ford continually passed on to the public. Prices fell as fast as sales rose, dropping from barely under $1,000 in 1909 to $355 (roughly $2,800 today) by 1920.

Ford's revolutionary vision included hiring thousands of handicapped workers, including bedridden patients who screwed nuts and bolts together in mini-assembly lines in their rooms. He believed this issue, along with minimum wages, maximum working hours, and the production pace, were the responsibility of entrepreneurs, not government. He said: "Our help does not come from Washington, but from ourselves. The government is a servant and never should be anything but a servant."

John Philip Holland
Ideas Man

"Mr. Holland climbed in, closed the hatch and started the engine . . . and before we realized it the boat was under twelve feet of water."
Mr. Dunkerly, Holland's engineer.

As the inventor of the submarine, he changed the way naval warfare was conducted forever. He secured the first investment for his "submersible vessel" from the Irish Republican Brotherhood (IRB), who hoped to use the craft against England, but he ironically ended up being commissioned to design two submarines for the Japanese during their war against Russia. It took eight years before he saw his first vessel launched successfully, but John Holland will forever be known as the "father" of the modern submarine.

Born February 29, 1840, in Liscannor, County Clare, to John Holland and Mary Scanlon, Holland began his career as a teacher. Reading about underwater transport and the works of various inventors, he became fascinated with the whole concept, and worked on the problem until he finally came up with his own design in 1870.

Needing financial backing, Holland moved to the U.S. and settled in New Jersey in 1873, where he taught until 1879. The IRB supplied him with $23,000 for his efforts, and the aptly named *Fenian Ram*, at 30 feet long and six feet wide, looked promising during test runs. The vessel managed to stay submerged for an hour at a depth of 60 feet. Writing about its launch, U.S. Admiral Philip Hichborn noted that "after the completion of this boat, Holland led the world far and away in the solution of submarine problems."

Holland's next move was to work on improving his design, but when the next vessel was constructed without his direct supervision it was badly damaged on its launch. In 1895, Holland's company won its first contract from the U.S. Navy to build a submarine, but after supervision of the project was handed over to a Navy admiral, the craft failed.

The astute inventor, not to be dissuaded, began to work on his own vessel in New Jersey, and its success inspired the federal government to quickly hand in an order for six more. Orders followed from all over the world, and Holland's reputation was secured.

He was married to Margaret Foley and the couple had four children. Holland died on August 12, 1914.

Ellis Island Immigration Museum

Corbis / Bettmann – UPI

William Mulholland
Water Titan
"There it is. Take it!"

His methods may have brought him in for some sharp criticism, but William Mulholland changed the way the Los Angeles of the late 1800s looked, and ensured that the City of Angels would prosper forevermore. A self-made man, Mulholland achieved this by rerouting the Owens River, sited more that 200 miles from L.A., in the process creating one of the engineering marvels of its time.

Born in Belfast in 1855, Mulholland was raised in Dublin. He left home when he was 15 and arrived in New York in the early 1870s. Working his way across the country, he arrived in San Francisco in 1877, and shortly afterwards moved to L.A.

Within eight years of being hired as a ditch-cleaner at a private water company, Mulholland had risen to the post of superintendent. After the city took over the company, he was made head of the Department of Water and Power, a position he remained in until 1928.

As the city continued to boom, Mulholland and a former L.A. mayor named Fred Eaton became convinced that more water would be needed to sustain growth. The Owens River

looked like L.A.'s best chance of survival, and in 1905 Mullholland began organizing the construction of the Los Angeles Aqueduct, which when built was considered second only to the Panama Canal as an engineering masterpiece. On November 5, 1913 Mulholland raised the Stars and Stripes and before a crowd of 40,000 onlookers opened the metal gates. As the water flooded through he spoke the memorable words, "There it is. Take it!"

While he deserved credit for this feat, and for his work in securing the continued prosperity of Los Angeles, the resulting drain on Owens Valley resources left local farmers reeling and they united to fight back, blowing up the Los Angeles Aqueduct at a critical point. They also commandeered control of an aqueduct gate, earning the support of media outlets from as far away as Paris. When their battle ran out of steam, Mulholland's woes looked like they were over.

It was to be a temporary reprieve, however. On March 12, 1928, the St. Francis Dam collapsed, resulting in a 15-billion-gallon flood that killed almost 500 men, women and children. Mulholland, who had supervised construction of the dam, was held accountable for the disaster by a board of inquiry and forced to resign. He died in 1935.

Louis Henri Sullivan
King of the Sky

"Form ever follows function, and this is the law. Where function does not change, form does not change."

His pioneering work in the field of high-rise design cannot be overestimated, and he is remembered as the creator of one of the world's first skyscrapers. Louis Henri Sullivan, together with engineer partner Dankmar Adler, was responsible for such notable buildings as the Auditorium and Stock Exchange buildings in Chicago and the Wainwright Building in St. Louis.

History has long recognized the contribution of the Irish to the building of American infrastructure, whether it be roads, canals, skyscrapers or churches. But Sullivan was the Irish American whose contribution to the skylines of various cities climbs tallest of all.

Born September 3, 1856 in Boston, Massachusetts, to Patrick Sullivan and Adrienne List, Sullivan was raised on the farm belonging to his maternal grandparents. His father was a dancing instructor who had immigrated from Cork; his mother had also recently arrived in the States from Geneva with her parents, and was of mixed French, German and Swiss ancestry.

Sullivan did not have a close relationship with his father, and wrote in his memoir that Sullivan senior was "a free-mason and not even sure he was a Catholic or an Orangeman." However, according to an article by Adolf K. Placzek, the young Louis Sullivan was "the most Celtic of Celts, if there is such a thing."

After studying at the Massachusetts Institute of Technology, Sullivan served apprenticeships with architects in Philadelphia and Chicago. He also studied in Paris for a year, but returned to Chicago where, in 1881, he established Adler and Sullivan. In what was to be an extremely efficient partnership, Sullivan designed the buildings (over 100 in all) and Adler built them.

Among Sullivan's young associates was Frank Lloyd Wright, who once described himself as the "pencil in Sullivan's hand." The relationship between the two was at times stormy, however, and when Sullivan discovered that Wright was moonlighting on different projects, he fired the younger man. "This bad end to a glorious relationship," remarked Wright, "has been a dark shadow to stay with me the days of my life."

Towards the end of the 19th century, architectural taste returned to neoclassicism, a trend Sullivan was unwilling to follow. In 1895, he and Adler went their separate ways, and Sullivan turned his attention to smaller buildings in small towns. He also authored two books on architecture – *Autobiography of an Idea* and *Kindergarten Chats and Other Writings*. He died in a Chicago hotel room on April 14, 1924, separated from his wife and virtually bankrupt.

Corbis / Bettmann – UPI

Leaves of Pain

BY JIMMY BRESLIN

At first, it seemed to be nothing. It was a curled-up dark brown leaf about the size of a good lock of hair and it was preserved in glass in a room in the Fairlow Herbarium in Cambridge, Massachusetts. A typewritten card alongside the leaf said that it was taken from an infected potato plant in Ireland during the famines of 1845–50. I looked at the leaf, read the card and began to walk away and, of course, did not leave. Here in this glass case was the weapon used by the earth when it turned against man and nearly ended a nation, the leaf that determined the character of its people, wherever they were, for generations at least.

Behind the glass case, on long shelves, was an impressive line of books. There also was in the room a man who could help me decipher some of the written matter. I decided to forget about taking one of the morning shuttles to New York. I sat at a table. Usually, when you are around relics of things Irish, you hear in your mind a song or have the feel of a smile.

This time, the hand went for a book. At the time of the famine, the man in charge of the room observed, mycology, the study of fungi, was only beginning. People from a couple of places in the world went to Ireland to collect blighted plants and then took them back to their laboratories to study. But they could give Ireland no help.

By the time the famine was ending, the potato fungus was only being given a name: "phytophthora infestas." One of the things most vile about the use of a dead language is the manner in which the message of horror becomes lost in the struggle to absorb the habitual syllables.

The man in the Fairlow Herbarium suggested one of the books, *The Advance of the Fungi* by E.C. Large. The author noted that in good weather the potato fungus reproduced sexually. However, when conditions were constantly wet and chilly, the fungus reproduced asexually, and at great rapidity. On two occasions during the famine years, there was a chill rain that did not seem to end. Fungus appeared wherever the land was wet. Potato leaves became brown and started to curl up and the potato underneath became purple and mushy. With no food, over a million died and millions fled.

The book says that experiments over the years show that the blighted potato was edible. Because of the fungus causing the inside of the potato to break down, much of the starch turned into sugar, thereby giving the potato a strange, sweet taste. This is something that can be said in the safety of a laboratory. But while a million were dying, people tried to eat the potatoes and found they could not.

The potato originates in the Andes Mountains of Peru, where it grows in many varieties. However, the English, who introduced it to Ireland in the 16th century, planted only one variety, the clone, and it is susceptible to the wet fingers of fungus. With no second variety of potato plant to withstand the disease, the blight became total. The Irish, ignorant of all this, planted any eyes which seemed even vaguely uninfected and prayed that the next crop would be clean. But the new plants were as infected as the ones from which they came.

As I was reading this, I began to think of the crumbling stone building on Bantry Bay, in Cork. The ruin stands right on the bay, at a point where the rocky shore builds up to great cliffs that go along flat, deep water until the water begins to rise and fall in great swells and suddenly the land ends and now it is ocean, not bay, slapping against the bottom of the cliff and sending spray high into the air, up to the top of the cliff. The ruins sit in a tangle of rough brush and are difficult to reach.

In 1845, at the height of the famine, the place was a granary. Each day, while Irishmen died with their mouths stained green from eating grass, the British worked this granary and filled sacks that were placed on ships and sent to England. Near the end, when there were no people able to work in the fields and supply the granary, the British announced that the building would be donated to the people. It could be used as a Children's Home, which is a twisted way of saying what it actually became: a morgue for children who died of not having food. The bodies of children were stacked floor to ceiling in the granary.

And now, in this room in Cambridge, with the time passing and the man in charge finding you still more to read about fungus and famine, the line in the English language I always think of first walked through my mind in all its stateliness and wisdom: "Too long a sacrifice can make a stone of the heart."

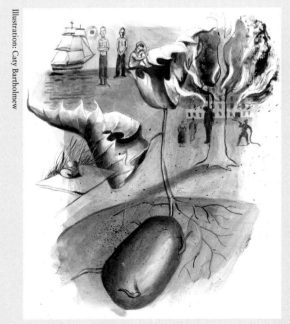

The sons of this famine burned an orphanage in New York City. It was called the Colored Orphan Asylum, of course; when the maimed poor anywhere lash out, they seek not the blood of dukes and earls, but rather victims such as they. The Colored Orphan Asylum was on Fifth Avenue, between 43rd and 44th Streets.

At three p.m. on Sunday, July 12, 1863, a crowd of nearly 4,000 Irish broke through the front gate of the orphanage, rushed across the lawns and broke inside. The orphanage officials managed to sneak 400 terrified black orphans out of the back door and take them to the safety of a police station. The mob of Irish, meanwhile, ransacked and burned the orphanage. And throughout the city, mobs of Irish, their hearts shale, their souls dead, rioted and killed blacks.

I always thought it was important to know what happens to men when their insides become stone. The violence, the illegal acts are not to be condoned. But I always want to know why it is that all people, even those of your own, lose control of the devils inside them. Perhaps something can be learned.

The riots in New York are called in history books "The Draft Riots." But at the time the newspapers referred to them as the "Irish Riots." The government in 1863 set up a military draft for New York, a lottery, but one from which any citizen could buy himself out for $300. Which excluded the Irish, who barely had money for dinner.

The first drawing was held on Saturday, July 11. When the names were published in the Sunday morning newspapers, growls ran through the tenements where the Irish lived. Soon, people were out in the streets, carrying anything that would hurt, and with their first violence, their first beatings, their first fires, the word struck them, as similar words have sunk into any thrashing crowds throughout history.

In Odessa, the crew of the Potemkin mutinied and the people were fighting the troops on the steps rising from the harbor and then somebody screamed the word: "Jews!" It became not a fight against authority anymore; it was a pogrom. And in Manhattan, in 1863, here were the Irish, the sons of famine, out in the streets against the injustice of a system that would allow the rich to buy out of a danger in which the poor must perish. And suddenly, inevitably, as the water of a wave turns to white, the word races through the crowd: "Niggers!"

On 32nd Street between Fifth and Sixth Avenues, a black was hung from a tree and his house burned. An army officer who had tried to stop the mobs was trapped on 33rd Street, between First and Second Avenues. He was beaten to death and the mob played with his body for hours, as a kitten does with a spool.

At six p.m. on the second night of the rioting, a mob of 600 Irish attacked a corner of Baxter and Leonard Streets in which 20 black families lived. The police arrived at this point, two platoons of them, led by three sergeants, listed in the records as Walsh, Quinn and Kennedy. The patrolmen under them all were Irish. At this time, 90 percent of the police force was Irish: Irish with their trait of loyalty. And loyalty was stronger than stone. There was no question what the police would do: protect the black families and then attack the mob, this mob of Irish. Attack them and beat them and club them and force them to break and run, and chase them down the streets and beat them so they would have no stomach to return for more.

During the three-day riot, the rioters killed 18 blacks. There could have been thousands killed without the police intervention. The police and army units killed 1,200 rioters. Seven thousand were injured. General Harvey Brown, in charge of the army troops, said of New York's Irish police department: "Never in our civil or military life have I ever seen such untiring devotion or such efficient service."

In the history of the Police Department of the City of New York, it was the act that first caused people to call them "The Finest." That it came as the result of having to quell savage assaults by other Irish is something that should neither be hidden nor explained away. Remember it. It happened 114 years ago, which is a short time as the history of the earth is measured.

Remember it, and do not condone it. But at the same time know about it. Know by being told what Yeats knew by instinct: the effect of something like this leaf in the glass in the room in Cambridge.

I gave the man back his books, said thank you and left the Herbarium and went to the airport in Boston for the shuttle to New York. I had to be at a wake in Brooklyn, in the Bedford Stuyvesant neighborhood. My friend Mabel Mabry's nephew, Allen Burnett, had been murdered. He was walking along Bedford Avenue and somebody shot him in the back because Allen would not give up his new coat. After the wake, I rode in the cab past the place where Allen was murdered. Bedford Avenue at this part, Kosciusko Street, is empty. The buildings have been burned and the sidewalks are covered in glass. In an empty lot alongside a boarded-up building, a pack of dogs rooted through garbage that had been thrown there during the day. Weeds grew in the lot. The weeds made me think of the curled-up dark brown leaf I had seen earlier that day.

This article was written by Jimmy Breslin in 1977 and republished by Irish America *in 1986 and October/November 2000.*

Business

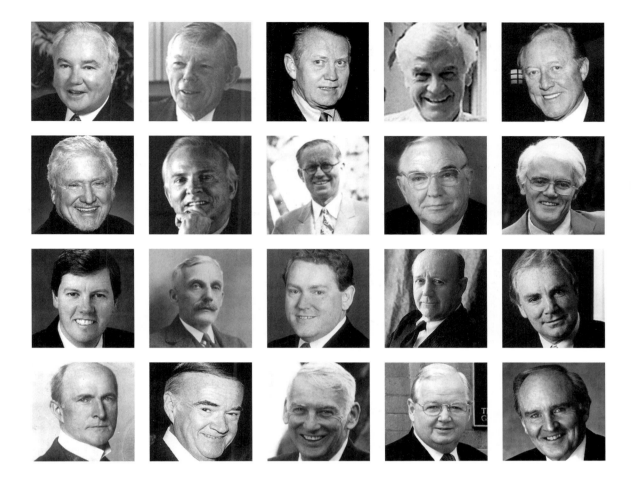

Brian P. Burns
Art Collector

He's a man of many talents – business executive, attorney and philanthropist – but it is perhaps for his extensive and unequaled art collection that Brian Burns is best known. Through his efforts, the work of dozens of Irish artists is exhibited regularly at various locations through-out the U.S. In 1996, an exhibition titled "America's Eye: Irish Paintings" was shown both at Boston College and in Dublin, courtesy of Burns' own private collection.

Burns is the chairman and president of BF Enterprises, Inc., a publicly-owned real estate holding and development company. A nationally regarded business executive, he has been the moving force behind some 40 corporate mergers.

He is also a director of the American Ireland Fund and the founder and principal benefactor of the John J. Burns (named for his father) Library of Rare Books at Boston College. The library houses more than 100,000 rare books, the largest archive of rare books in the U.S., and three million manuscripts. Burns is vice chairman of the Irish American Fulbright Commission and is a member of the Trinity College Foundation Board in Dublin.

In 1990, the Burns Foundation endowed the library with a Visiting Scholar in Irish Studies

chair. His art collection was the subject of a major exhibition for several months in 1997 at the Yale Center of British Art in New Haven, Connecticut.

Burns was a principal benefactor of the first Irish Famine memorial in Cambridge, Massachusetts, which was dedicated in July 1997 by former Irish President Mary Robinson. He currently serves as a member of the Irish Prime Minister's Economic Advisory Board.

Burns traces his roots to County Kerry. His wife Eileen is a member of the Advisory Board to the National Gallery of Ireland.

Chuck Dolan
Cable Giant

A giant in the television industry, Charles "Chuck" Dolan is the founder and chairman of Cablevision Systems Corporation, one of the nation's largest television operators, as well as a multi-faceted business providing specialized TV programming and telecommunications services.

A native of Cleveland, Ohio, Dolan is the son of an inventor and spent his childhood in Cleveland before serving in the Air Force and studying at John Carroll University. In his earliest professional endeavors, he and his wife Helen worked from home, editing and producing short film reels of sports events for syndication to television stations.

Dolan went on to found Home Box Office Inc. (HBO) in the 1970s. He then sold it to Time Life Inc. and established the Cablevision Systems Corporation in 1973. In 1997, Cablevision purchased a majority interest in the Madison

Square Garden properties, which include the arena complex, the NBA New York Knicks, the NHL New York Rangers, as well as the MSG Network.

Dolan and his wife have six children. Their son James is chief executive of Cablevision. Two other sons, a nephew and son-in-law also hold senior management posts in the company.

Dolan, who serves on several boards, is chairman of the national Academy of Television Arts and Sciences. He was the 1998 recipient of the American Irish Historical Society's gold medal.

Charles Feeney
Generous Soul

"Nobody can wear two pairs of shoes at one time."

The publicity has died down somewhat in the intervening years (which is how he prefers things), but New Jersey businessman Charles "Chuck" Feeney will always be remembered as the man who gave his millions away . . . quietly.

Feeney sprang into the public eye in 1996, when it emerged that he had donated over $600 million, a huge portion of his personal wealth, to create the fourth-largest philanthropic organization in the U.S.

William Nelsen, the president of Citizens' Scholarship Foundation of America, which has received support from Feeney's Atlantic Foundation for over a decade, told the *New York Times* that his organization had received "the most valuable kind of assistance" from Atlantic. He added: "As an organization, we've more than quadrupled in size since getting support from this anonymous donor."

And *Times* columnist Maureen Dowd, writing after Feeney addressed the *Irish America* Business 100 luncheon in 1997, a rare occurrence for one as publicity-shy, described his desire for anonymity as "startling in an age when people stamp their names on every available surface."

Feeney was unmasked as the anonymous donor who had given huge sums of money to educational institutions and charitable foundations only after the chain of Duty Free Shops he had co-founded was sold.

He holds both Irish and American citizenship and is well known for his support of Irish causes. Less known is his huge role in bringing American involvement to bear on the Irish peace process. He was a key behind-the-scenes figure also in helping Irish immigrants win legal status in the United States. Three Irish universities – Trinity College Dublin, Dublin City University and the University of Limerick – benefited from Feeney's magnanimity, and he also funded the setting up and initial running of the Sinn Féin office in Washington, D.C.

Thomas J. Flatley
Boston Benefactor

Thomas Flatley was born in Kiltimagh, County Mayo and like many Irish emigrants of his era arrived in America in 1950 with little money and few prospects. He started off working in a German delicatessen in New York and later served in the Korean War, after which he moved to Boston.

At age 26 he became founding president of the Flatley Company, which eventually became the largest sole-proprietor business in the U.S. with multi-million-dollar real estate and construction holdings.

He has made the *Forbes* 400 Richest Americans on several occasions and continues to be a real estate and construction powerhouse in Boston. He is best known in Irish America, however, for his extraordinary charitable works. A huge benefactor of The American Ireland Fund, he also personally underwrote the Boston Irish Famine Memorial, the only major full-scale commemoration in that city of the event that defined the Irish in America. The richest Irish-born immigrant of his generation, Thomas Flatley is a man who has never hesitated to give back. He has certainly come a long way from the penniless immigrant who arrived on America's shores all those years ago.

William J. Flynn
Peace Broker

"No pessimist ever set foot on Ellis Island, no pessimist ever crossed the prairies, and no pessimist built cities from one end of the continent to the other. These things were done by people with vision and hope."

William J. Flynn will always be remembered as the man who dispensed with a great taboo – the notion that American business should not get involved in bringing peace to Ireland. He broke the mold when he set out in tandem with a few others to change the reality that American business had nothing to offer on peace in Ireland. The Irish peace process is the result.

Thus, the name of the genial Mutual of America Chairman has become as well known in Irish political circles as it has in the business world. Flynn helped build Mutual from a small struggling organization in 1971 into the industry leader and insurance giant it is today.

He was a key figure in the U.S. delegation that worked tirelessly to broker the first IRA ceasefire in 1994. In recognition of his leadership and diplomacy on this front, Flynn was the inaugural recipient two years ago of the Initiative for Peace Award from the National Committee on American Foreign Policy. As chairman of the committee, Flynn's advice was instrumental in

persuading President Clinton to grant a U.S. visa to Sinn Féin president Gerry Adams in 1994. He has also led two delegations to Northern Ireland to push for economic investment and peace in the region. This year, he was back again as part of a team of American observers at Drumcree.

A native New Yorker, whose parents came from Counties Mayo and Down, Flynn is president of the board of Flax Trust America and a member of the Ireland America Advisory Board. He is a past chairman of the Ireland Chamber of Commerce in the U.S.A. and has been a board member of several organizations, including the American Cancer Society Foundation, Co-Operation Ireland and the Catholic Health Association of the United States. *Irish America* magazine chose him as Irish American of the Year in 1994, and in 1996, as Grand Marshal, he proudly led the New York St. Patrick's Day Parade up Fifth Avenue.

Flynn holds an MA from Fordham University. He is married to Peggy and they have four children and ten grandchildren.

Merv Griffin
Entertainer

"My background first drew me to Ireland, but now I have a reason to be here for many years to come."

Entertainer, entrepreneur, producer, gourmet – is there anything Merv Griffin hasn't done? Millions of Americans remember him as the host of *The Merv Griffin Show*, but his reputation as producer, entrepreneur and hotelier is rapidly growing as well. Merv Griffin is a force to be reckoned with.

Of all his undertakings, the one dearest to the hearts of the Irish and Irish Americans is his purchase and renovation of St. Clerans, the centuries-old manor house in County Galway that was once the residence of the director John Huston and his family. Griffin's own Irish

background initially drew him to Ireland, and now St. Clerans gives him a reason to keep coming back. Of the many jewels in Griffin's crown of hospitality, St. Clerans is the first Merv Griffin Hotels property in Europe.

Born in San Mateo, California, Griffin started out in entertainment by entering talent contests, writing songs, singing on the local radio station and later touring with "Freddy Martin and His Orchestra." Increasingly popular with nightclub audiences, he struck gold in 1950 with his recording of "I've Got a Lovely Bunch of Coconuts."

Doris Day saw his nightclub performance and was so impressed she arranged a screen test for him at Warner Bros. Studios. After starring in several hit movies, he crossed over into television, appearing on *The Arthur Murray Show*, *The Jack Paar Show* and others. In 1962, NBC gave him his own hour-long talk show – *The Merv Griffin Show*.

Through Merv Griffin Entertainment, he continues to develop and produce successful game shows like *Jeopardy!* and *Wheel of Fortune* along with other television programs and feature films.

Griffin also has a private vineyard in California where he oversees bottling of wines distributed under his "Mont Merveilleux" label. What will he try his hand at next?

Denis Kelleher
Wall Street Success Story

One of the great Irish immigrant financial success stories of the century, Denis Kelleher, the son of a shoemaker, left his native Kerry in 1958 and landed on Wall Street as a messenger boy with Merrill Lynch soon afterwards. The night before emigrating he had come home late from a dance in the nearby village of Rathmore and found a letter from his sister saying that a ticket to America was waiting for him at Shannon Airport. That was all it took, and the next day he left his old life behind forever.

Starting out as a runner at Merrill Lynch, he spent the next seven years working his way up from the ground floor. After a stint in the U.S. Army, he left the company and joined the legendary Rune Connive firm run by his close friends Bill Rune and Rick Connive. It was to become one of the most successful money-managing companies on Wall Street.

In 1981, Kelleher went out on his own, starting the Wall Street Clearing Company, which provided clearing services for over 70 brokers and 900 banks. Hugely successful, it was bought out by Alex Brown and Sons in 1989.

Soon after, Kelleher founded Wall Street Investor Services, which was soon managing the investment portfolios of some of the biggest pension funds and private investors in the United States. Now called Wall Street Access, it specializes in discount brokerage, asset management and bank brokerage programs. It processes billions of dollars annually and is listed on the U.S. Stock Exchange. If it ever went public its net worth would likely be over the billion dollar mark.

Despite his extraordinary success, Kelleher has never lost sight of his humble roots. When the issue of Irish illegal immigration became a major problem in the 1980s, he was one of the chief underwriters of organizations seeking to legalize the undocumented. He has also been a major contributor to the American Ireland Fund and has his own special scholarship fund in his native Kerry to help promising students. He was awarded the Ellis Island Medal of Honor in 1995.

Joseph Patrick Kennedy
Patriarch
"He may be president, but he still comes home and swipes my socks."

Apart from breaking new ground for Catholic Irish Americans in finance and politics, Joseph P. Kennedy should be remembered for shaping a family whose generations of public service throughout this century continue to inspire all Americans. As patriarch, politician and financier, his accomplishments have made the path into society for Irish Americans that much easier.

Only one generation removed from the Famine ship that carried his family to America, Kennedy became the first truly great Irish American success story on Wall Street, using his legendary ability to talk, spin a deal and weave a vision to create a financial and political legacy that reaches down to his great-grandchildren today.

Kennedy's ancestors emigrated to the United States in 1848 from Dunganstown in County Wexford. Joseph was born in Boston in 1888 to Patrick J. and Mary (Hickey) Kennedy. Patrick

Kennedy, a saloon keeper, made it a point to send his son to "proper Bostonian" schools, and so Joseph attended Boston Latin School and Harvard College.

In 1914, Kennedy married Rose Fitzgerald, the daughter of John F. "Honey Fitz" Fitzgerald, the mayor of Boston. The couple had four sons and five daughters.

Kennedy began his career as a bank examiner, and by the age of 26 was president of the Columbia Trust Company. During World War I, he was assistant general manager of the Bethlehem Shipbuilding Corporation. He later turned his attention to investment brokering and Hollywood, where he integrated the Keith-Albee-Orpheum movie-house chain and reorganized such major film companies as Paramount Pictures. In 1934, at the height of the Great Depression, Kennedy was a multi-millionaire, and his fortune was growing.

He also directed his business acumen to benefit the Democratic Party, serving as fund-raiser and adviser to President Franklin D. Roosevelt during the 1932 campaign. In 1934, Roosevelt appointed him chairman of the newly-formed Securities and Exchange Commission, which led to the chairmanship of the U.S. Maritime Commission. In 1937, he was assigned to England as Ambassador to the Court of St. James, making him the first Catholic and the first Irish American to hold the position.

When Kennedy arrived in England with his wife and nine children, his charming, informal ways endeared him to the British media. The honeymoon did not last, though. As the threat of World War II loomed larger and larger, Kennedy lost popularity for advocating accommodation with Hitler. When England entered the war, Kennedy expressed his doubts about the country's prospects for survival, estranging him further from the English and from Washington.

Kennedy returned to the United States in October 1940, and resigned his position as Ambassador one month later. But the damage done to his political career by his wartime stance was not to be remedied. Realizing this, he turned his attention to his sons, grooming them for political office. He originally had hopes of his eldest son Joseph winning the Oval Office, but when Joseph was killed during World War II, he redirected his attentions to the next son in line, John. John's entry into national politics energized Joseph in his later years. His influence on the political careers of his children is immeasurable, but it is Rose's maxim that has proved to be their guiding principle: "To whom much is given, much is expected."

In 1961, Kennedy suffered a stroke that left him an invalid for the remaining years of his life. He died in his beloved Hyannis, Massachusetts on November 18, 1969.

Joseph and his wife, Rose.

Irish Memories

BY THOMAS FLEMING

My County Mayo-born grandfather, David Fleming, could not read or write. He had a brogue so thick I couldn't understand a word he said. But I knew one thing: he was Irish and proud of it. He had a favorite poem that he made me memorize and recite when I was six. It was called "Why I Named You Patrick." I can only remember one verse of it.

When you wear the shamrock, son,
Be proud of your Irish name.
No other one I know of
Can stand for greater fame.

Old Davey was a big bulky man, with thick arms and solid shoulders. He looked like he could put his fist through a door if he got mad. He liked jokes about fighting Irishmen. One of his favorites was about the Irishman who got shipwrecked and drifted up to the shore of an unnamed country. "Is there a government in this place?" he asked the natives. They said yes. "I'm agin it," the Irishman said.

The joke had some personal meaning to Davey. In 1870, when he arrived in Jersey City, the place was run by Anglo-American Protestants, better known these days as WASPS. "No Irish Need Apply" signs were plentiful. During World War I, when an Irishman was promoted to foreman at the Colgate factory, it made headlines in the local paper.

Old Davey, as I called him privately, was an angry man. He would not tolerate a bag of Lipton's tea in the house. He disliked Thomas Lipton because he was English and flaunted his wealth, winning all sorts of prizes on his famous racing yacht.

Davey also disliked insurance men. Around the turn of the century, there was a big exposé about how the insurance companies had cheated millions of poor people by collecting 50 cents a week from them long after they had paid up their little policies.

Fifty cents was real money to David Fleming. It was what he had gotten paid for a day's work at Standard Oil when he started out there as a laborer. He told my Aunt Mae, with whom he lived after his wife died, that he never wanted to see an insurance man in the house.

My Aunt Mae used to meet the insurance man out on the corner. One day someone's schedule got confused. The insurance man came to the door of their second-story flat.

"Metropolitan Life!" he chirped as Davey opened the door.

Wham! Davey punched the poor guy down a whole flight of stairs. Aunt Mae had to change insurance companies.

My father always referred to Davey as "the old gent." He never said "the old man" or "my old man." I sensed there was a lot of respect in his choice of words. Now I think I know why. The old gent got up and went to work at Standard Oil every day for 50 years. He never drank his pay. He cared about his wife and kids.

When my publisher, W.W. Norton, started a series called *The States and the Nation*, they asked me to write the history of New Jersey. My agent, a WASP from California, said he didn't think the money was good enough. I said: "My grandfather couldn't read or write. Now they're asking me to write the history of the state. I'll do it for nothing."

My mother didn't like Davey very much. She called him a thick mick. She never said that to my father, of course. But that's what she called him to me and my brother. My mother was what they used to call lace curtain Irish. She was a beautiful dark-haired woman, a stylish dresser. Her father had been a pretty prosperous carpenter. Her mother was the daughter of a schoolteacher in Ireland. She could read and write and my mother was one of the few Irish-Americans to graduate from Dickinson High School and spend a year in normal school to earn a teaching certificate.

My mother considered culture more important than a well-decorated house – though she liked that, too. She read the latest novels; she loved the theater, especially the plays of Eugene O'Neill. She started taking me to shows when I was seven or eight. She had a lot to do with making me a writer.

The kind of Irish jokes she liked were about thick micks. One told how this Irishman, just off the boat, was invited to a banquet. They served a consommé. He had never seen anything like it, but he drank it. They served a salad. This baffled him too, but he ate it. Then came a lobster. He threw down his napkin and left the table. "I drank your water and I ate your grass," he said. "But I'll be damned if I'll eat that bug!"

My father, Thomas J. Fleming, whom everyone called Teddy – that was my Jersey City name, too – was built like my grandfather, big hands and arms and the same shoulders, but somewhat shorter.

His side of the family told me what it meant to grow up Irish and poor in Jersey City. During the summer, while he was still in grammar school, he and his brothers Dave and Charlie used to work in a watch factory next door to their tenement on Pacific Avenue. Each morning they faced a clerk in a high white collar who looked down at them from a tall desk and asked: "Protestant or Catholic?"

If you said Protestant, even though the map of Ireland was on your face, you got a job. If you said Catholic, the clerk said: "No work today."

You can imagine what David Fleming thought of this Protestant supremacy act. It gives you a glimpse of why the Irish supported a politician

Thomas Fleming, right, his father Thomas J. "Teddy" and brother Gene at the beach.

named Frank Hague, who took over the city in 1917 and soon made it clear that no one was going to push the Irish around any more.

Before Hague arrived, my father's ambition when he was a kid at All Saints School was to become a major league baseball player. He loved the game. Some mornings he and his friends would get up in the dawn and play a few innings before school began. Sometimes in March they had to shovel snow off their field down in Lafayette. I've always liked the name of the field – The Happy Nines.

Watching them on many mornings was a big black-robed figure – Monsignor Michael Meehan, the pastor of All Saints. When my father graduated from the eighth grade he called him into the rectory.

"What are you going to be, Fleming?" he asked. "A major leaguer," my father said. "No you're not," Monsignor Meehan said. "You can't hit a curve. We've got too many tramp Irish athletes already. You're going to business school."

Thirty years later, when my father became the leader of the Sixth Ward, Monsignor Meehan was still there. He called my father into the rectory again. "I suppose you're going to work your head off to make good down here," he said.

My father allowed that he was going to do

something like that. "Well, just remember this," the Monsignor said. "Jesus Christ himself couldn't keep these people happy."

My father never became the businessman Monsignor Meehan envisioned. History had other ideas. In 1917 he found himself in the U.S. Army on the way to France to fight the Germans. He went because Monsignor Meehan and other leaders said it was a way to prove the Irish were good Americans.

He and other Irish Americans in Jersey City were not exactly worshipers of President Woodrow Wilson. They elected him governor in 1910 on his solemn promise that he would allow Boss James Smith of Newark and Boss Bob Davis of Jersey City to have the okay on patronage. The minute he got to Trenton, Wilson went back on his word.

That was a mortal sin to an Irish American politician. They might pad the voting rolls, tolerate gambling, cut a deal or two with a local contractor. But your word was your bond. Then Wilson made a speech in 1915 in which he accused Irish and German Americans of "pouring poison into the veins of American life" because they did not like the way he sided with the English in the war that was killing millions of people in Europe.

But the Irish, including Teddy Fleming and a lot of his friends from Jersey City, went to Europe and fought the Germans. In the gigantic battle of the Argonne in 1918, all the officers in my father's company were killed or wounded. He was the top sergeant and they made him an instant lieutenant.

In 1968, on the 50th anniversary of Argonne, my wife and I went to France and I followed my father's struggle through the Argonne, using his regiment's diary. I saw the price the Irish in the 78th Division paid to prove they were Americans.

We got to a place where the diary said they attacked La Ferme Rouge – the red farmhouse. It was still there. We went to the door and with the help of an interpreter introduced ourselves. The farmer, a guy built like my grandfather, had been there when my father's regiment attacked! He had been sixteen at the time.

He took us to the trenches around the farm's perimeter. He pointed out a nearby wood, the Boise des Loges, which the Germans had filled with machine guns. The regiment lost almost a thousand men attacking it. It was as bad as Belleau Wood, but it never got the publicity the Marines got for that show.

My father, like most doughboys, utterly despised the Marines for the way they bragged about themselves.

Back at La Ferme Rouge, the farmer broke out a bottle of Moet et Chandon and he offered a toast: "To the son of the man who freed the Bois de Loges."

That was one of the proudest moments of my life.

My father never made a big deal about his combat days. His favorite Argonne story was about four Irish Americans, led by a corporal named Delaney, that he sent out to patrol no man's land one night. The two previous patrols had not come back. These guys didn't either.

In 1920, my father was walking down 33rd Street in New York. Who comes toward him but Corporal Delaney? "I thought you were feeding the worms in the Argonne," my father said. "Lieutenant," Delaney said. "Do I look crazy? The minute we got out there, we found a break in our trenches and ran like hell for the rear. After about a mile, we yelled 'gas' and started coughing our brains out. They put us in nice comfortable beds at the hospital and sent us home on the next ship."

My father always shook his head over that one. "I might have done the same thing if I was in his shoes," he said.

When he got back to Jersey City, my father discovered that getting commissioned in the Argonne had changed his life. Frank Hague was looking for war heroes to give his organization

The author at age two and his father, Thomas J. "Teddy" Fleming.

The author Thomas Fleming.

voter appeal. Teddy Fleming soon became a politician. Doc Holland, the leader of the Sixth Ward, made him his right-hand man.

In private, my father always strenuously denied he was a war hero. He never had much use for guys who won promotions or medals. He said he had seen too many people do things under fire to save the life of a friend and get nothing for it – except maybe get themselves killed. But he let the organization add "commissioned officer" in his biography every time they ran him for office.

He meant what he had told Monsignor Meehan. He worked hard at being a politician, especially during the Great Depression. Night after night, he sat in the ward clubhouse talking to people who were desperately looking for jobs. He never promised a job he could not deliver. That was basic to his Irish American code. The people knew his word – plus his handshake – was his bond.

One night that saved his life. A man with a Slovak name appeared for the third or fourth time. My father said he would go all out to get him into the ironworkers. The man wept – and put a loaded pistol on my father's desk. "If you turned me down again, I was going to kill you," he said.

Almost every night after the clubhouse closed, he would spend a couple of hours in the ward's bars, listening to political opinions, complaints, pleas for promotion at city hall or on the cops or fire department.

I remember, after he retired, trying to tell him what a good job I thought he'd done as a leader. How the kind of work he did kept a city together.

He looked at me as if I'd gone nuts. "But, Teddy," he said. "You had to listen to an awful lot of baloney."

When I was a teenager, I used to go down to the ward for political rallies. My father wasn't much of a speaker. He had a short set piece, which mostly consisted of telling the voters: "You are my people. Never forget that. If you need something, come to me and I'll try to get it for you."

He meant that, too. He was one of the few ward leaders who was willing to go head to head with Mayor Frank Hague to get promotions and raises for his people. This often led to screaming arguments and threats of exchanging punches.

It was one way – probably the only way – to win Mayor Hague's respect. I remember the first time I met the mayor, who was about six-foot-two and looked as if he could eat you for breakfast. He mashed my hand and said: "Your old man's one in a barrel."

What does it add up to? I think – or hope – it's a kind of window on what being Irish American was all about in Jersey City. It's a rather surprising mix of pride and anger and a kind of ongoing conflict between the two sides of that hyphen, between Irish and American.

It wasn't always pretty or noble. It was hard to be pretty or noble when your father made 50 cents a day – and you had to deny your religion to get a job. Things happened that made you mad

– that made you want to get even.

One day when my father was a teenager he came out of All Saints Church and he met a local Protestant who said: "Hey, Fleming, did you tell the monsignor what you do to your sister?"

In ten seconds the guy was on his back in the street with about a thousand dollars' worth of new bridgework ruined. My father had to leave town for a few weeks while Monsignor Meehan cooled off the law.

But going to France, commanding men in battle, dealing with people in the ward made my father and a lot of other Irish-Americans outgrow that early anger. I'll never forget the night I realized this.

Answering the doorbell, I confronted a small snub-nosed man in a velvet-collared coat that had seen better days. He asked to speak to my father. I said I would see if he was at home.

My father was upstairs in his bedroom, dressing to spend the evening at the Sixth Ward Club. When I told him the man's name, he frowned. "He's the son of the guy that owned the old watch factory," he said. "They went bankrupt last year. He' s looking for a job."

My father went downstairs. I hung over the second-floor railing above the stairwell, expecting to hear a parable of Irish vengeance acted out. I was totally disappointed. My father greeted the man courteously and they discussed where he might find work. My father finally decided the man's training as an accountant might win him a slot at the IRS. He promised to put in a word for him at City Hall.

I asked my father why he hadn't made the ruined Protestant scion crawl. Had he forgotten what they made him do at the watch factory? My father looked at me with mild disapproval. "That happened a long time ago," he said.

Many years later, while I was writing books about the American Revolution, I came across the motto of the greatest Irish-American of 1776, Charles Carroll of Maryland. He said as Irish "we must remember – and forgive." I was stunned to realize I had seen my father, who never got beyond the eighth grade in All Saints School, act out that profound – and profoundly difficult – advice in Jersey City.

When I was finishing my novel *Rulers of the City*, I found myself in a bind. The mayor of my imaginary city, which has strong resemblances to Jersey City, is trying to cope with a busing crisis. He's the son of the old era's ward leaders. His liberal Protestant wife is giving him hell from one side and his ethnic Democratic supporters are doing the same thing from the other side. The mayor finds himself wishing for the good old days, when the Organization could settle things with orders from City Hall and a few nightsticks.

In the book, the mayor digs out his father's papers and starts to read the letters he got as a ward leader, the speeches he made. I did the same thing in real time. There were letters of thanks for favors, from canceling a bill at the Medical Center to reports on how a son or daughter was doing in a new job in Trenton or Washington. There were copies of those speeches telling the voters of the Sixth Ward, a mix of Irish, Poles, Czechs, Slovaks, Italians and blacks, "You are my people."

The mayor, in concert with the author, realizes the only thing worth preserving from the old organization was the caring. The rest of it, the world where all the answers were written in advance in the Baltimore catechism and the okay from City Hall – they were probably well rid of it.

The caring. Caring about people of every race and creed, because they're fellow Americans – and hopefully – but not necessarily – Democrats.

I like to think that idea, that political and spiritual reality, is what the Irish-American years have left as a heritage for Jersey City.

Thomas Fleming's most recent novel, Dreams of Glory, *set during the American Revolution, was published in October 2000. "Irish Memories" first appeared in* Irish America *in November 1998.*

Donald Keough
Philanthropist

"Suddenly an Irish door has been opened in America, and across the country people with Irish in their blood have become not just more aware of it, but more interested in and proud of it."

Don Keough represents something fundamental in Irish American business – he is in many ways its chieftain and his involvement has had huge economic benefits for the Emerald Isle.

He has used his position, first as president and COO of Coca-Cola and then as chairman of investment bank Allen & Company, to tirelessly promote and encourage American involvement in Irish affairs, including philanthropy and the peace process.

As one of the most highly respected figures in American business, his word on these issues carries major sway. As a typical example of his quiet business diplomacy, he recently arranged for Microsoft chief Bill Gates, Berkshire Hathaway supremo Warren Buffet and other leading businessmen to visit Ireland.

Keough's love of Ireland and all things Irish has led to his continuing deep involvement in that country's economic development, and he went on to serve on the Taoiseach's (Irish Prime Minister) Economic Advisory Board, visiting Ireland several times in the process.

He is currently chairman of the board of Allen & Company, a New York investment banking company, having previously served as president of the Coca-Cola Company. He retired from Coca-Cola in 1993, after over 40 years of service.

A graduate of Creighton University and a navy veteran, Keough has been awarded an honorary doctorate from Trinity College Dublin, and is former chairman of the University of Notre Dame. He and his wife Marilyn endowed a chair of Irish Studies at Notre Dame in 1993. In October of last year, the Keough Notre Dame Center of Irish Studies was officially opened in Dublin.

Keough is a past recipient of the Laetare Medal, the highest award that can be bestowed by the home of the Fighting Irish. He has also been honored with the American Irish Historical Society's medal and was *Irish America's* Irish American of the Year in 1993.

Peter Lynch
Giver

"Investing is a passive business. You can't control the market. You just have to sit back. You have to understand you'll make mistakes. It's not your fault. If you're consistent and you keep doing it, you'll win."

Peter Lynch is much more than a smiling face on a billboard or in a television ad – he is the most successful money manager in the history of Wall Street. His know-how led the Fidelity Magellan Fund to grow an astonishing 2,800 percent over 13 years, a feat which has afforded him the fiscal freedom to do what he likes best: give his money away.

Lynch retired from the Magellan Fund in 1990 to devote his time to non-profit work and spend

Scott G. McNealy
Sun King

"I want Sun to be controversial. If everyone believes in your strategy, you have zero chance of profit."

Sun Microsystems, a company that Scott McNealy helped to found in 1982, is the quintessential Silicon Valley success story. In just 16 years, the company has become the leading global supplier of networked computer systems, and for more than a decade, McNealy has been advancing Sun's vision and slogan – "The network is the computer."

The company is listed in the Fortune 500, and was described by *Fortune* as the best qualified company to "seed the growth of the Internet." According to *Business Week*, Sun Microsystems "can claim to be the only pure play in the business."

The Wall Street Journal says the California computer company "has long been praised for its accomplished, if cocky, management team and a history of innovation." This is mainly attributable to Java, says the *Journal*, the computer language that Sun is pushing to challenge Microsoft.

McNealy is a native of Columbus, Indiana, and graduated from Harvard with a degree in economics. He also earned an MBA at Stanford University and is married with two young sons.

more time with his wife and family. Earlier this year, he and wife Carolyn donated more than $10 million to Boston College's School of Education, easily the largest individual gift ever made to the College.

A 1965 graduate of Boston College and a member of its board of trustees, Lynch is also a best-selling author. Two of his titles, *One Up on Wall Street* and *Beating the Street*, sold over one million copies and have been translated into several languages, including Chinese, German, Korean, Polish, Swedish, Spanish and French.

Lynch's great-grandparents, on both his father's and mother's side, are from County Kerry. He and his wife have three daughters.

Andrew Mellon
Philanthropist

One of the most prominent and certainly one of the wealthiest businessmen of the century, Andrew Mellon played a major role in the development of industry, balancing the national economy and the development of philanthropic institutions.

The son of Thomas Mellon, a native of County Tyrone, Mellon was born in 1855, in Pittsburgh, Pennsylvania. He studied at Western University of Pennsylvania, but left school to run his father's lumber and building business. Observing his son's business acuity, Thomas Mellon transferred ownership of his private banking firm, T. Mellon and Sons, to Andrew in 1882.

Under Andrew Mellon's leadership, the firm flourished by identifying and investing in companies with growth potential at a time of huge technological advances. The bank became the principal stock holder and developer of such Company of America (Alcoa), Gulf Oil, United States Steel and the Standard Steel Car Company. Mellon also contributed to the building of the Panama Canal, the George Washington Bridge and New York's Waldorf-Astoria Hotel. In 1902, T. Mellon and Sons incorporated as Mellon Bank.

Mellon became financially involved in conservative Republican Pennsylvania politics and when Warren G. Harding was elected President in 1920, he asked Mellon to become Secretary of the Treasury, a position he kept into the Hoover administration. In 1932, President Hoover appointed Mellon Ambassador to Great Britain, where he assisted in implementing the war debt moratorium and advised on international finance.

A private art collector, he left his collection of classic paintings and sculpture to the federal government in 1937 to establish the National Gallery of Art in Washington, D.C. The collection was valued at more than $35 million. Mellon did not wish the institution to bear his name in the hopes that it would prompt the giving of others. He died in 1937, four years before the gallery's completion.

Library of Congress

Thomas J. Moran
Community Leader

"When the scientists finish the human genome project, I am certain that they will find a gene that calls us back to the home of our ancestors, no matter how long we have been gone."

He is passionate about the ongoing struggle to find peace in Northern Ireland, and about the importance of securing adequate economic investment in the troubled area, but Tom Moran has also taken the time to ensure that he sees the issue from both sides.

To this end he was one of the people who invited Democratic Unionist Party leader David Ervine to speak at a National Committee on American Foreign Policy luncheon in 1999.

honors, he has been awarded the Calvary Medal, the Ellis Island Medal of Honor and the Terence Cardinal Cooke Award.

His ancestors come from Kesh in Fermanagh and Carrick-on-Suir in Tipperary, and Moran travels to Ireland frequently for both business and pleasure. A dedicated Harley Davidson enthusiast, he lives in New York City with his wife Joan.

Thomas Murphy
Media Giant
"I think it's an Irish thing, this ability to sell and get along with everybody."

One thing is certain, Thomas Murphy has mastered the art of making a deal. After building a bankrupt television station in Albany into the Capital Cities empire, he ended up taking over media giant ABC in 1985 in a $3.5 billion deal. Ten years later, he turned around and sold Capital Cities/ABC to Disney for $19 billion. To illustrate the magnitude of Murphy's business success, a $10,000 stock investment in his nearly bankrupt Albany company all those years ago would have yielded $10 million today. What happened in those intervening years to explain such a turnaround? Quite simply, Murphy and the media revolution.

Ervine is widely regarded as one of the most impressive speakers on the Northern Ireland issue, and the event held at the New York City headquarters of Mutual of America ensured that he would be exposed to member of the community who may not previously have had a chance to hear his thoughts.

As president and chief executive officer of Mutual of America, one of the nation's preeminent insurance companies, Moran is a familiar face in the business world, and also in philanthropic circles, where he is well known for his long-time dedication to several Irish American humanitarian and community causes.

Concern Worldwide, the Irish relief organization, and Project Children, which every year brings children from Northern Ireland to the U.S. on vacation, have long been on the receiving end of his quiet assistance and generosity. Moran serves on several boards, including the National Center for Disability Services, the National Committee on American Foreign Policy, and the United Way of New York City. He is also a member of the Ireland Chamber of Commerce in the U.S.A. and the chairman of the North American Board of the University College Dublin Graduate School of Business. Among other

Murphy was born in Brooklyn, the son of a New York State Supreme Court Judge, and a descendent of natives of Birr, County Offaly. He attended Princeton University for a year before he joined the Navy in 1943. They Navy sent Murphy to Cornell University to study engineering. After his Navy tour ended, he tried to enroll at Harvard Business School but was told, because of his tender age (he was 21 at the time), to go and work for a year and then reapply. His second attempt was more successful: Murphy ended up a Baker Scholar and he graduated with the class of 1949, famed for its extraordinarily high percentage of success stories.

Murphy spent some time at an advertising agency and as director of new products for Lever Brothers, but he really wanted to run his own company. So when the opportunity came for him to take over a bankrupt UHF station in Albany he jumped at it.

Under Murphy's leadership, the station turned around, eventually buying stations in Raleigh/Durham, North Carolina and Providence, Rhode Island and becoming Capital Cities. It was to be the start of an empire.

Tony O'Reilly
The CEO

"I never really left Ireland. I feel a sense of loyalty, commitment and, indeed, debt to Ireland."

With an estimated personal fortune of over a billion dollars, Dr. Anthony J.F. O'Reilly is Ireland's richest man; his influence in business and control in the Irish media is matched only by his desire to give something back to his homeland.

One way he seeks to repay his sense of indebtedness to Ireland is through his commitment to contributing to a peaceful resolution to the conflict in Northern Ireland, and he hopes the aid supplied through the various Ireland funds will do just that. And indeed they have helped as no Irish fund has – last year The American Ireland Fund alone awarded more than $12 million in grants to almost 250 organizations throughout Ireland.

As chairman and former chief executive officer of international food group H.J. Heinz, O'Reilly is also one of the most influential men in Ireland through his stake in the Independent Newspaper Group. But it is his involvement as co-founder of The American Ireland Fund and the other Ireland Funds in Canada, Australia, Great Britain, France, Germany and New Zealand that affirms his continuing loyalty to his native Ireland.

Born in Dublin in 1936, O'Reilly studied law at University College Dublin. At age 25, he became the general manager of An Bord Bainne, the Irish state-owned dairy processing group. During his tenure there, he launched Kerrygold, the most successful Irish brand name ever. O'Reilly left to work for Heinz in 1968, and within 11 years became CEO of the Pittsburgh-based group, which has 38,000 employees worldwide.

O'Reilly also has other extensive business interests, including roles in Fitzwilton and Waterford Wedgewood, both internationally branded companies. Married to Greek heiress

Chryss Goulandris, he has homes in Dublin, Kildare, Cork, Pittsburgh and the Bahamas. The father of six children, he is a keen rugby fan, having played as an amateur for Ireland in his youth.

John Quinn
Patron of the Arts

"Ulysses may not be the final thing. But it may lead to a new literary form."

In the correspondence of W.B. Yeats, Lady Gregory, John Millington Synge, Ezra Pound and James Joyce one name is continually repeated – John Quinn. When this New York lawyer died in 1924, there were few people in the world of art who didn't know his name. Today, unfortunately, there are few who do.

Quinn was, quite simply, one of the driving forces behind the Irish literary renaissance, alternately supporting, advising and sometimes protecting the luminaries of Irish art and literature in the early part of the century. He was also an avid collector of art and original manuscripts. Along with his collection of paintings, be owned all of Joseph Conrad's manuscripts and the first draft of T.S. Eliot's *Waste Land*.

But what is most remarkable about this accomplished man was his unstinting generosity to Irish artists. When the American public did not know what to make of the work of Yeats, Synge or Joyce, Quinn served as the writers' interpreter and champion.

The Yeats family were undoubtedly the ones who benefited most from Quinn's generosity. He arranged W.B. Yeats' first North American tour in 1903–04, providing the poet much-needed exposure. He was also supporter and adviser to J.B. Yeats, the poet's father, supporting him in his declining years. In fact J.B. Yeats is buried in the Quinn family plot in Chestertown, New York. Quinn also supported Jack Yeats' career and

Cuala Industries, run by the Yeats sisters.

But Lady Gregory, John Millington Synge, James Joyce and other Irish artists also enjoyed Quinn's support. When Lady Gregory and her touring company's production of Synge's *Playboy of the Western World* ran into censorship difficulties in Pennsylvania, Quinn was their defense lawyer. Quinn also bought and exhibited several paintings by George Russell (A.E.).

Quinn advised John Millington Synge about navigating the business of publishing, secured copyrights and settled contracts for the young writer. He also provided moral and financial support for Douglas Hyde, founder of The Gaelic League, who became the first president of Ireland. It seems that no member of the Irish literary revival went untouched by Quinn's insight and generosity.

James Joyce also benefited from Quinn's patronage, gladly selling him original manuscripts. At one point Joyce expressed concern that Quinn had paid him too much for the manuscript of *Portrait of the Artist as a Young Man*. While Quinn found Joyce difficult, he was continually drawn to his writing, and so he kept sending the checks. He tried to advise Joyce as well, but was usually ignored.

It was Quinn who also argued the case for the publication of *Ulysses* in the U.S., developing the highly unusual defense that the book could not corrupt because it was incomprehensible. While he did not win the case, his argument was later the basis for the decision 12 years later to allow *Ulysses* to be published in the U.S.

When Quinn succumbed to cancer at the age of 54, his will stipulated that all of his holdings of art be sold at public auction, allowing other art lovers to enjoy these treasures the way he had. For his vision of the future of art, and generosity with both time and money, all lovers of literature and art owe John Quinn an immense debt of gratitude.

Michael J. Roarty
Marketing Wizard

"I hope that as Irish Americans we will always be mindful of the heritage of our ancestors, and know that we too suffered our discriminatory phase and that the knowledge will help us understand others."

Michael Roarty was one of the pioneering Irish American businessman who forged new links between America and Ireland and created a philanthropic and business connection which is flourishing today. Before it became popular or fashionable, Roarty began doing business in Ireland.

As executive vice president and director of marketing at Anheuser-Busch, Inc., Roarty was the key figure behind Anheuser-Busch's sponsorship of the Irish Derby and the beer company's expansion into Ireland, where Budweiser now has the leading market share.

Though now retired from Anheuser-Busch, Roarty continues to have a positive influence on business in Ireland through his leadership of the

Ireland – United States Council for Commerce and Industry, Inc.

Founded in 1963 to assist in the exchange of views and ideas between key businesspeople and policy makers in the U.S. and Ireland, the Council brings together leading business-people from the Irish American community and also funds an internship program which brings Irish students to the U.S. each summer to work with participating companies.

Roarty, born in Detroit to Mayo and Donegal immigrants, is also a member of the Taoiseach's (Irish Prime Minister) Economic Advisory Board in the United States. A wonderful master of ceremonies, he is known for his good humor and wit.

He and his wife Lee have three children and live in Missouri.

Dan Rooney
Silent Hero

The highly respected owner of the famed Pittsburgh Steelers, Dan Rooney's example – the pursuit of excellence, not glamour – has had a positive influence throughout the National Football League. Even though the Steelers haven't reached the Super Bowl in recent years, Rooney's stature within the league continues to grow. Why? Because in the money-driven

madness that surrounds sports in this country, Rooney has remained a voice of reason, a reminder that the game and the people are really what it is about.

In his 44 years with the Pittsburgh Steelers, Dan Rooney has distinguished himself as one of the most active, and present, executives in the NFL. He goes to the stadium every day, and unlike many owners, he genuinely likes the players. A central figure in the NFL for almost 30 years, his league functions have included membership on the board of directors for NFL Trust Fund, NFL Films and the Scheduling Committee.

Rooney was appointed president of the Steelers in 1975, and has a reputation for having developed and molded a model professional sports franchise with his characteristic low-key approach.

His dedication to the Steelers is matched by his dedication to Ireland. A co-founder of the Ireland Fund (1976), he has served on the board of the Ireland Fund and The American Ireland Fund. One of the hardest-working members on the board, he is credited with building The American Ireland Fund from the ground up.

He is also the driving force behind the Rooney Prize for Literature, a prize awarded annually in

Newry, County Down, for academic merit. Rooney and his wife Pat have also established and supported two named funds in The American Ireland Fund. They recently gave $1 million to The American Ireland Fund to support educational efforts throughout the island of Ireland.

John T. Sharkey
Benefactor

John T. Sharkey retired from MCI in 1999, but not before making a lasting contribution to the company. As vice president for Corporate National Accounts, Sharkey has played an integral role in the steady inroads MCI has made into the global telecommunications market.

But MCI isn't the only place that Sharkey has left his mark. Ireland is a better place for his involvement there.

Sharkey's grandparents came from Counties Tyrone and Roscommon, and the importance of his heritage is reflected in his involvement with several Irish organizations, including Belfast's Flax Trust and The American Ireland Fund. In fact, The American Ireland Fund was recently the recipient of Sharkey's generosity in the form of a $1 million gift. He is also a founding charter member of the Ireland Chamber of Commerce in the U.S.A. The Smurfit Business School at University College Dublin has named Ireland's

first Chair in Electronic Commerce in his honor in recognition of his long-time commitment to charitable causes in Ireland and the U.S.

Sharkey was also a member of the delegation which traveled to Ireland for President Clinton's historic trip in 1995 and he headed a delegation from 30 American companies which traveled to Dublin and Belfast in 1998.

Raised in New York's Hell's Kitchen, Sharkey is a graduate of Iona College and the Management Institute at New York University. He and his wife Helen live in New York City.

Jack Welch
Electric Leader

"Tell people the truth, because they know the truth anyway."

Jack Welch is, in a nutshell, the world's greatest business leader. *Business Week* magazine has extolled him as "the gold standard against which other CEOs are measured."

A second-generation Irish American, Welch was born in Peabody, Massachusetts. His father worked for the Boston & Maine Railroad, while his mother was a homemaker. Welch believes he benefited from being an only child, that he was loved, praised and nurtured more than many children, and as a result developed the confidence necessary to succeed.

Welch was especially close to his mother, and it was from her that he learned three important lessons that have contributed to his wild success: to communicate candidly, to face reality, and to control your own destiny.

Welch earned a degree in chemical engineering from the University of Massachusetts. He recalls his years at UMass as crucial in bolstering his self-esteem. He made the dean's list four years in a row and at his professors' encouragement went on to earn a Ph.D. in engineering.

After finishing graduate school, Welch joined General Electric in 1960. Through his aggressive

marketing of the company's plastics, materials, and consumer goods services, he steadily moved up the corporate ladder until he was appointed GE's youngest-ever chairman and CEO in 1981. Understanding the demands of a new high-tech, global environment, Welch immediately sought to bring about dramatic and swift change at GE. In a step that some have described as ruthless, but others call "masterful strategic planning," Welch redefined GE's areas of concentration and mandated that the company rank number one or number two in everything it did. Enterprises that did not measure up were sold. The negative impacts of this mandate were 132,000 layoffs, 73 plant closings and more than 200 sales of products or businesses. The positive results were the acquisition of RCA in 1985 and the overall transformation of an industrial giant into a flexible, entrepreneurial organization widely regarded as the best-managed company in the world, and one of the most profitable. The numbers tell the whole story: Since Jack Welch became chairman in 1981, GE's market capitalization has grown from $12 billion to nearly $260 billion in 1998.

Welch takes great pride in his Irish heritage and is a past recipient of the Ellis Island Medal of Honor.

Two Grandfathers

BY WILLIAM KENNEDY

Grandfather Peter McDonald is fifth from right.

My grandfathers, George Kennedy and Peter McDonald, died before I was born. I came to know something of them through talks with my parents and other relatives, a few artifacts, death certificates and obituaries, and two photographs that defined them for me forever. Both photos are working-class portraits.

The portrait of George Kennedy is with three other men who are, I believe, from the Albany Water Department. They are pausing in their work on the granite blocks and water lines of an Albany street to pose with their tools – shovel, pickax, two-handed valve wrench, wheelbarrow – and George, second from left, holding a pry bar. He has a stubble of white whiskers in the photo, looks hunched and grizzled, and was probably near the end of his life. He is wearing a vest and a gold-plated chain for his pocket watch. I inherited the chain, perhaps also the watch, but I can't be sure the watch was his. The chain is functional;

the watch (whoever owned it) doesn't work.

George had come to Albany in 1880 at age 20 from County Tipperary, worked as a laborer and risen to become yardmaster at the George H. Thatcher & Co. foundry, which made railroad car wheels for the New York Central Railroad. He eventually brought over two of his brothers and two sisters, who all settled in Albany. He died in March 1923 of lobar pneumonia at age 63. His wife, Hannora Ryan (remembered as the sweetest of women, and who came from the next town over from George in Tipperary), had died in February 1896, also of lobar pneumonia, at age 29. My father, William, said she never recovered from the birth of his sister, Mary, some months earlier.

The Kennedys lived on Van Woert Street, a long, almost solidly Irish block at the edge of Albany's Arbor Hill but considered part of North Albany, when my father was born in 1887.

Grandfather George Kennedy is second from left.

They later moved to a house next door to an ice house. In 1890, when my father was three, somebody torched the ice house; the Kennedy house went with it and the family lost everything. George moved from yet another home on Lawrence Street so my father wouldn't have to cope with the horse and carriage traffic when he went to school, and finally, he moved back to Van Woert Street and stayed there.

In George Kennedy's photo with the work gang his days of authority as yardmaster are behind him, as is his time as foreman at the Rathbone, Sard & Co. foundries (500 men employed, among them my father, who did piece work as a stove mounter, but quit when the wages per piece dropped from $1.35 to $.55). The iron and steel business went west toward the coalfields, and the coal stoves my father was mounting were made obsolete by the advent of gas. The times turned against George Kennedy, and in his late days he was again a simple laboring man.

I have a photo of a slightly younger George with his daughter, Mary, taken in 1917 when she was 22. George is at his social best: clean shaven, hair tidily combed, wearing a dark suit, striped shirt with white collar, dark tie and the watch chain. He looks strong; he is square jawed and handsome in this photo, but there is a grimness to his mouth and his eyes are sad. He lived the last 27 years of his life without his sweet wife, without a woman in the house, except when one of his sisters came by to clean the place. He could not raise the baby Mary and also work, so he raised only my father, a wild, electric boy who was nine when his mother died. Hannora's maiden sister raised Mary until she married.

The street photo of George came to me from Mary in the 1960s, and I was so moved by it that I thought of having it blown up to poster size as a way of advertising my origin, but that seemed as pretentious as trying to deny an origin. So I let it go unsung until now, when the chance to write about it thrust me into a search of the family archives and led to my first conversation with Mary Craig Hurley, 89, who lived on Van Woert Street, directly across from George.

Mary remembers George from 80 years gone. She sees him about 1912, when she is nine and he is 52, at a Van Woert Street house party – "all of Van Woert Street would be there" – and again at the annual clambake in Donovan's backyard. George is always dancing and singing "The Stack of Barley", an Irish reel.

"He did a marvelous dance," Mary says, "and he had a good singing voice. I remember the words that he sang: 'Oh my little stack of barley was the cause of all my misery . . .' He was a wonderful man, a good-livin' man."

I am sure George Kennedy knew my mother's father, Peter McDonald, who was born in Albany and lived on Colonie Street, a block away from Van Woert.

Peter's photo, which hung in a reverential space in our kitchen all my early life, is with a train and track crew, all standing with Engine 151 of the Central. (Everybody in the family played 151 when Clearing House, the numbers game, was vogue.) Peter is fifth from right, handsome, wearing a stylish scarf under his jacket and overalls, the only man in the photo so garbed. Swift Mead, an old-time boxer and saloonkeeper, said of Peter: "He was a dressed-up guy, always with a clean uniform. A hardworkin' man."

Peter began as a laborer and rose to become passenger locomotive engineer on Engine 151. He was given a medal for making a record-breaking run with the Twentieth Century, the Central's greatest train, from Albany to Buffalo. The medal has been lost and the record of the run I haven't yet found. But I believe it was a true record, for his children – my mother, Mary, my Uncle Peter, and my Aunt Katherine – would not have invented such braggadocio.

Peter fathered five children, two of whom did not survive infancy. He took sick in April 1916; the sickness lingered and he died in January 1918 of pleural pneumonia and myocarditis at age 43. His widow, Annie Carroll, the only grandparent I knew, lived with us and helped raise me. She died of complications after a stroke in 1951. I can't remember her mentioning Peter, but I believe they had a very good marriage.

I inherited Peter's scuffed black leather wallet in which he kept a record, during his illness, of his 107 visits to and by an Arbor Hill doctor, Marcus D. Cronin. In the last seven days of Peter's life Dr. Cronin came to the house twice a day. The doctor bills came to $96, which my grandmother paid in two installments, in May and December 1918.

At the time of Peter's death, both of his daughters were working in an office and supporting their mother and rambunctious young brother, Pete. I have very few memories from any of the three about their father. They were effusive in their love for him, but his death was four decades gone when I began to ask questions. I did inherit that wallet and his railroad pass for 1913, and military enrollment papers for World War I; also a postcard he sent to my mother in 1913 when she was at Camp Tekakwitha on Lake Luzerne in the Adirondacks. "Howdy toots," he wrote her. "Don't get drowned." He said he was taking an engineer's exam Monday and signed it P.A.P.

A clipping with his obituary was also in the wallet. "Mr. McDonald was stricken with an attack of pleural pneumonia about six months ago and it greatly weakened his heart. He had made a wonderful fight against great odds for the past few months, but his condition had been gradually growing worse up to yesterday when his heart finally gave out." They don't write obits like they used to.

The photographs of Peter and George are close to being terminal images: George, old in his 60s; Peter in his prime, at his career summit, a few years from a wasting early death. If you block off the chin stubble, George looks like my father. Peter looks like his son, Peter. My father inherited from George the love of song and dance (he was a prize waltzer), and Peter and his sisters inherited the wit that kept me laughing all my life. Neither inheritance shows up in the photos, but what is there are starting points for a continuity of family and meaning. These men – widower and widow-maker – are emblematic of what their children became and of what they passed on to us, the next generation: a veneration of ancestors, an appreciation of the working class, a bemusement with genetic gifts.

We really can't know how guardedly, how limitedly, they lived, any more than they could have imagined life in the space age.

Even my father didn't believe it when men walked on the moon. "You damn fool," he told me when we were watching them on television in 1969, "you can't get to the moon."

The streets and houses and people my grandfathers knew, the jobs they held – most are gone now, or obsolete. But George and Peter aren't. There they are, standing for their portrait photos, offering up the gift and the challenge of creative memory. They look into the camera and say to us, "We were, now you are." Anything after that is found gold.

William Kennedy won a Pulitzer Prize for Ironweed, *one of his six novels. Other novels in his 'Albany cycle' include* Legs *and* Billy Phelan's Greatest Game.

Community

Educators

Explorers

Margaret Tobin Brown
The Unsinkable Molly Brown

"I'm unsinkable."

Margaret Tobin Brown was reading a book in her first-class cabin on the *Titanic* when she heard a crash and was thrown to the floor by the impact. Pulling herself up, she went out into the corridor to investigate and saw her fellow passengers standing around in their nightwear. It was then she noticed that the engines had stopped. She went up on deck and was flung into a lifeboat with thirteen other people, three men and ten women. Amid the confusion and fear, Maggie promptly took command, organizing the other passengers of the small boat to row and buoying their spirits with her indomitable personality.

After her boat was picked up by the *Carpathia* shortly after dawn the next day, Maggie continued to help with rescue efforts. Even before the *Carpathia* docked in New York, she had nearly $10,000 worth of pledges. She later helped to form a committee of other wealthy survivors to help destitute victims of the disaster.

When she finally arrived in New York, she told a reporter that she attributed her survival to "typical Brown luck . . . We're unsinkable." Years later, she gained the nickname "Molly Brown," and was immortalized as "The Unsinkable Molly Brown" in Meredith Willson's Broadway musical.

The daughter of Irish immigrants, Brown was born Margaret Tobin on July 18, 1867 in Hannibal, Missouri. She received little formal education and found work in her early teens as a waitress. Around 1884, she moved to Leadville, Colorado, after having purportedly been told by one of her customers, Samuel Clemens (Mark Twain), about the wealth that could be found in the Rockies. In Leadville, she met James Joseph (J.J.) Brown, the manager of a silver mine. The two married in 1886 and had two children, Helen and Lawrence.

J.J. made a small fortune in a gold find and he and Maggie moved to Denver. Maggie sought to enter Denver society but met with little success. After she and her husband separated, she began traveling throughout Europe with her son, Lawrence, where through her persistence and flamboyant personality she gained acceptance into the society of a group of wealthy Americans.

In 1912, she was touring Europe when she received word that her grandson, Lawrence Palmer, Jr., was ill. Brown immediately made arrangements to return to the States, booking her passage on the *Titanic*.

After the disaster, Brown used her money and newfound fame on behalf of a variety of causes, including women's suffrage and local Catholic charities. She also led one of Denver's first preservation projects when she spearheaded the movement to save the home of Denver poet Eugene Field. She even ran for the U.S. Senate three times, failing to win each time. Brown's declining years were spent traveling between Denver, New York and Newport, Rhode Island. At age 65, she suffered a stroke and died on October 26, 1932 at New York's Barbizon Hotel.

Corbis / Bettmann - UPI

Photo courtesy Marquette University Archives

Dorothy Day
Heroine

"Don't call me a saint. I don't want to be dismissed so easily."

From time to time there comes an individual whose life exposes the limitations of the written word. Dorothy Day was such a person. Her strength, singularity and ability to nudge humankind a little further up the ladder of emotional and spiritual evolution goes beyond language.

As a journalist, peace activist and founder of the Catholic Worker movement, Day's combination of radical politics and commitment to social justice broke new ground for the American Catholic Church. While her unyielding pacifism provoked criticism during her lifetime, she has now come to be considered heroic, even holy, for her steadfast commitment to non-violence, so much so that there is a movement to have her canonized.

Day was born in Brooklyn, New York on November 8, 1897 but spent most of her childhood in Chicago. Her father, John Day, was a newspaperman and when Dorothy was about eight years old, he went through a period of unemployment. The family was forced to move into a tenement flat over a tavern in Chicago's South Side. Day was so ashamed of her home that on leaving school in the evenings she would enter a fancier, more impressive building so that her classmates would not know where she really lived. Her father eventually found work again and the family moved to a large, comfortable house on the North Side, but Dorothy's memories of the grinding shame of poverty would never leave her.

Of Presbyterian Irish stock, Day became interested in Catholicism as a child. A formative moment came when she went to the house of a Catholic friend and found her friend's mother, Mrs. Barrett, on her knees in prayer. Remaining on her knees, Mrs. Barrett told Dorothy where her friend was and returned to her prayer. In her autobiography, *The Long Loneliness*, Day recalled, "I felt a burst of love toward Mrs. Barrett that I have never forgotten, a feeling of gratitude and happiness that warmed my heart." This memory fueled Day's own spiritual search and played a large role in her later conversion to Catholicism.

At the same time, books like *Les Miserables*, *Bleak House*, *Little Dorritt* and Upton Sinclair's *The Jungle* were increasing her awareness of social injustice and suffering of the poor. Prompted by her reading, Day began to explore the poorer neighborhoods of Chicago, and discovered in poverty a wealth that went beyond money. She was only 15 years old with a social awareness that went beyond her years.

An excellent student, Day won a scholarship to the University of Illinois at Urbana and enrolled at the age of 16. Refusing her family's financial assistance, she supported herself through a variety of jobs, washing, ironing and caring for children. When she was 18, she left school and moved to New York to work as a journalist for various socialist and left-wing publications.

It was in New York that Day's social activism truly began. In 1917, she was one of 40 women arrested in front of the White House for protesting women's suffrage. It was the first of many visits to the interior of a jail cell.

Meanwhile, her fascination with the spiritual discipline of the Catholic Church continued to grow. The turning point occurred in 1926. She was living on Staten Island with her common-law husband, Forster Batterham, when she found out she was pregnant. She had undergone an abortion several years previously and it proved to be the greatest regret of her life.

She believed that the damage her womb sustained left her incapable of carrying another child. To Day, this second pregnancy was nothing short of a miracle and she could think of no better way to express her gratitude to God than to raise her child a Catholic.

When Tamar Theresa Day was born, Day went against the wishes of her common-law husband and had the baby baptized. "I did not want my child to flounder as I had often floundered. I wanted to believe, and I wanted my child to believe, and if belonging to the church would give her so inestimable a grace as faith in God . . . then the thing to do was have her baptized a Catholic."

The baby's baptism ended Day's relationship with Batterham. While she still loved him, her now unshakable faith in God could no longer coexist with his complete lack of faith. On December 28, 1927, Day herself was baptized a Catholic.

In the years that followed, Day tried to find a way to combine her Catholic faith with her radical social values. Her chance came in the winter of 1932 when she met Peter Maurin, a French immigrant strongly influenced by the teachings of St. Francis of Assisi. Maurin encouraged Day to start a paper that would publicize Catholic social teaching and promote a peaceful transformation of society. *The Catholic Worker* was born.

A combination of the radical and the religious, *The Catholic Worker* challenged capitalism and the existing social order while remaining rooted in the Bible and Catholic teachings. Around the paper grew a national movement that combined works of mercy, such as feeding the hungry and housing the homeless in "hospitality houses", with working actively for peace, labor and civil rights.

Unlike many charitable houses, the Catholic Worker houses made no attempt to convert those who came through its doors. When a social worker once asked Day how long "clients" were allowed to stay, Day responded, "We let them stay forever. . . Once they are taken in they become members of the family. They are our brothers and sisters in Christ."

What earned Day the greatest amount of criticism, but has proved to be her greatest contribution, was her commitment to pacifism. During the Spanish Civil War, the Catholic Church by and large threw its support behind Franco, the fascist who styled himself the defender of the Catholic faith. *The Catholic Worker* refused to support either side and lost two-thirds of its readership as a result. Throughout World War II, the Cold War, the Korean War and the Vietnam War, Day continued to speak out against violence, leading acts of civil disobedience and often getting arrested. During the 1950s, Day led the Catholic Worker community in its refusal to participate in civil defense drills. Day believed that preparing for nuclear attack prompted the belief that nuclear war was winnable and that it justified military spending. "We do not have faith in God if we depend upon the Atom Bomb," one *Catholic Worker* leaflet explained.

In 1963 and 1965, Day traveled to Rome to encourage the Vatican to speak out against violence. She and her fellow pacifists had reason to celebrate when in December 1965 the church issued the Constitution on the Church in the Modern World. The Constitution described any act of war that indiscriminately destroyed vast areas with their inhabitants as "a crime against God and humanity." It also called for legal provisions for conscientious objectors while describing "criminal" those who obey commands which condemn the innocent and defenseless.

For her achievements Day received many honors. As part of the Council of the Laity in 1967, she was one of two Americans invited to receive Communion from the hands of the Pope. For her 75th birthday, the Jesuit magazine *America* devoted a special issue to her, celebrating her as the individual who best exemplified "the aspiration and action of the American Catholic community during the past forty years." Notre Dame University awarded her its Laetare Medal for "comforting the afflicted and afflicting the comfortable." When she was no longer able to travel, she received a visit from Mother Teresa of Calcutta, who pinned on her the cross worn only by fully professed Missionary Sisters of Charity.

Day passed away in 1980, and since her death she has been credited with restoring the Gospel's teachings on nonviolence to a place of prominence within the Catholic Church. She once remarked, "If I have achieved anything in my life, it is because I have not been embarrassed to talk about God." But more than that, she is one of the few who had the courage to act on their beliefs.

Loretta Brennan Glucksman
Keeping the Home Fires Burning

"I feel so welcomed and drawn in by my friends in Ireland. The more I know, the more I want to know."

"There has not been a great tradition of giving to Ireland – possibly because no one has asked,"

Loretta Brennan Glucksman once remarked. As national president of The American Ireland Fund, Glucksman has changed all that, and is personally leading a campaign to raise $100 million to promote peace and cultural and business opportunities in Ireland.

Glucksman credits her husband, Lewis, as the inspiration behind her commitment to serving Ireland's people. Together they donated $3 million to the center for Irish studies at New York University. Ireland's universities have also benefited from the Glucksmans' philanthropy, including Trinity College, University of Limerick and University College Dublin.

Brennan Glucksman – whose career has included teaching, television production and running her own public relations firm – also serves on the board of several Irish-related organizations, including the Irish American Cultural Institute, Cooperation Ireland and the Ireland-U.S. Council for Commerce and Industry.

She and her husband have five children and five grandchildren. They reside in Manhattan and also keep a home in Ireland.

Ellis Island Immigration Museum

Fr. Flanagan on arrival at Ellis Island.

Father Edward Flanagan
Saving Grace
"There's no such thing as a bad boy."

Spencer Tracy won an Academy Award for his stirring portrayal of Boys Town founder Father Edward Flanagan, but Flanagan surely earned something even greater for his three decades of public service: a place in heaven.

Born on July 13, 1886 in Leabeg, County Roscommon, Flanagan left Ireland for the States shortly after finishing high school in Sligo. His brother Patrick was a priest in Omaha, and Flanagan hoped to follow in his footsteps, but it was to take longer than he anticipated. Poor health delayed his vocation by a couple of years. He was finally ordained to the priesthood in 1912 in Innsbruck, Austria.

Within four years of his return to Omaha, he turned his eye to the disadvantaged youth of the area. In 1917 he opened his first shelter for less fortunate children. Originally called Father Flanagan's Boys' Home, it soon became known as Boys Town, and moved to larger facilities in 1922. Several new branches were to pop up across the state as the reputation of Boys Town spread.

While Flanagan did not believe in spoiling his young charges, he really cared for them and truly believed his oft-repeated maxim that there was "no such thing as a bad boy." At the request of President Harry Truman, he traveled internationally to study problems of juvenile welfare. Among his stops were Japan, Korea, Austria and Germany. It was on May 15, 1948, during a visit to Berlin, that he died of a heart attack.

In 1979, some 30 years after Flanagan's death, Boys Town finally caught up with the times, and young women began to be admitted. After his death the haven he established ceased to attract as much publicity, but Boys Town is still active today. Flanagan was buried at Boys Town's Dowd Memorial Catholic Chapel, where his epitaph reads: "Father Flanagan, Founder of Boys Town, Lover of Christ and Man."

John Cardinal O'Connor
Shepherd
"If my father had one passion above all else it was one of justice towards the working man. That's in my blood."

When John Cardinal O'Connor was elevated to the position of Archbishop of New York in 1984, he was a breath of fresh air for many Irish Americans. His concern and active participation in the affairs of Northern Ireland ran counter to the widespread sentiment that the Catholic

Church in the U.S. had withdrawn from any substantial involvement. His refusal to be cowed by politicians assured Irish Americans that in O'Connor they had a staunch ally.

Two examples stand out in particular: the Joe Doherty case and the 1985 New York St. Patrick's Day Parade. Joe Doherty, a member of the IRA, had been arrested in New York and held on an extradition warrant. Once, when Doherty was transferred to a remote prison in upstate New York, away from his friends and lawyers, it was O'Connor who demanded, and got, his return to New York City.

When Peter King, then comptroller of Nassau County, and a supporter of Sinn Féin and Noraid, was elected grand marshal of the St. Patrick's Day Parade in 1985, the Irish government tried to persuade O'Connor to boycott the parade. But the Cardinal clearly saw that his responsibility was to the people of New York, not a foreign government, and he participated in the parade after all.

Under O'Connor's leadership, the Archdiocese of New York has been the quickest to respond to the plight of illegal Irish immigrants, providing free counseling, medical care and social services.

Even though outspoken in his conservative views, he has won the respect of many liberals, including Paul O'Dwyer, the human rights advocate. "The strength of his leadership, so freely given in freedom's name, was never more needed," he once said. "His example lit the way for the timid and the fearful."

O'Connor was born in Scranton, Pennsylvania, and his childhood was once described as that of a "typical poor Irish kid of the Depression." His father, Thomas, the son of Roscommon immigrants, was very passionate about his Irish heritage. In an interview with *Irish America* magazine, O'Connor recalled, "You'd have thought Parnell was his brother-in-law the way he talked about him."

O'Connor's own interest in Ireland expanded while he was in the seminary. He read the works of Patrick Pearse, Joseph Mary Plunkett and Padraic Colum and the Irish poets of the time. As he rose through the ecclesiastical ranks, he visited his relatives in Ireland several times. Since being appointed Cardinal he traveled to Ireland as chairman of the committee for social developments and world peace of the National Conference of Bishops.

From 1979 to 1983, O'Connor served as bishop at the military vicariate in New York City. He spent a year as Bishop of Scranton, Pennsylvania before being called to return to New York to succeed Cardinal Cooke. And he wasted no time in distinguishing himself as a sincere and powerful advocate to New York Irish Americans.

Cardinal O'Connor passed away in May 2000 after battling brain cancer.

Richard Cardinal Cushing

One of the most influential and popular church leaders in America, Richard J. Cushing reined as Archbishop of Boston for 25 years. During this time Catholics emerged from the immigrant ghetto to break the barrier of prejudice with the election of John F. Kennedy to the office of president. Cushing gained national recognition as a friend and adviser of the Kennedy family and participated in the 1961 presidential

inauguration. But he was first and foremost a friend of the poor. He had genuine respect and love for the sick, the elderly and especially children in need and throughout his life he sought to improve their lot.

He was born in South Boston on August 23, 1895, the third of five children of Patrick and Mary Dahill Cushing. His parents were Irish immigrants and his father worked as a blacksmith. Cushing attended public elementary school and graduated from Boston College High School in 1913. After two years at Boston College he entered the seminary and was ordained in 1921. Assigned to the diocesan office of the Society for the Propagation of the Faith, he quickly gained a reputation for his ability to raise funds for the foreign missions.In 1939, he was ordained an auxiliary bishop, and five years later in 1944, he succeeded Cardinal William O'Connell as Archbishop of Boston. Immediately upon assuming office, he established the Archbishop Cushing Charity Fund, stating: "Our hospitals, schools, asylums for the aged and underprivileged must be cathedrals of the modern age."

Cushing was extremely inventive in his fundraising efforts, and Bostonians of all faiths supported his efforts by participating in the Archdiocesan Waste Paper Drive. He held benefit performances enticing popular stage and screen stars to take part. And whether it was a society ball or a parish bazaar, he offered citizens of every social class a chance to become involved in giving. Cushing was named cardinal in 1958. He died on November 2, 1970.

Paul O'Dwyer
Civil Rights Champion

"If you take my kind of position you expect to be defeated much of the time. It's as simple as that."

Paul O'Dwyer was one of this century's most outspoken, progressive defenders of the cause

of civil rights and justice, continually standing up in defense of the downtrodden, regardless of race, gender or creed. Time and again O'Dwyer stood up for what was right, regardless of the personal cost he would suffer. At the height of the Cold War when the country was seized by the Red scare, he was accused of having "Red sympathies" for speaking out against the "national witch-hunt" and for defending people accused of Communist sympathy.

His next battle was for the civil rights movement. In 1963, he was asked by the National Association for the Advancement of Colored People (NAACP) to defend a college teacher accused of inciting riot. O'Dwyer argued that her arrest violated her civil rights, and she was freed on a reduced charge. He also participated in the drive to give the vote to black residents of Mississippi.

In the late 1960s, O'Dwyer once again found himself at odds with the political establishment in his vigorous opposition to the Vietnam War. His stance cost him a U.S. Senate seat when he was branded as unpatriotic.

In spite of opposition from regular Democrats and *The New York Times*, O'Dwyer won the seat of City Council President in 1973 after the reform Democrats, trade unions and the Irish weeklies and minority papers rallied to support him.

Born in the parish of Bohola, County Mayo, O'Dwyer grew up during a time of immense turmoil in Ireland as the Easter Rising, the Black and Tan war, the partition of Ireland and the subsequent Civil War all played out.

The youngest of eleven children, he immigrated to New York City in the spring of 1925. He had been preceded by his four brothers, one of whom, Bill, he had never even met.

One year after his arrival, O'Dwyer enrolled in St. John's University Law School, paying his way with some assistance from his brothers and out of his wages working in the shipping department of a silk mill. He was admitted to the bar in 1931 and went on to become a partner in the prestigious New York law firm O'Dwyer and Bernstien.

Throughout his long career, O'Dwyer championed the underdog. Back in Ireland he co-founded the Cheshire Homes, to look after handicapped children and adults. The center in his native Bohola was a particular delight to him.

O'Dwyer was a driving force behind the election of David Dinkins as New York City's first black mayor. On an international level, he helped supply the Irgun in the battle for the creation of Israel. He represented the Iranian government after the Ayatollah Khomeini took power when no one would take their case; he made an issue of the rights of Native Americans; and of course, in his beloved Ireland he fiercely proclaimed the right to Irish unity. His republicanism, however, did not stop him being a pioneer in reaching out to loyalists and he helped draft the seminal Ulster Defense Association document "Common Ground", which played a major role in the politicization of paramilitary loyalism in Northern Ireland.

His brother Bill was Mayor of New York and later Ambassador to Mexico. Paul O'Dwyer died on June 26, 1998 in New York. At his wake his nephew Frank Durkan, also a civil rights attorney, said simply, "The fire never went out."

Margaret Higgins Sanger
Birth Control Pioneer

"No woman can call herself free until she can choose consciously whether she will or will not be a mother."

Historian H.G. Wells, writing in 1931, said: "When the history of our civilization is written, it will be a biological history, and Margaret Sanger will be its heroine."

Like many Irish and Irish American working- and middle-class women of her time, Anne Purcell Higgins had a tough life, gradually worn down by 18 pregnancies and the birth of 11 living children. She died at the young age of 40. This dilemma had a profound affect on her sixth child, Margaret, who would go on to do sterling work in family planning and on behalf of oppressed women everywhere.

Born September 4, 1879 in Corning, New York, to Purcell and Irish immigrant stone mason Michael Hennessy Higgins, young Margaret attended college in the Catskills and went on to train as a nurse at White Plains Hospital. Her first marriage, to architect William Sanger, ended in divorce after 18 years and three children. She subsequently married millionaire J. Noah Slee.

But Sanger was far from a lady of leisure, as she could well have afforded to be. She became active in socialism and the women's labor movement in 1912, and worked like a Trojan in the tenements of New York's Lower East Side, an experience which opened her eyes to the connection between poverty, premature death and lack of family planning.

It was Sanger who coined the term "birth control", and she was one of the most vociferous advocates for the legalization of contraception. In 1916, with the help of her sister Ethel Byrne, Sanger opened a birth control clinic in Brooklyn, a "crime" which earned her a 30-day prison sentence. Her second husband's wealth aided her in the establishment of the American Birth Control League and the Birth Control Research Bureau. In 1942, these two organizations came together to form Planned Parenthood, a group which is still going strong today, and believes strongly in birth control and legal abortion. Sanger was also behind the development of a contraceptive pill.

Sanger died on September 6, 1966, less than a year after the Supreme Court had repealed a Connecticut law that prohibited the use of contraception by married couples.

Andrew Greeley
Man of Many Collars

"The Irish are the most likely of all American ethnic groups to be in constant communication with their sister and their mother. And somewhat less so, but still ahead of everybody else, with their brothers and their father."

Sociologist, priest, historian, best-selling author, there's really no easy way to pigeonhole Chicago native Andrew Greeley, and that's just the way he likes it. "If you want to know what's happened to me, read the memoirs," he said in a 1999 interview. "But if you want to know me, read my novels."

The fact remains that he has done some of the most extensive research and analysis into the ethnic make-up of this country, and particularly into the history and role of the Irish in America. His book about the American Irish, *That Most Distressful Nation: The Taming of the American Irish*, is a groundbreaking work.

Born February 5, 1928 on Chicago's West Side, Greeley is the grandson of County Mayo immigrants. In a 1995 interview with *Irish America* he remarked that his sister traced his Irish consciousness back to his days at the University of Chicago, when he began to define himself as Irish in reaction to fellow sociology students who failed to see the importance of ethnic groups.

A Catholic priest since 1954, Greeley has been writing novels for over 20 years, with sales reaching 20 million plus. Many with Irish characters and themes, his books have entertained millions of readers for years. "I have to feel inside the skin of my characters," he told *Irish America* in 1986, "that's why they are all Irish."

But it is his tireless work as a sociologist which

really earns Greeley a place in the top Irish Americans of the century. His research has focused on such topics as contemporary issues facing the Catholic Church – including celibacy and female priests; and the decline of Irish Americans as an ethnic group.

Through his work as a research associate with the National Opinion Research Center (NORC) Greeley found in the late '70s that "in terms of education, occupation, and income, Irish Catholics are notably above the national average for other whites" and were more likely "to attend graduate school and choose academic careers" than were white Protestants.

Greeley is professor of social sciences at the University of Chicago, his alma mater, and at the University of Arizona. He holds an M.A. degree and a Ph.D. In 1986 he established a $1 million Catholic Inner-City School Fund, providing scholarships and financial support to schools in the Chicago Archdiocese. Two years earlier, he contributed a $1 million endowment to establish a chair in Roman Catholic Studies at the University of Chicago.

His numerous awards and honors include the 1993 U.S. Catholic Award for furthering the cause of women in the church and the 1987 Mark Twain Award from the Society for the Study of Midwestern Literature.

with his late wife Jeanette. His current pet project is Irish Educational Services, a program that enables Irish Americans to support children in education in Ireland.

Born to Irish parents from Counties Clare and Cavan in Manhattan, McKiernan has had a life-long immersion in all things to do with Ireland and education. Since the establishment of the Irish American Cultural Institute in 1964, the organization has been responsible for countless services, including the donation of hundreds of thousands of dollars to the arts in Ireland and the setting up of the Irish Way Program, which gives American high school students the opportunity every year to study and travel in Ireland.

McKiernan's honors from Ireland include an honorary doctorate from the National University of Ireland and the UDT Endeavor Award for Tourism. He is also the only American ever to have been made an Honorary Life Member of the Royal Dublin Society (RDS). He has also been honored by organizations such as the Wild Geese, the AOH and the Eire Society.

On this side of the Atlantic, he holds honorary doctorates from three American universities, all in addition to his earned doctorate in English literature from Pennsylvania State University. McKiernan has nine children. He now lives in Wisconsin.

Eoin McKiernan
Champion of Education

"We can give no greater evidence of our love for Ireland than to join in the race to further the achievement of Irish children."

Eoin McKiernan is widely acknowledged as one of the foremost authorities in the U.S. on Irish affairs, and includes on his resumé such job descriptions as author, lecturer, script writer, TV presenter, columnist and consultant. But Dr. McKiernan's best-known contribution is perhaps the Irish American Cultural Institute he founded

Helen Keller (left) and Annie Sullivan

Annie Sullivan
The Miracle Worker

"Children require guidance and sympathy far more than instruction."

The dynamic partnership of Annie Sullivan and Helen Keller is one that has inspired many books, movies and even a stage play.

When Helen Keller was born in Tuscumbia, Alabama, she was quite precocious, speaking her first word at only six months and taking her first steps at age one. Her early promise was cut down when at the age of 19 months she was stricken with what is now believed to be encephalitis. She pulled through, but her parents were horrified to learn that she was now blind and deaf.

Without any proper education, young Helen ran wild, and she was seven before someone was found to help her. That someone was 21-year-old Annie Sullivan, the daughter of Irish immigrants from County Limerick. Herself poorly sighted, Sullivan quickly proved to be an able teacher for Helen. In the early years of their work, she was both eyes and ears for Keller.

Before teaching Keller how to communicate, Sullivan first had to teach her young charge some simple discipline. They worked tirelessly together, and Keller finally, haltingly learned how to communicate again.

Sullivan taught her pupil by spelling words into Keller's hand. The two developed a language that grew very extensive and Keller also learned to read Braille. When she was ten, Keller also learned to speak clearly enough to be understood.

At the age of 19, with Sullivan's help, Keller took the entrance exam for Radcliffe College. The older woman sat beside her, spelling the questions into her hand. Keller graduated with honors from Radcliffe in 1904.

The two worked and traveled together for 50 years, during which time Sullivan married John Macy. Sullivan died in 1936, three decades before her young pupil. The highly regarded play *The Miracle Worker* by William Gibson tells her story. She is also portrayed in a book written by Keller, entitled *Teacher: Anne Sullivan Macy* (1955).

NASA

Eileen Collins
Rocket Woman

"I didn't get here alone. There are so many women throughout the century that have gone before me and have taken to the skies . . . Without them I wouldn't be here today."

On July 22, 1999, two days after the 30th anniversary of the first moonwalk, U.S.A.F. Col. Eileen Collins became the first woman to command a space shuttle. When she and her crew flew into space to launch the Chandra X-ray Observatory, the most advanced X-ray telescope ever flown, she, in the words of Hillary Clinton, took "one big step for women and one giant leap for humanity."

The second of the four children of Rose Marie and James Collins, both immigrants from County Cork, Eileen was born in Elmira, New York in 1956. She fell in love with flying while watching planes taking off and landing at a local airport. As a teenager she held various odd jobs to pay for her flying lessons, which she took while studying at Corning Community College. She received an ROTC scholarship to Syracuse University, earning a B.A. in mathematics and economics in 1978. She went on to earn an M.S. in operations research from Stanford University in 1986 and an M.S. in space systems management from Webster University in 1989.

Through ROTC, Collins joined the Air Force in 1976, the first year that women pilots were accepted. After completing training as a test pilot in 1990, she was accepted for an astronaut class and became an astronaut in July 1991. In 1995, she made history as the first woman to pilot a space shuttle, when NASA chose her to pilot the first U.S.-Russia Shuttle/Mir rendezvous. For this historic flight, Collins took along a scarf worn by Amelia Earhart and keepsakes from 13 female astronauts who never made it into space. "Women helped pioneer aviation," Collins told a news briefing, pointing out that since the 1930s, "women were not given the same opportunities as men."

Collins is married to Patrick Youngs, a Delta Airlines pilot, and they have one daughter, Bridget Marie. Her hobbies include running, hiking, camping, reading, photography and astronomy. She and her husband both play golf and they traveled to Ireland in 1993 to participate in the Irish Open.

Well aware of the important place she takes in history and of her status as role model for young women, she is a frequent visitor to high schools, encouraging girls to pursue the study of math and science. At St. Charles School in Orlando, Florida, where her niece and nephews are students, she helped start a Young Astronauts Club. An active member of the Catholic Church, her faith has obviously played an integral role in her life. As she told one newspaper, "I believe God gives us hopes and dreams, the desire to do certain things with our lives and the ability to set goals."

General Michael Collins
Rocket Man

"Man has always gone where he has been able to go, it is a basic satisfaction of his inquisitive nature, and I think we all lose a little bit if we choose to turn our backs on further exploration."

As the 17th American in space, Michael Collins was the first astronaut to walk out twice during a single mission. He began his six-year career as an astronaut in 1964, and just two years later was commander of the Gemini 10 mission.

NASA

In January 1969, Collins was named Command Module pilot on Apollo 11, the first mission to land on the moon. As the pilot in command, he circumnavigated the moon's surface on July 22, 1969, while astronauts Neil Armstrong and Buzz Aldrin took those first historic steps.

Born in Rome, Italy in 1930, Collins graduated from the Military Academy in 1952. Shortly after the Apollo 11 mission, he resigned his commission in the Air Force to take the position of Assistant Secretary of State for Public Affairs. In this position he was responsible for liaising between the State Department and the American public, with a particular emphasis on communicating with the youth population.

Collins will perhaps be best remembered, however, for his involvement in the construction and early operation of the National Air and Space Museum in Washington, D.C. In his seven years as the director of the Museum he was able to combine two of his lasting passions: his love of space and desire for greater education of this country's youth. In 1978, Collins was named Under Secretary for the Smithsonian Institution. When he left that position in 1980, his commendation stated that ". . . the Smithsonian and the Nation are forever indebted to him for his service."

Collins authored several books on space, including 1974's *Carrying the Fire* (with a foreword by Charles Lindbergh), which remains a classic today. Among his honors and citations are the Presidential Medal of Freedom, the Collier Trophy, the Harmon Trophy, the Thomas D. White Trophy and the Goddard Trophy. The Air Force awarded him the Distinguished Service Medal with Oak Leaf Cluster and the Distinguished Flying Cross. NASA awarded him its Distinguished Service Medal and Exceptional Service Medal.

In 1998, the West Point Military Academy presented its Distinguished Graduate Award to Collins. The citation read, in part: "General Collins' career exemplifies the purpose of the Military Academy: to produce graduates who will give a lifetime of service to this country . . . No one has served his country better in a wide variety of difficult and challenging assignments than General Collins."

Kathryn Sullivan
Space Walker

Dr. Kathryn D. Sullivan became the first American woman to perform a space walk, also known as extravehicular activity (EVA). She did this on the STS-41G Space Shuttle Challenger mission in October 1984. Her space walk, the purpose of which was to demonstrate the feasibility of satellite refueling, lasted three and a half hours.

The shuttle crew (Sally Ride was also on this mission, the first flight to include two women) also successfully deployed the Earth Radiation Budget Satellite (ERBS)

In April 1990, Dr. Sullivan flew on the STS-31 Space Shuttle Discovery mission. The purpose of this mission was the deployment of the Hubble Space Telescope (HST). The Hubble turned out to be nearsighted but was given a corrective lens on a later shuttle mission.

Dr. Sullivan also flew on the STS-45 Space Shuttle Atlantis mission in March 1992. This mission carried the first Atmospheric Laboratory for Applications and Science (ATLAS-1) into space. The laboratory was carried in the shuttle cargo bay.

Born on October 3, 1951, in New Jersey, Sullivan earned a Ph.D. in Geology at Dalhousie University in Nova Scotia, Canada in 1978. Her research included oceanography expeditions. She joined the U.S. Navy and became a Naval Astronaut in 1978. In 1992, she assumed the post of chief scientist, National Oceanic and Atmospheric Administration, having been nominated by both the Bush and Clinton administrations. She remained at NOAA through 1996, when she took up her current position as president and chief executive officer of COSI (Center of Science and Industry.)

In Pursuit of My Ancestral Heritage

BY JOSEPH MCBRIDE

Once when I was a child I asked my mother to let me dye my entire body green for St. Patrick's Day. She refused, sensibly enough, or I would still be trying to scrub the food coloring from my fingernails. That memory tells me I must have had a strong enough desire to proclaim my Irish roots from an early age.

But those were the days when the "melting pot" ethos was dominant in America and it was not fashionable to take ostentatious pride in one's ethnic background. We have come a long way since then, thanks in large part to an African American writer, the late Alex Haley, whose *Roots* made us all more aware of the need to pay homage to our ancestors.

I was named Joseph Pierce McBride after my maternal grandfather, Pierce Joseph Dunne, a miner and truckdriver in Idaho and Washington. My parents reversed my grandfather's first two names for mine because he always had trouble with people thinking "Pierce" was his last name. I had my own problems with the name. One day when I was eight years old, my psychotic third-grade teacher, a nun who enjoyed locking me in the closet, called me before the class and asked what my middle name was.

Photo courtesy of Joseph McBride

The author's great-great-grandparents Bridget Foy and Patrick Flynn, who emigrated from County Mayo in the 19th century.

Sensing that I was being set up for mockery and embarrassed to admit to what I thought was a strange-sounding middle name, I replied, "Peter." Today, thanks to the Irishman playing James Bond, a kid would be proud to bear such a grand Gaelic name as Pierce, but I felt humiliated, not least because I had sheepishly denied my own ethnic identity.

Eventually I learned to take pride in my colorful and rebellious lineage. My mother, the former Marian Dunne, who worked as a Milwaukee newspaper reporter, was our family historian. But she was not always timely with her revelations, preferring to spin them out gradually, like an Irish-American Scheherazade.

As she recorded, the first of our family to emigrate from Ireland to North America, James Gavin of County Armagh, arrived in Newfoundland in 1820. After being conscripted into the British navy, he jumped ship when it docked in Newfoundland, assuming his mother's maiden name, Carey, to avoid recapture.

Several of my ancestors worked as coal miners in Newfoundland and Idaho, and Pierce Dunne toiled in a silver mine. My great-grandfather Jimmy Dunne, an activist in the miners' union during Idaho's labor turmoil of the late 19th century, died of "miner's con" (consumption) soon after my birth in 1947. When I took my first train trip to meet my mother's family at the age of eight months, I was not allowed to see Grandpa Jimmy but I did get to meet my great-grandfather Dominic Flynn, who delighted in teaching me how to spit. Two weeks later he was dead.

My mother's family always had an acute awareness of political issues. She remembered sitting in front of her Grandpa Flynn's radio during the 1928 presidential campaign and "listening, at age five, to the months and months of debate over whether a Catholic could be elected U.S. president. I was over there with them listening to the election returns, and I will never forget the tears trickling down the men's cheeks –

first-generation Irish-Americans – as they learned that Al Smith had been defeated by Herbert Hoover.

"Like many other ethnic and religious groups then and now, they wondered if true equality would ever come; by then the Irish [Catholics] were OK, but not good enough to be president." Grandpa Flynn did not live long enough to see John F. Kennedy elected president in 1960. But my mother and I worked in Kennedy's campaign during the Wisconsin primary while she was vice chairman of the state Democratic Party.

My father, Raymond McBride, a newspaper reporter born in Superior, Wisconsin, had mostly Irish heritage, along with some French and Bohemian blood from his mother, Genevieve Garceau. The name McBride is Scottish, but it is derived from a cult devoted to St. Brigid who immigrated to Ireland in ancient times to practice their religion freely. My McBride ancestors began arriving in the U.S. during the mid-19th century. My great-grandfather Edward McBride, born in Iowa, traveled with his older brother to Nebraska in a covered wagon in 1881.

My grandfather John McBride reported a memorable incident that occurred during his father's journey: "While camped for the night he and his brother were awakened by the barking of their dog. Getting up and walking out in the moonlight they came face to face with the Jesse James gang, a band of bank robbers who were on the move. The bandits' only request was an exchange of horses as theirs were tired and spent. There was nothing else to do for the two startled young men but to comply. The exchange was made and it turned out to be a fair one as the horses they got were just as good, if not better than their own.

"Eventually they came to the tiny settlement O'Neill [Nebraska], founded by a hardy band of Irish folk headed by General John O'Neill, who led about 20 families from Pennsylvania." In that wagon train was a 17 year-old girl named Hannah Gallagher, whose father had died in a

The author's mother, Marian Dunne McBride, in her high school graduation portrait. Spokane, Washington, 1940.

coal mine accident. Hannah married Edward McBride and became my great-grandmother.

When I trace the evolution of my Irish consciousness, I realize that my life choices pushed me along that path, sometimes unconsciously. Among the strangest and most revealing experiences I had while working as a reporter for the Hollywood trade paper *Daily Variety* came in 1977 when I wrote the obituary of the legendary B-movie producer-director Bryan (Brynie) Foy. I did not realize at the time that he was my great-uncle.

As a child, Brynie was a member of the popular Irish American vaudeville act *The Seven Little Foys*, who were celebrated in a 1955 film of that title starring Bob Hope as the paterfamilias, Eddie Foy, Sr. Shortly after I wrote Brynie Foy's obit, my mother informed me that her Grandpa Flynn "was the eleventh of the twelve surviving children of Bridget Foy (sister of the vaudeville star Eddie Foy, Sr.) and Patrick Flynn, who emigrated from County Mayo, Ireland, and homesteaded on forty acres near Sauk Center, Minnesota."

Luckily I gave Brynie an affectionate send off,

although I couldn't resist poking some fun at his bizarrely eclectic Hollywood career. Known as the King of the B's, Foy directed the first all-talking film, Warner Bros.' truly execrable gangster film *Lights of New York* (1928), and produced an early nudist documentary, *Elysia* (1934), with himself and his crew also nude behind the camera. He produced the blacklist-era feature *I Married a Communist* and the awful JFK biopic *PT-109*. Along the way Foy made a comedy-horror film with the wonderful title *Sh! The Octopus*. (Years later I was mortified to learn that Brynie was one of the people who advised RKO to cut 45 minutes from my favorite film, Orson Welles' *The Magnificent Ambersons*.)

My growing awareness of Irish history and culture was intensified by my fondness for the films of the great Irish American director John Ford, the master of the Western genre, whose work I have been writing about since the late 1960s. But nothing brought my ethnic identity to the forefront more than the donnybrook over my 1992 review in *Daily Variety* of the Paramount film *Patriot Games*. I called it an "ultraviolent, fascistic, blatantly anti-Irish" adaptation of Tom Clancy's novel, "a right-wing cartoon of the current British-Irish political situation." History has borne out my assessment, but *Daily Variety*, which at the time was owned by a British publishing conglomerate, disowned me and my review after Paramount withdrew its ads from the paper.

I was gratified by the unanimous support of fellow journalists and critics who defended my First Amendment rights.

I was also backed by Irish American groups and many individuals of all backgrounds, typified by an anonymous man who left a heartening message on my voicemail: "Don't let the bastards grind you down." Most pleasing of all was *Irish America* naming me one of the top 100 Irish Americans of 1993 and editor Patricia Harty inviting me to write for the magazine.

In *The Book of Movie Lists* (1998), I wrote, "The quintessential romantic fantasy of every Irish-American male is to move to Ireland, buy a cottage in Connemara, and marry a woman who reminds him of Maureen O'Hara." Imagine my consternation when I married an Irish woman named O'Hara who told me she hated *The Quiet Man!* Although people in Ireland get their Irish up over what they consider to be the movie's corny ethnic stereotypes, while visiting the places where *The Quiet Man* was filmed in County Mayo with my new bride in 1985, I found that everybody there behaves exactly like a character out of *The Quiet Man.*

I married Ruth O'Hara after she came to Los Angeles to do graduate work in psychology at the University of Southern California, where she earned her Ph.D.; today she is an assistant professor at the Stanford University School of Medicine. Over the years we have had many spirited discussions about Ford films, and she now says she has come to like *The Quiet Man* a little.

Ruth's family, formerly of County Wicklow and now of the San Francisco Bay area, come from a proud Irish republican background, and my 16 years of knowing them have given me a much deeper understanding of Irish history and culture. Ruth's late grandmother Sheila Smyth Harris joined the republican movement in 1919 after her 19 year-old brother Patrick, on his way home from serving Mass, was shot in the back by the Black and Tans. She was jailed for nine months during the civil war that followed the signing of the Anglo-Irish Treaty. When Mrs. Harris died in 1983, she was given a state funeral, complete with full military honors.

Ruth and her mother, Hetty, helped me research Ford's roots in Spiddal, County Galway, for my forthcoming biography of the filmmaker. One blustery night outside the Spanish Arch in Galway, I was following the path of a Ford tracking shot in *The Rising of the Moon* when I tripped over an anchor that wasn't seen on camera and almost fell backward into the Irish Sea.

Noel O'Hara, Ruth's late father, had a lifelong fascination with American history and culture. His favorite films were Ford's *The Searchers* and George Stevens's *Shane*, and he was delighted to have family ties to someone whose great-grandfather had been robbed by Jesse James. One of Noel's fondest memories was the time he and I went to see *Shane* at the Academy of Motion Picture Arts and Sciences Theater in Beverly Hills, where he was able to see the film's reptilian bad guy, Jack Palance, in the flesh.

Noel provided invaluable advice and research assistance for my Ford biography. One of his scholarly coups was finding documentation to support Ford's account of traveling to Ireland in December 1921 on the same boat with Michael Collins, who was returning from London with the draft of the Treaty for consideration by his colleagues in Dublin. I was delighted that Noel's research helped me disprove British critic and filmmaker Lindsay Anderson's patronizing description of this story as "typical Ford – poetically true, no doubt." As Noel wrote me,

Hetty and Noel O'Hara in his Irish American literature class at New College of California, March 2000.

"It is a very colorful anecdote with republican overtones, or undertones, and will provide a nice little adventure in your account of Ford's travels."

Noel spent many years as an electrical engineer and union representative on the board of directors of the Electricity Supply Board in Ireland, but he was at heart a man of letters. Early retirement allowed him to pursue his literary passions full-time. He did groundbreaking research on Irish-American writers, parts of which were published in publications including the *Los Angeles Times* and *The Recorder: A Journal of the American Irish Historical Society*. He taught Irish and Irish American literature at New College of California in San Francisco, as well as lecturing on his research to that city's Irish Literary and Historical Society.

Gary Holloway, a past president of the society, called Noel "probably the finest Renaissance man I ever knew. He had a very devout following of people who just hung on his every word." Daniel Cassidy, director of the Irish Studies program at New College, considered Noel "a man with tremendous soul and intellect, and that's a rare combination. He was part poet, part academic, and part humorist. He had an incredible impact on his students at New College. If Noel had a mission in life, it was that of a man from Ireland who really had respect for the Irish diaspora. He had that kind of vision, a wide vision."

Noel's book manuscript *In Pursuit of the Irish-American Writer*, which I am now editing for publication, has expanded my own sense of what it means to be Irish American. Describing his work as "a sort of literary travel book through Irish America", Noel experienced America by following the trails of many of the country's greatest writers.

With his generous, ecumenical perspective, Noel admired the stimulating, if often fractious, mixture of religious and ethnic cultures in the United States. What prompted him to begin writing the book was a 1989 article by Mary Gordon in the *New York Times Book Review* expressing astonishment that despite Ireland's rich literary tradition, Ireland had "produced so little in its American branch."

"The majority of the classic Irish writers whom Gordon named were Protestants," Noel points out in the introduction to his book. "Yet when she shifted to the 'American branch', she confined herself to writers who were or are Catholic.

There was nothing unusual in this, for she was conforming to the apparently universal practice of only acknowledging Catholic Americans of Irish descent as Irish-Americans. But such a definitive statement by an American writer of renown, who has Irish ancestry herself, caused me to reflect on the truth of that universal perception . . .

"I had been fascinated by the United States since childhood, and Mary Gordon's observations stayed on my mind, and in time gave me an excuse to view the country for myself, from the perspective of an Irishman who didn't exclude any American with significant Irish ancestry, irrespective of religion, from the category 'Irish-American.' My adventure would be a way of looking at the United States on the ground, through the places, lives, and works of famous American writers with Irish ancestry.

"Certain writers seemed important to me because of the unique nature and impact of their work. Gore Vidal is unique as a writer who has written novels which span the whole history of the Republic. Edgar Allan Poe was the literary pioneer in so many ways, and Thomas Wolfe exemplified his own contention that Americans are exiles in their own land. Flannery O'Connor is the extraordinary Christian of American literature, whose fiction challenges the hegemony of science in our age. Margaret Mitchell is the outstanding talebender, and William Faulkner the foremost homesteader, the writer whose considerable number of masterpieces were written in and inspired by a postage stamp of soil in Mississippi. John Kennedy Toole is the serious comedian, the artist whose hilarity is an expression of his dismay at his own age. Raymond Chandler made literature out of mere detective stories, and Scott Fitzgerald is the

misunderstood moralist who turned a tatty tale into one of the most beautiful novels in the English language.

"Eugene O'Neill created the first real tragedy in America, and so radically changed the theater in the United States. William Kennedy has probed the existential pain of being Irish in America, and in the process has identified a pathological past that needs to be buried as quickly as possible. No family of Irish provenance has made such a contribution to American writing as the Jameses from County Cavan. No American writer is held in higher regard than Henry James, and his brother, William, is the country's most famous philosopher and psychologist. One of America's most popular and enduring writers is John Steinbeck, whose masterpiece has a haunting and unique resonance with Irish history. Other writers would be encountered en route, some with Irish ancestry with whom I would linger a while…"

Noel O'Hara died unexpectedly in May 2000 of leukemia, which came as a terrible shock since he seemed so uncommonly vigorous for a man of 64.

As I teach my own course on Irish and Irish American literature and film at New College this fall, I know I can never replace Noel but am proud that by following his tradition and that of my Irish ancestors, I am able to "stand on the shoulders of giants."

Joseph McBride's biography Searching for John Ford *will be published in 2001 by St. Martin's Press and Faber and Faber. A revised edition of his 1992 biography* Frank Capra: The Catastrophe of Success *was published in September 2000 by St. Martin's.*

Labor Leaders

Law

Medicine

Teddy Gleason
The Great Negotiator

"God be with the days when if you didn't vote Democrat you weren't allowed to go to church on Sundays."

For almost a quarter of a century, spearheading a period of immense growth and change, Teddy Gleason headed up the International Longshoremen's Association. In his book *Dreamers of Dreams*, Donal O'Donovan wrote: "Whatever the marks of a shrewd and talented negotiator, Teddy Gleason has them." After Gleason's death in 1992, ILA president John Bowers said: "We have lost a great leader and a great man. I've noted before that Teddy Gleason will go down in history as the president who was able to get the most for his members. His memory will long endure."

Born November 8, 1900 in New York City to Thomas Gleason and Mary Quinn, immigrants from Nenagh, County Tipperary and Omagh, County Tyrone respectively, Thomas W. Gleason was quickly nicknamed Teddy to distinguish him from his father and grandfather.

By age 15 he was working alongside his father on the West Side piers in Manhattan, the start of a career that was to span 77 years. Gleason worked various jobs on the docks, all the while further cementing his close ties to the ILA. His union activity saw him cut off from his job during the Great Depression, and he was forced to take on two jobs to support his wife and young family.

With the arrival of President Franklin D. Roosevelt's "New Deal" and the increasing respect for unions, Gleason was able to pick up his career as a longshoreman and labor leader. He rose steadily in union ranks and became president of the ILA in 1963. The International Transport Workers' Federation later elected him as vice president.

Gleason's achievements in the ILA include securing a guaranteed annual income for workers hurt by increasing automation. He was also vice president on the executive council of the AFL-CIO and his expertise was often called on around the world to help out in labor disputes. His investigation into the movement of wartime cargo in Vietnam earned him a Medal of Merit in 1967 from the U.S. Veterans of Foreign Wars. He received countless other awards from such bodies as the United Seamen's Service, the Catholic Youth Organization and The Carmelite Sisters for the Aged and Infirm. A true Irishman, however, he was most proud of being chosen as Grand Marshal of the New York St. Patrick's Day Parade in 1984. Gleason said at the time: "It took me 80 years to get from 12th Avenue to 5th Avenue."

Gleason was married to Emma Martin, and the couple had three sons, Thomas, Jr., John and Robert. He died on December 24, 1992 at the age of 92.

International Longshoremen's Association – AFL-CIO

Elizabeth Gurley Flynn
Powerhouse

"The awareness of being Irish came to us as small children, through plaintive song and heroic story."

Born to a Galway mother, Annie Gurley, and a father whose roots lay in Mayo, Tom Flynn, Elizabeth Gurley Flynn was the oldest of four children. Raised on a strict diet of her father's socialist and Marxist principles, it's hardly surprising that she turned out to be both an active labor organizer and later a Communist official.

Talking about her ancestors, Gurley Flynn said all of her great-grandfathers had been United Irishmen. Her great-grandfather Flynn was deeply involved with the "Races of Castlebar", and led General Humbert's French troops from Ballina to Castlebar. His son, one of 18 children, was Gurley Flynn's grandfather. He left his native Ireland during the Famine era for Maine, from where he later took part in the Fenian invasion of Canada.

Gurley Flynn was born in Concord, New Hampshire on August 7, 1890, and later moved with her family to the South Bronx. A bright student, she showed promise as a public speaker, and on leaving school turned to socialism and labor agitation. One magazine editor dubbed her "an East Side Joan of Arc."

A stalwart of the Industrial Workers of the World, Gurley Flynn traveled from Montana to Washington to Chicago, speaking on behalf of workers everywhere and earning herself a spell behind bars in Spokane for her troubles. She was behind two huge demonstrations, one in Massachusetts in 1912, the other in New Jersey the following year. Her first marriage and a later common-law relationship failed. Gurley Flynn had two children, one of whom died shortly after birth.

It was in the last three decades of her life that Gurley Flynn took up her second cause, that of

Communism. Elected to the party's national committee in 1938, she wrote a regular column for the *Daily Worker*. A second prison sentence was to follow in the 1950s when Gurley Flynn was convicted under the Smith Act, which made it illegal to advocate forceful overthrow of the government. She served over two years at the Federal Penitentiary for Women in Alderson, Virginia. Never one to waste time, she used the jail term to write her autobiography, a record of her first 36 years. A memoir of her time in prison, *The Alderson Story*, was also published after her release.

In 1961, Gurley Flynn became the first woman chairperson of the American Communist party. A planned second volume of her autobiography never came to fruition, due to her untimely death in Moscow on September 4, 1964. In a final fitting tribute, the woman who embraced Communism with all her heart was accorded a state funeral in Red Square.

Library of Congress

Mary Harris "Mother" Jones

Miners' Angel

"Pray for the dead and fight like hell for the living."

Mother Jones was one of America's most effective union organizers. At a time when few women were activists, she was a fearless crusader for the rights of American workers and became the champion of child laborers. But most of all, she was the "miners' angel" often risking arrest and her own safety in her support of the miners' struggle for safer working conditions and better pay. It was the miners who dubbed her "Mother" Jones.

A tiny woman in a black dress with a lace collar, steel-rimmed spectacles and snowy hair pulled back in a bun, Jones could have been mistaken for someone's genteel, soft-spoken grandmother, until she opened her mouth. Her speeches appealed to laborers' sense of justice and self-respect and rallied them to action.

Ridiculing their bosses and the politicians, she told the miners that they had the power to change the world.

She herself was no stranger to sorrow and oppression. Born Mary Harris in Cork, Ireland in 1837 to a poor Irish Catholic family in a country governed by the Anglo-Irish Protestant minority, she knew what it was like to be a second-class citizen. Her family had a history of activism: her grandfather was hanged as a traitor to the crown for fighting against British rule, and her father, Richard, was forced to leave Ireland for defying British rule. Richard Harris and his family settled in Canada, where he found work on the Canadian railroads. After finishing her secondary education, Mary trained to become a teacher and also learned dressmaking.

Alternating between dressmaking and teaching, Mary moved around a great deal before settling in Memphis, Tennessee, where she met and married George Jones, a union iron molder, in 1861. They had four children.

In 1867, a yellow fever epidemic swept through Memphis' Irish section, killing George and their four children. Mary Jones returned to Chicago only to suffer more loss. In 1871, the Chicago Fire destroyed her home and her dressmaking business. Her father died in Toronto only two months later.

Working for the affluent as a dressmaker while living among the poor, Jones grew enraged at the disparities between the classes. She began to attend political and labor protest meetings, ultimately launching her own campaign for workers' rights, first for Irish railroad workers and miners, then for all laborers. Over the next 25 years she crisscrossed the country, fueling workers' hopes and inciting their strikes. In 1901, she was a commissioned organizer in West Virginia for the United Mine Workers. She walked miles of railroad, scaled cliffs and waded across streams to attend secret meetings. She was arrested in 1902 for her efforts and was declared "the most dangerous woman in America."

The following year, she led a Children's March from New Kensington, Pennsylvania to Oyster Bay, Long Island, the summer home of President Theodore Roosevelt. She wanted to show the President what happened to victims of child labor. Roosevelt refused to meet the marchers.

In 1913, she returned to West Virginia to participate in the Paint Creek strike. She was arrested, court-martialed and sentenced to house arrest for three months. She also testified at several congressional hearings on behalf of miners, Mexican political prisoners and industrial workers. Her last major strikes were among the steel workers in Pittsburgh, Pennsylvania in 1919 and the coal miners of West Virginia, 1921.

In 1930, only months before her death, she remained as outspoken as ever, making her debut on newsreel cameras protesting the Prohibition Act. She died on November 30 and was buried in the Union Miners Cemetery in Mount Olive, Illinois.

George Meany
Labor of Love

"The yearning for freedom – the insistence on human dignity – are forever enshrined as part of the Irish character. Similarly, they are the wellspring of the American trade union movement."

Bronx native George Meany followed his father into a plumbing trade, but he saw the work only as a means to an end. His real ambition was to become involved in the labor movement, a goal he achieved with spectacular results. By the time he died, at age 85 and only weeks after he retired, Meany had held the top positions of both the American Federation of Labor (AFL) and its eventual incarnation on merging with the Congress of Industrial Organizations, the AFL-CIO. His name is synonymous with the labor movement in the U.S., and especially in his beloved New York City.

Born August 16, 1894, Meany was one of ten children, and the grandson of Irish immigrants from Counties Longford and Westmeath. His father, Michael Meany, was president of Local Two of the plumbers' union, but was adamantly opposed to having his sons follow in his footsteps. His antipathy was lost on George, who became an apprentice in his teens and soon followed on to membership of Local Two. After his father died and his older brother enlisted in the army, Meany became the family breadwinner, a fact which delayed his wedding to Eugenie McMahon by a couple of years.

By 1952, Meany was president of the AFL, and subsequently he led the AFL-CIO. He was widely admired as a plain-speaking, scrupulously honest man, with a remarkable memory and a tough, forceful personality. He is also remembered for his tireless rooting out of corruption.

The years which preceded his election as president of the AFL involved lobbying for the New York State Federation of Labor, of which he served as president for a term in 1934. In his position as president of the AFL-CIO he was accustomed to dealing with the U.S. presidents of the time, including Eisenhower, Kennedy, Johnson and Carter. He retired in November of 1979, and died less than two months later.

The George Meany Memorial Archives

Transport Workers Union of America

Mike Quill
Himself

"I never stopped being a farmer's son. The only thing really worth owning is a piece of land."

It was to become one of the most powerful unions in America but when the Transport Workers Union (TWU) was established in New York City in 1934 its prospects looked bleak. Conditions were dreadful for the workers, who often had to work a seven-day week. Few gave the union any hope of getting established.

But the transit bosses reckoned without the willpower of the TWU's nucleus of founders, eight or nine IRA veterans from the Irish Civil War including 29-year-old Kerry native Michael Joseph Quill. The new union was formed, and the following year, Quill was elected president.

Quill and his family in Ireland were well known in their local village for their staunch support of republicanism, and tales of young Mike's daring exploits in foiling the Black and Tans were legendary. Several members of the family joined anti-treaty forces in the Irish Civil War, and were forced to leave their native land when the war ended.

Born September 18, 1905, Quill left for America when he was just 19. He worked at various odd jobs – doorman, elevator operator, sandhog – before gaining employment with the New York subway system as a ticket clerk.

Although the transport body was deeply resistant to organized labor, Quill and his fellow Irishmen persisted and succeeded in forming the TWU.

On the occasion of the 25th anniversary of the TWU, Quill remarked that he considered its greatest successes to be "the restoration of the rights of citizenship and dignity to the individual worker . . . I mean freedom from fear, freedom from want, freedom to speak one's mind." Throughout his long association with the TWU, and organized labor in general, Quill remained an active and outspoken advocate of workers' rights. His work helped secure better working hours and conditions for the union's laborers. He also served as a member of the New York City Council at various times during his life.

In 1959, Quill's wife of 22 years, Mary Theresa "Mollie" O'Neill, died of cancer. He married Shirley Uzin in 1961 and almost 20 years after his death her biography of him, *Mike Quill: Himself*, was released.

In 1965, Quill led a massive strike against New York's bus and subway lines. His efforts brought the city to a standstill for 12 days and resulted in him being sent to prison. While behind bars, he suffered a heart attack, not his first, and he died less than a year later. Friends and admirers from Monsignor Charles Owen Rice to the Reverend Martin Luther King, Jr. lined up to pay tribute to his memory.

King described him as a pioneer of the modern trade movement and a pioneer in race relations. Said King: "He was a fighter for decent things all his life – Irish independence, labor organization and racial equality . . . When the totality of a man's life is consumed with enriching the lives of others, this is a man the ages will remember – this is a man who has passed on but who has not died."

John Sweeney
Labor Leader

"America needs a raise."

John Sweeney, president of the AFL-CIO, America's largest labor union, has long been active in Irish affairs, and is a member of several Irish organizations. In 1995, he accompanied President Clinton on his first visit to Ireland.

Sweeney's election as president of the American Federation of Labor-Congress of Industrial Organizations (AFL-CIO) in 1995 ushered in a new era in the labor movement. On the day of his electoral win, he led an impromptu march up Manhattan's Fashion Avenue protesting wages and work conditions in the garment industry. Within weeks, he had established a multi-million-dollar fund to finance television and radio commercials, town rallies and telephone campaigns to hammer away at the evils of wage discrimination, job insecurity and union-busting corporations.

Born May 5, 1934 in New York's Bronx to Irish immigrant parents from Leitrim, Sweeney studied economics at Iona College, and took a job at IBM after graduating. He had worked at a union job to pay his way through school and soon left IBM to take a lower-paying job with the International Ladies Garment Workers Union, a move that would set the course for his life's work.

As president of the Service Employees International Union (SEIU) from 1980 until taking his current position, Sweeney doubled union membership and recorded countless other successes. Since his election to the helm of the AFL-CIO, he created new management posts to create leadership positions for women and minorities, all part of his goal to abolish the long-held concept of the labor movement as the domain of white males. In 1996, he wrote a book titled *America Needs a Raise: Fighting for Economic Security and Social Justice*. He also co-authored *Solutions for the New Work Force* in 1989. He and his wife, Maureen Power, have a son John and daughter Patricia.

William J. Brennan, Jr.
Defender of Justice

"The law is not an end in itself, nor does it provide ends. It is preeminently a means to serve what we think is right."

Considered one of the most influential shapers of public policy in the nation, the late Justice William Joseph Brennan, Jr. was best known for his support of civil rights, and particularly freedom of speech. He was a figure of immense importance in modern law, and it was his guiding hand that spurred the revolution in constitutional law in the 1960s and '70s.

In a rare interview with *Irish America* magazine in 1990, Brennan discussed his background. Born April 25, 1906 in Newark, New Jersey to Roscommon immigrants William Joseph Brennan and Agnes McDermott, Brennan was the second of eight children. His parents were reluctant to talk of their lives in Ireland, leading Brennan to conclude that "their memories were of hardships", but they brought up their family with a strong sense of Irishness.

Brennan and his siblings were raised to be aware of the Friendly Sons of Saint Patrick and the Ancient Order of Hibernians. The senior Brennan also subscribed to the *Irish World* and other such publications, and St. Patrick's Day was a big occasion for celebration in the household. "Everything I am, I am because of my father," Brennan once said.

Brennan graduated from Harvard Law School in 1931 and started his career with the New Jersey firm of Pitney, Hardin & Skinner. He was named a judge of the State Supreme Court in 1949, and three years later was elevated to the New Jersey Supreme Court. In 1956, President Dwight D. Eisenhower appointed Brennan to the Supreme Court, and he became its youngest member. During his 34 years on the Supreme Court bench, Brennan published over 1,250 opinions, including several landmark decisions on such issues as the rights of racial minorities and women and the protection of freedom of expression.

His Catholicism proved no barrier to Brennan's fervent belief in the strict separation of church and state. He was married to Marjorie Leonard and the couple had three children. After Marjorie died in 1982, Brennan married Mary Fowler, who had worked as his secretary for over 25 years. He died on July 24, 1997 in Arlington, Virginia at the age of 91.

Vincent Hallinan
The Great Defender

"We're not fallen angels. We're risen apes."

He's probably the only lawyer who appeared before the courts and defied the defense to prove the existence of heaven. As well known in his native San Francisco as Clarence Darrow was in Chicago, Vincent Hallinan helmed a number of high-profile cases, often ending up behind bars himself for his troubles. A 300-page biography of Hallinan by James P. Walsh is titled *San Francisco's Hallinan: Toughest Lawyer in Town,* which gives some idea as to his reputation. He

One of Hallinan's most notorious cases involved his spirited defense of Pacific Heights society matron Irene Mansfeldt, charged with killing her husband's mistress. Mansfeldt confessed to the police, but Hallinan refused to let her sign it, and advised her to say nothing further. In an explosive trial, during which he completely destroyed the prosecution's medical expert, Hallinan did a splendid job of convincing the jury that Mansfeldt had killed the other woman during a haze brought on by drugs her husband, a doctor, had prescribed for her. He saved his client from the gas chamber and she got off with a comparatively light custodial sentence of 25 months. In a 1989 interview with *Irish America*, Hallinan told writer Frank McCourt, "It was far and away the best victory I've ever won in court."

Asked where he picked up the dramatic flair he employed to such good use in the courtroom, Hallinan said: "A lot of things I've said I've extracted from books. When I was a little fellow, only seven, my father used to give me money to memorize Irish poems and recite them. I'd give the money to my mother, of course. It helped me build a tremendous memory."

Married to Vivian, Hallinan was a devoted father to the couple's six sons, many of whom are carrying on the family legal tradition in San Francisco today, including Terence, the city's District Attorney. His wife wrote a book in the 1950s entitled *My Wild Irish Rogues*, which focused on her raising her staunchly leftist political sons in the midst of political turmoil. Vincent Hallinan, a lifelong socialist who described himself as a "roaring atheist", died in 1995.

was almost as well known for his strident politics, and once ran for President.

Born to Irish immigrants on December 16, 1896, Hallinan learned his first legal lesson at his father's knee and remembers it as "the incident that determined my career." Hallinan senior, facing eviction with his wife and seven children from their Western Addition apartment, enlisted the help of attorney Charles Heggerty, who first counseled his client of the necessity to keep the process servers at bay for as long as possible. He then had the eviction case thrown out of court on the grounds that the notice to vacate was "fatally defective."

Heggerty cited the case of *Spivolo v. Mahoney* as grounds for his argument. Hallinan remembers his father marveling at the judge's ignorance of this landmark case, but it was only years later that the son, then a learned attorney, "saw the thousands of books and recognized that there were numberless decisions [and] realized the wonder would have been if [the judge] had heard of *Spivolo v. Mahoney*."

Sandra Day O'Connor
Supreme Court Justice

"I don't know that there are any shortcuts to doing a good job."

On September 25, 1981 Sandra Day O'Connor took the oath of office as a Justice of the United States Supreme Court, becoming the first woman ever to serve on the court. Given the curious chemistry of the current court on which she sits, she has garnered enormous power, as hers has proven to be the key swing vote on a wide range of contentious issues, from affirmative action to abortion to the death penalty. In 1993 the *American Bar Association Journal* hailed her as "arguably the most influential woman official in the United States."

O'Connor is the descendant of Famine immigrants named O'Dea, but her grandfather changed the name to "Day." Sandra Day O'Connor was born in 1930 in El Paso, Texas on an isolated ranch. Located too far from any schools, Sandra's mother taught her to read,

and at the age of five, Sandra was sent away to attend school. She returned to the ranch at age 13, and made a 22-mile trip each day to attend high school. After finishing high school, she enrolled at Stanford University, receiving her law degree in 1952. That same year she married her classmate John Jay O'Connor III.

O'Connor applied for jobs at several law firms, but they were reluctant to hire a woman. O'Connor turned instead to public service, working as deputy county attorney in San Mateo, California.

The O'Connors moved to Arizona in 1957, and there Sandra opened her own law firm in order to have time to spend with her three sons, Scott, Brian and Jay. In 1969, she was elected as a Republican to the Arizona State Senate. Three years later she was elected Senate Majority Leader, becoming the first woman to hold that office in any state senate in the country. That same year, she also served as Chairman of the State, County and Municipal Affairs Committee. She also served on the Legislative Council, the Probate Code Commission and the Arizona Advisory Council in Intergovernmental Relations.

In 1974, O'Connor was elected county judge, and five years later, the governor of Arizona appointed her to the state court of appeals. In July of 1981, she was nominated by President Reagan as Associate Justice of the United States Supreme Court, taking the oath two months later. From making history to interpreting the law of the land to raising three boys, O'Connor has done it all and remains a shining example for women in this country.

When asked during her confirmation hearings how she wanted to be remembered, she replied with the same unflappable evenhandedness that has characterized her career: "Ah, the tombstone question. I hope it says, 'Here lies a good judge.'"

Dr. Kevin Cahill

Born in the Bronx, New York, Dr. Kevin Cahill is the president general of the American Irish Historical Society, as well as a distinguished doctor whose patients have included Pope John Paul II, Ronald Reagan, and several UN Secretary Generals. He was the first American ever to receive the Grand Cross Pro Merito Melitersi, a papal award. Among his many other citations is a Georgetown University Bicentennial Medal.

On awarding him this honor in 1989, Georgetown paid Cahill a rare tribute. "He has ministered to the sick and suffering in Nicaragua, Libya, Lebanon, Somalia as well as to AIDS patients in New York City, recognizing that we shall save our fragile world only by relieving the pain and privation of individual men and women. . . For his distinguished work as a physician, for his generous ministry to the suffering and destitute of the Third World, for his commitment to use his skills to bring peace, justice, and a decent life to all people on earth, Georgetown University . . . is honored to present its Bicentennial Medal to Dr. Kevin Cahill."

In a review of his most recent book, *A Bridge to Peace*, *The New York Times* said, "Dr. Cahill . . . commands our attention with the unmistakable authority of a journeyer returned from scenes of great suffering."

In his 25 years as president general of the American Irish Historical Society, Cahill has refurbished its prestigious brownstone home on New York's Fifth Avenue and has continued the effort to raise the awareness of Irish Americans of their cultural history and ancestry.

He and his wife Katherine have five sons and four granddaughters. His son Christopher serves as editor of *The Recorder*, the journal of the AIHS.

Kathy and William Magee

During the past 17 years 45,000 children have received surgery for disfigurements such as cleft lip and palates, burn scars and clubfeet, thanks to Operation Smile. Founded in 1982 by plastic surgeon William P. Magee and his wife, Kathy, a nurse and social worker, Operation Smile now has a worldwide network of some 12,000 volunteers spanning 75 cities and nine countries and is headquartered in Norfolk, Virginia.

"Looking at a child with an ugly cleft lip and knowing that a 45 minute operation will change this life from one of rejection and shame to one of acceptance and joy deepens our commitment to work harder to raise public awareness, to recruit more volunteers, to develop more financial supporters, to train more surgeons in developing countries, and to heal more children," said Dr. Magee.

In 1999, the organization's World Journey of Hope '99 brought an international team of 1,000 medical volunteers on a nine-week mission to the U.S. and 17 other countries to treat and transform the lives of some 5,000 children.

Dr. Magee, son of a doctor, brother of two doctors, and the second of 12 children, was born in Hoboken, New Jersey. His maternal grandmother, a Murphy from Valencia Island, settled in Pennsylvania in the 1800s and married another native Irishman named Sugrue.

Working as a team, the Magees, who have five children, have made it possible for thousands of children to smile again.

The Perils of Pat

BY PETER QUINN

The man on the horse is my paternal grandfather, Patrick Francis Quinn. The date is September 5, 1904. Pat is about to take his place as Grand Marshal of the New York City Labor Day Parade. The horse was rented for the occasion. I have the sash he is wearing in the photograph, a piece of faded blue silk embroidered with gold lettering: P.F. Quinn – President – Central Federated Union.

The place is outside the old Fifth Avenue Hotel, which stood at the corner of 23rd Street, across from Madison Square Park. Somewhere out of view of the camera, my grandmother attended with her three children, Gertie, John, and my father, Peter, born the previous May.

Pat was just short of his 45th birthday. He'd been born outside Thurles in County Tipperary, on September 27, 1859, barely a decade after the famine that had ravaged much of Ireland. At the height of it, Colonel Douglas, a relief inspector in Tipperary, had written his superior, "Nobody who has not personally seen the state of matters in this country can form to himself any idea" of the horrors. Pat must have heard a good deal of those horrors as a boy.

Although Pat was dead when I was born, he was fixed in my mind by my own father who – for better and worse – has been dominated and driven by Pat. This is how Pat taught my father to swim: took him out to Coney Island, walked him to the end of the pier and threw him in. Later, he would discourage my father from the acting career he wanted to pursue, and push him into Democratic politics (a theatrical career of a kind, I guess, and one my father followed with some success, becoming a state assemblyman, a U.S. congressman and a judge).

I have some idea now, as both a son and father myself, of the tensions that must have existed between the two. I know also that this must have been aggravated by the radically different experiences and expectations: the father, unschooled, making his way in the world through brawn and bravado, a born wanderer; the son, lithe, with none of his father's workingman's bulk, a graduate of Manhattan College and Fordham Law School, a young man who loved to dance and read Shakespeare, and who was at home in New York.

Left: The author's grandfather Patrick F. Quinn, 1904. Right: The author's father Peter A. Quinn, 1936.

There was between Pat and his son, I'm sure, a touch of the shadow that demarcated the lives of James and Eugene O'Neill – that perhaps falls between every immigrant and his son. But his own private long day's journey was something my father never spoke about. Instead, he held us spellbound with tales of the public Pat. The bones of the story are contained in the obituary printed in the *Bronx Home News* in October, 1941. Pat, the boy who went West, who fought in Cuba, who played a prominent role in the union movement. On these bones my father put flesh and blood, a chronicle of serialized adventures beside which even Davy Crockett (cynosure of every red-blooded Bronx kid in the 1950s) seemed to pale.

Pat landed in New York in 1873 with his parents and siblings (their passage paid by a relative who'd come out in the 1840s). He attended school only briefly before he was put to work. Sometime around 1880, Pat set out on his own, got a job on the railroads and headed to the frontier. It was at this point the sketchy details of Pat's early life gave way to the full-blown talents of my father's abilities as seanchai and raconteur. Pat wasn't merely one of the army of Irish laborers stoking furnaces on the hundreds of trains crisscrossing the continent. Pat's train was pursued through the Wildest West by the most ferocious of the Apaches, and as the engine struggled up a steep incline, it was Pat's epic coal shoveling that gave the train the steam it needed to escape.

The irony of an Irishman helping drive forward the same process of colonization in America that had dispossessed his own people in Ireland was one we never considered. Yet, though caught like everyone else in the contradictions of history and marked by his own inconsistencies, Pat was a man with a gut-seated hatred of injustice. "I know what it's like to be hungry," he once told my father. "And that changes a man."

By the 1890s, Pat was fully immersed in the struggle of organized labor. He was an early member of the Knights of Labor. In 1894, he went to Chicago to help support the famous Pullman strike and was threatened at gunpoint by railroad detectives. He was set upon one night in Tompkins Square Park in New York by anti-labor goons. He earned his place at the head of that 1904 Labor Day Parade.

Pat was married twice. When his first wife died in childbirth, Pat left his infant daughter, my Aunt Gertie, with his sister and went to Cuba to bury his grief by digging for gold. He ended up fighting alongside Cuban insurrectionists. Back in America, he married a new love, my grandmother, and became the leader of the Coppersmiths Union and an organizer for the AFL. Pat's union work kept him on the road part of the year, and sometimes he took my father along.

My father remembered one time in particular, in the summer of 1916, when they traveled from a labor convention in Detroit for a day's outing in Toronto. It was at the time of the British offensive on the Somme, and the imperial patriotism of many Canadians was running high. Pat and my father were crossing a public square at dusk when a band began to play "God Save the King." Silent, reverent men removed their hats as the Union Jack came down. My father went to take off his cap. Pat stopped him. "That flag is a symbol of royalty and aristocracy," he said in a loud voice. "It stands for empire and greed. Never doff your hat to it."

There were shouts from the crowd, and threats. My father was scared but kept his eyes on Pat, who wouldn't be cowed. Pat stood there with my father at his side, hats unremoved, heads unbowed. And that's how I most like to think of them: the Irish immigrant laborer and his son, together in that one moment, afraid perhaps, but refusing to bend a knee before emperors or empires.

Peter Quinn is the author of Banished Children of Eve, *a historical novel based on the Irish in Civil War-era New York. "The Perils of Pat" was first printed in* Irish America *in November 1993.*

Nationalists

Politics

Eamon de Valera
The Long Fellow

"I am in America as the official head of the [Irish] Republic, established by the will of the people in accordance with the principles of self-determination."

Given that nobody born outside the United States can ever hope to become President of the nation, it is ironic that a humbly born New Yorker was elected President of Ireland in 1959 and went on to serve two seven-year terms. Eamon de Valera, or 'Dev', as he was commonly known, had a long association with Ireland and Irish causes, an association which predated his presidency by five decades.

Born October 4, 1882, at the Nursery and Child's Hospital on Lexington Avenue in New York (a plaque commemorates the spot, now a Loews Hotel), de Valera had a difficult childhood. His mother, Kate Cull, had emigrated to New York from County Clare some three years earlier and worked as a domestic for a wealthy French family. The family's Spanish

music teacher, Vivian de Valera, was to father her child, but it is not known whether he died shortly after his son's birth or simply abandoned mother and son.

Christened Edward, the youngster was put into the care of another Clare woman, and when he was three he was sent to live with relatives in Ireland. His mother later married an Englishman named Charles Wheelwright, and she continued to live in New York.

A promising student, de Valera later became a teacher. He also immersed himself in Irish nationalism, joining the Gaelic League, the Irish Volunteers, and later the Irish Republican Brotherhood. One of the leaders of the 1916 Rising, he escaped execution and changed his name to Eamon, the Irish version of Edward.

The year after the Easter Rising, de Valera was chosen as leader of the newly formed Sinn Féin party and served as a member of Parliament. When his party boycotted the British parliament and set up their own Dáil (Parliament), de Valera became its leader. After the founding of the Irish Free State in 1922, and the Civil War which followed, he founded his own political party, Fianna Fáil.

In 1932, de Valera became leader of the Irish Free State, or Taoiseach (Prime Minister). He continued to dominate Irish politics for decades, serving as Taoiseach in 1932-48, 1951-54 and 1957-59. Loved and hated in equal measures, he certainly did much for the preservation of the Irish language. He is also the only politician to have served as both Taoiseach and President of Ireland.

De Valera died at the age of 92 on August 29, 1975. His granddaughter, Síle de Valera, followed in his political footsteps and serves as the current Fianna Fáil Minister for the Arts, Culture, Gaeltacht and the Islands. A grandson, Eamon O Cuiv, is another member of Fianna Fáil and the Dáil (Parliament).

John Devoy
Rebel with a Cause

"The land of Ireland belongs to the people of Ireland and to them alone, and we must not be afraid to say so."

John Devoy was only a boy, no more than nine or ten years old, when he decided he could no longer in conscience join his classmates when they sang "God Save the Queen" at school. It was to be only the first rebellious act in a long life filled with them.

Born on September 3, 1842 in County Kildare to William and Elizabeth Devoy, John Devoy moved with his family to Dublin when he was seven. In 1861, he joined the Irish Republican Brotherhood and swore an oath to the Irish Republic, promising to bear arms "to defend its integrity and independence." He learned the soldier's trade during a brief stint with the French Foreign Legion, spending a year in Algeria.

In 1866, during a strong clampdown on the IRB, Devoy was arrested and sentenced to 15 years penal servitude. A special deal five years later saw him released from prison on condition he leave Ireland forever. He arrived in New York on January 18, 1871, along with O'Donovan Rossa. After finding work as a reporter with the *New York Herald*, Devoy turned his hand to more serious business. He joined Clan na Gael and helped mastermind the rescue of soldier prisoners from Australia on board the ship *Catalpa*.

During his time in New York, Devoy founded two newspapers, the *Irish Nation* and *Gaelic American*, and helped greatly with work on the *United Irishmen*, edited by Arthur Griffith. In 1879, Devoy and Michael Davitt worked together on the "New Departure", which had as its goals the promotion of tenants' rights, the achievement of self-government, the exclusion of sectarian issues from politics, and support for struggling nationalities.

Devoy visited his native Ireland in 1924, for only the second time since his exile. Four years later, he died in Atlantic City, New Jersey, at the age of 86. He would no doubt have reveled in the obituary published by the *Times* of London, which referred to him as "the most bitter and persistent, as well as the most dangerous, enemy of this country which Ireland has produced since Wolfe Tone."

Patrick Ford
Patriot

"[America} is Ireland's base of operations. Here, in this Republic . . . we are free to express the sentiments and to declare the hopes of Ireland."

One of the great Irish American newspapermen, Patrick Ford published the *Irish World* in New York in the late 1800s and early 1900s and wrote sympathetically of the plight of American Indians and African Americans at a time when it was highly unpopular to do so. He was also a committed advocate of freedom in Ireland.

Although he could remember little of his life in his native Ireland, having moved to Boston at the age of seven, Ford devoted his life to Irish causes, specifically the issue of independence. "I might as well have been born in Boston," he told a reporter in later years. "I brought nothing with me from Ireland . . . nothing tangible to make me what I am."

There might not have been anything tangible about it, but the fact remains that through his incarnations as both a dedicated newspaperman and a diehard nationalist, Ford brought plenty with him from Ireland, and spent his adult years making sure he was in a position to give back to the country he loved so much.

Orphaned young and educated in Boston, Ford was inspired to support the Irish struggle for independence after encountering the anti-Irish sentiment that riddled his adoptive city.

During the Civil War he served with the Ninth Massachusetts Regiment.

Stints at newspapers such as *The Liberator*, the *Boston Sunday Times* and the *Charleston Gazette* were followed by Ford's decision to start his own publication, the New York-based *Irish World*, which quickly became the most widely read Irish American newspaper of its time.

According to historian Thomas Brown, Ford was "moralistic and shrill, given to expressions of righteous violence that were thick with the Old Testament. He oscillated wildly between the two extremes of universal humanitarianism and Irish terrorism."

In the 1880s, Ford organized 2,500 branches of the Irish Land League, and raised $300,000 for its efforts. British Prime Minister Gladstone reportedly said at the time: "But for the work the *Irish World* is doing, and the money it is sending across the ocean, there would be no agitation in Ireland."

In his 40s, Ford published two books which further illustrated his antipathy towards Britain: *A Criminal History of the British Empire* and *The Irish Question and American Statesmen.* Up until two years before his death, Ford remained editor of *The Irish World*. He died at his home in Brooklyn in 1913.

Joe McGarrity
Celtic Warrior

". . . the general awakening that was taking place in Ireland seemed to make us forget everything else for the time and think only of the fight in prospect."

Joe McGarrity was Eamon de Valera's right-hand man in America, and was once described by poet Padraic Colum as "a gallowglass ready to swing a battleaxe with his long arms." It was an apt description for the old warrior.

McGarrity was born in Carrickmore, County Tyrone in 1874. Legend has it that as a penniless

all problems until the mid-1930s, when de Valera, then Taoiseach (Prime Minister), suppressed the IRA under the Offences Against the State Act and used military courts to jail them. McGarrity ended all contact with de Valera.

Almost two decades earlier McGarrity had exposed a plot against de Valera by his enemies in New York, which, if successful, would have forced his return to Dublin in disgrace and ended in his defeat because he had incurred the wrath of Judge Daniel Cohalan and the aged Fenian veteran, John Devoy, as Dáil Eireann's spokesman in the U.S.

Devoy in the *Gaelic American* denounced de Valera for a published interview with a British correspondent in which the politician had said Britain should declare a "Monroe Doctrine" for Ireland, as the U.S. had done for Cuba. Devoy's point was that the Monroe Doctrine had made Cuba a dependency of the United States. De Valera, however, seemed ignorant of Cuba's real status.

Discussion of the issue at a large meeting in the Waldorf-Astoria Hotel turned into an indictment and trial of de Valera. McGarrity, who had letters proving this was a plot, saved the day for de Valera. "From the day I landed in America, I had the absolute cooperation of Joe McGarrity," de Valera declared. "If I were dying tomorrow and had the power to hand over the cause of Ireland to one man, that man would be Joseph McGarrity."

On December 9, 1920, on the eve of his return home to Ireland, de Valera did exactly that. He nominated "Joseph McGarrity of 3714 Chestnut St., Philadelphia, as my substitute, entitled to act with all my powers in case I am incapacitated by imprisonment or death or any other cause. I anticipate to be absent from the U.S. for some time. During my absence I wish you to act for me as Trustee of Dáil Eireann in regard to such funds as are at present in the U.S." McGarrity died on September 4, 1940.

16-year-old he walked to Dublin, boarded a cattle boat to Liverpool disguised as a drover, and sailed to America on someone else's ticket. He settled in Philadelphia and made a fortune selling liquor and real estate.

He joined Clan na Gael, the Fenian movement in America, and devoted his life to the cause of Irish independence. He conferred the title "President of the Irish Republic" on Eamon de Valera when the latter landed in New York in June 1919 to seek U.S. support for the Irish Republic declared by the first Dáil in January 1919.

De Valera's title was "President of Dáil Eireann." Joe argued that Americans had no idea what "Dáil Eireann" meant but that "President of the Irish Republic" was analogous to the title "President of the United States" and its use by de Valera would make that clear.

Henceforth, McGarrity was de Valera's first lieutenant in America and a fount of wisdom on

Hugh Carey
The Gov

"Blessed are the Irish of St. Patrick because you can remain poor all your life and yet participate through our faith in the richest legacy that a human being may have. May we extend that legacy for peace in the world through the next millennium."

His two terms as Governor of New York have singled out Hugh Carey as a man whose name will go down in history. Over a dozen years after he last held the office, he is still remembered as the man who, against all odds, did so much for his native city and state.

Born in Brooklyn to Dennis and Margaret Carey, the son and daughter of Galway and Tyrone immigrants, Carey served during World War II, receiving the Bronze Star, the Croix de Guerre with Silver Star and the Combat Infantrymen's Badge for his bravery. His mother once worked as a secretary for Nellie Bly, the world-famous reporter who made history when she traveled around the world in record time.

A year after he returned from service, Carey married Helen Twohy and by 1966 they had 14 children. After graduating from St. John's University with a J. D. degree Carey was called to the bar in 1951, but by 1960 his attention was

focused more on politics. He sought and won the Democratic nomination for Congress in Brooklyn, and resided in Washington for the next 14 years.

Carey's wife Helen passed away in 1974, but not before urging him to continue with his bid for Governor of New York. He was elected in November 1974, and took office the following January. Carey's two terms in office saw the launch of the "I Love New York" campaign and the Empire State Games. He is widely credited with having saved New York from bankruptcy and introducing sweeping fiscal reforms.

Bill Clinton
President

"The [Irish] people want peace; the people will have peace."

It is unparalleled in the history of the American presidency to have an occupant of the Oval Office who has worked so hard and so long to bring peace to Ireland.

Soon after entering office, Bill Clinton took a calculated risk for peace when he granted a visa to Gerry Adams, the leader of Sinn Féin, to come to America. He did so despite the advice of the Justice Department, FBI, CIA, State Department and the British government, who were furious at his step.

The visa played a huge role in sparking the first IRA ceasefire and the Irish peace process, the most hopeful development in Northern Ireland in generations. Without Bill Clinton it would simply not have been possible.

His first visit to Ireland in November 1995 was truly historic. Huge crowds turned out, evoking memories of John F. Kennedy's visit a generation before. In Belfast an estimated 50,000 people drawn from both communities saw him deliver a strong message for peace. It was the first ever visit North by a U.S. President.

He was there too during the crucial lead-up to

the Good Friday Agreement. Senator George Mitchell, the man he personally appointed as his peace emissary, was the man who brought all the parties together to sign the historic document.

In good times and bad Clinton has continued to persevere on the Irish issue, a fact which has made him hugely popular with Irish Americans. As the Northern Ireland political parties feverishly worked towards an acceptable compromise this July, and hoped to make the establishment of a new government a reality, Clinton was on hand once again to speak to party leaders and remind them of what they stood to lose if agreement was not reached. He interrupted several top-level meetings and remained in contact even during his personal time, ready to pick up the phone at a moment's notice if necessary.

The President's second visit, in September 1998, further earned him a place in the history books as the U.S. President who has done the most work for Ireland. British Prime Minister Tony Blair, who accompanied the First Couple

on a visit to the stricken town of Omagh, still reeling from the effects of the tragic bombing a month earlier, hailed the U.S. leader, saying no one had done more for peace in Northern Ireland. Added Taoiseach (Prime Minister) Bertie Ahern, during Clinton's visit to Dublin: "The helping hand of the United States was always there in the hour of need. And there were many such hours."

Throughout 1998, Clinton was also on hand to meet Northern Ireland politicians of all stripes. In December, the D.C.-based National Democratic Institute for International Affairs presented the W. Averell Harriman Democracy Award jointly to the President and the North's political leaders.

President Clinton traces his Irish ancestry to Fermanagh on his mother's side. His long-held ambition to play a round of golf at Kerry's famed Ballybunion Golf Club was finally realized in September 1998. The President was named Irish American of the Year by *Irish America* magazine in 1996.

Library of Congress

James Michael Curley
Boston Brave

"I never took a quarter from anyone who couldn't afford it."

James Michael Curley was born on November 20, 1874, the second son of Irish immigrants. When he died 84 years later, his was the biggest wake the city of Boston had ever seen. In between times, Curley rose to fame as a four-time mayor of his beloved city, Governor of the Commonwealth, congressman and jailbird.

Even as a youngster, Curley knew that politics would be his ticket out of the tenements of Roxbury Ward 17. At 24, he entered his first campaign for city government. In the spirit of Tip O'Neill's famous statement that all politics are local, Curley was a strong believer in keeping his constituents happy, and he helped out with many favors.

In 1902, Curley and another campaigning politician impersonated two campaign workers at a federal postal examination. Both were spotted and subsequently imprisoned. They ran their campaigns from prison and both were successfully elected. Prison sentence notwithstanding, Curley went on to enjoy huge successes in the political arena. When in 1914 he was elected mayor of Boston, it was at the expense of John F. "Honey Fitz" Fitzgerald, grandfather of President John F. Kennedy, who dropped out of the campaign after Curley threatened to expose his alleged liaison with a woman named Toodles Ryan.

During four terms as mayor, Curley, whose favorite nickname was "Mayor of the Poor", transformed his beloved city with an ambitious series of public works developments. His pet project was the rejuvenation of Boston City Hospital, and he ensured that millions of city dollars were poured into the endeavor.

In 1947, during Curley's final term as mayor, he was found guilty of defrauding the U.S. mail through his short-lived involvement with a firm called Engineers Group Inc. Sentenced to 18 months at Danbury federal prison, he served five before being pardoned by President Harry Truman. In 1958, his political career well and truly over, he died in his beloved Boston City Hospital. The city he had served so well dedicated a park near Faneuil Hall to Curley, erecting two statues there in his honor in 1980.

Richard Daley
Chicago Boss

"It has been my philosophy all my life that good government is good politics."

He was the last of the great city bosses in America and he may have delivered the White House to JFK. His strong roots in the Irish working-class neighborhood of Bridgeport, Chicago served Richard Daley well when it came to his life in public service and politics. The

common saying in his native city during his reign as mayor was that "Chicago is owned by the Jews, lived in by the blacks, and run by the Irish."

The son of second-generation Irish parents, Daley accompanied his mother as she frequently marched in suffragette demonstrations. Daley's father became involved in politics through his membership in the sheet metal workers' union, a career choice his son was to follow at a young age. After graduation from high school, Daley studied law by night at DePaul University. He also pursued his political leanings, working for the Eleventh Ward in the Democratic organization. A job in a councilman's office led Daley up through the ranks, and he ran for his first office – that of state representative – in 1936. He won that election, and was to win his next two – in 1939 when he ran for the state senate, and in 1955 when he ran for mayor.

As mayor, Daley was both loved and hated, but most agree that he was a fair dealer, and made decisions on a consensus basis after conferring with all the parties involved. During the Democratic National Convention in 1968 he came under heavy fire after anti-war protests drew a strong response from the city's police force, who reacted with batons drawn. Observers accused the cops of brutal tactics, but Daley stuck by his men in blue and defended their actions.

His influence was profound, and he played a large part in having John F. Kennedy elected as President in 1960, with both Cook County (Daley was chairman of the Cook County Democratic Organization for 23 years) and the state of Illinois giving their votes to Daley's fellow Irish American Catholic politician.

Richard Daley died in office on December 20, 1976, one year into his sixth four-year term as mayor. He was buried in his beloved Chicago, with the strains of his favorite marching song, "Garryowen", keening gently over the breeze. His legacy lives on today, with his son, Richard M. Daley, currently serving his fourth term as mayor of the Windy City.

Library of Congress

James Farley and James, Jr.

James Farley
Postmaster

"It occurred to me that it would be wise to have some little distinguishing mark that would induce the receiver to remember me as an individual. . . . Green ink did the trick so well that it was given the job permanently."

Without him, FDR may never have been President. James Farley was one of the pillars of the Democratic Party in the early part of this century, investing in it the fierce loyalty typical of many Irish Americans of the time. He dedicated this same loyalty to Franklin Delano Roosevelt, and in many ways he was the key to FDR's success, first as New York governor, then as President of the United States.

James Aloysius Farley was born in 1888 in Grassy Point, New York and graduated from Packard Commercial School in New York City. He began his business career in 1906 as a bookkeeper for Universal Gypsum Company. Between 1912 and 1919, he worked as a town clerk in Stony Point, New York, but returned to New York City to pursue his business interests and enter the political field.

Farley was elected a member of the New York State Assembly in the early '20s and over the next 20 years his stature within the Democratic Party steadily increased. In 1928, Farley organized FDR's successful campaign for governor of New York. Soon afterwards he was named chairman of the New York State Democratic Committee. Then in 1932, he led FDR's campaign for President as chairman of the Democratic National Committee. Upon assuming the presidency, Roosevelt appointed Farley United States Postmaster General.

Roosevelt knew that he had a good thing in Farley, and he was the obvious choice to head up Roosevelt's 1936 reelection campaign. However, the two parted ways over Roosevelt's decision to seek a third term in 1940. Farley was opposed to a three-term presidency because of tradition and also out of concern for Roosevelt's declining health.

Farley's growing popularity with the party continued unchecked. At the 1940 Democratic National Convention, he even received a nomination for presidency, which he declined. While he had the political and managerial skills necessary for the job, he was well aware that the public was not ready to elect someone of his working-class Irish Catholic background.

Farley remained in politics through the national elections of 1944, serving as New York State Democratic Committee chairman a second time. He moved away from politics after that, turning his attention back again to the world of business. He died on June 9, 1976 in New York City.

Edward Kennedy
The Senator

"I was always interested in politics and elective office. Some form of public service was always emphasized and stressed in the family."

When Senator Edward Kennedy was presented with the 1997 Irish American of the Year award by *Irish America* magazine, the citation stated that "Kennedy is a chieftain, which is what the old Irish word taoiseach actually means. He has led the cause of Ireland on Capitol Hill for over a generation now and has often received little recognition in return. However, when the history of this period is written he will loom largest of all."

No one played a larger role in persuading President Clinton to become a player in the Irish peace process than Kennedy, and to this day he remains an invaluable adviser to the president on the issue.

He has been involved in Irish issues almost since he joined the Senate in 1962. From the outset of the Northern troubles he became the major American player, and aligned himself firmly with constitutional nationalism and with SDLP leader John Hume, a long-time friend.

In 1992 Kennedy made the courageous decision to support a visa for Sinn Féin leader Gerry Adams, which became the linchpin of the American intervention in the then fledgling peace process. Without his support President Clinton would never have taken that risky step which transformed the peace process.

At every step since in the peace process Kennedy has led the American response and he remains as influential as ever. His announcement that he would seek another term in 2000 was greeted with relief in Irish circles, where there is a clear understanding that his influence and advice will be sorely missed when he eventually decides to retire.

Jean Kennedy Smith
The Ambassador

Ireland's President Mary McAleese praised Jean Kennedy Smith's "fixedness of purpose" during a ceremony in 1998 which conferred honorary citizenship on the U.S. Ambassador to Ireland as her four-year term came to a close.

Taoiseach (Prime Minister) Bertie Ahern and President McAleese had cleared the way for the honorary citizenship to be bestowed on Kennedy Smith, and announced the surprise news at a farewell party on July 4 at the ambassadorial residence in Dublin's Phoenix Park. Ahern paid tribute to Kennedy Smith's "immense service" during her tenure, saying, "You have helped bring about a better life for everyone throughout Ireland." The Massachusetts native described her ambassadorial term as "the most remarkable, most exciting, most rewarding years of my life." She stayed on in Ireland through President Clinton's visit in September, and returned to the U.S. shortly afterwards. In May 2000 she developed a cross-border Irish arts festival, featuring dance, music, visual arts, literature and theater.

Kennedy Smith's appointment to Ireland in 1993 earned her and the late Joseph Sr. a place in the history books when they became the first father/daughter combination to serve as ambassadors in U.S. diplomatic history. Her father had earlier served as Ambassador to Britain.

Our Jack

*Somewhere in the shadowy land between myth and history lies the domicile of
John F. Kennedy. The first United States president of Irish Catholic descent,
Kennedy was a man of many faces: war hero, orator, lover, creator, visionary.
He had it all, and it was all taken away, but in the end he gained immortality.*

PETE HAMILL writes on JFK, our Irish American of the Century

That day I was in Ireland, in the dark, hard northern city of Belfast. I was there with my father, who had been away from the city where he was born for more than 30 years. He was an American now: citizen of Brooklyn, survivor of the Depression and poverty, one leg lost on an American playing field in the late 1920s, playing a game learned in Ireland, father of seven children, fanatic of baseball. But along the Falls Road in Belfast in November 1963, he was greeted as a returning Irishman by his brother Frank and his surviving Irish friends, and there were many Irish tears and much Irish laughter, waterfalls of beer, and all the old Irish songs of defiance and loss. Billy Hamill was home. And on the evening of Novemher 22, I was in my cousin Frankie Bennett's house in a section called Andersonstown, dressing to go down to see the old man in a place called the Rock Bar. The television was on in the parlor. Frankie's youngest kids were playing on the floor. A frail rain was falling outside.

And then the program was interrupted and a BBC announcer came on, his face grave, to say that the president of the United States had been shot while riding in a motorcade in Dallas, Texas. Everything in the room stopped. In his clipped, abrupt voice, the announcer said that the details were sketchy. Everyone turned to me, the visiting American, a reporter on a New York newspaper, as if I would know if this could possibly be true. I mumbled, talked nonsense – maybe it was a mistake; sometimes breaking news is moved too fast – but my stomach was churning. The regular program resumed; the kids went back to playing. A few minutes later, the announcer returned, and this time his voice was unsteady. It was true. John F. Kennedy, the president of the United States, was dead.

I remember whirling in pain and fury, slamming the wall with my open hand, and reeling out into the night. All over the city, thousands of human beings were doing the same thing. Doors slammed and sudden wails went up. *Oh, sweet Jesus, they shot Jack!* And *They killed President Kennedy!* And *He's been shot dead!* At the foot of the Falls Road, I saw an enraged man punching a tree. Another man sat on the curb, sobbing into his hands. Trying to be a reporter, I wandered over to the Shankill Road, the main Protestant avenue in that city long ghettoized by religion and history. There was not yet a Peace Line; not yet any British troops hovering warily on the streets, no bombs or ambushes or bloody Sundays. The reaction was the same on the Shankill as it was on the Falls. *Holy God, they've killed President Kennedy:* with men weeping and children running aimlessly with the news and bawling women everywhere. It was a scale of grief I'd never seen before or since in any place on earth. That night, John Fitzgerald Kennedy wasn't "the Catholic president" to the people of the Shankill or the Falls; he was the young and shining prince of the Irish diaspora.

After an hour, I ended up at the Rock Bar, climbing a flight of stairs to the long, smoky upstairs room. The place was packed. At a corner

This photograph of JFK, taken in Coos Bay, Oregon, shortly after he addressed a group of tough, hostile longshoremen in their union hall, shows a pensive Kennedy, obviously preoccupied with his failure to reach the men.
Photograph © Jacques Lowe.

Robert Knudsen / John F. Kennedy Library / SIPA press

Kennedy with his children, John (in Newport, Rhode Island in September, 1963) and Caroline.

table, my father was sitting with two old IRA men; one had only two fingers on his right hand. They were trying to console him when he was beyond consolation. His grief was real. No wonder. For the Catholic immigrants of his generation, men and women born in the first decade of the century, Jack Kennedy was forever and always someone special. His election in 1960 had redeemed everything: the bigotry that went all the way back to the Great Famine; the slurs and the sneers; *Help Wanted, No Irish Need Apply*; the insulting acceptance of the stereotype of the drunken and impotent Stage Irishman; the doors closed in law firms, and men's clubs, and brokerage houses because of religion and origin. After 1960, they knew that their children truly could be anything in their chosen country, including president of the United States.

"They got him, they got him," my father said that night, embracing me and sobbing into my shoulder. "The dirty sons of bitches, they got him."

And then "The Star-Spangled Banner" was playing on the television set, and everyone in the place, a hundred of them at least, rose at once and saluted. They weren't saluting the American flag, which was superimposed over Kennedy's face. They were saluting the fallen president who in some special way was their president too. The anthem ended. We sat down in a hushed way and drank a lot of whiskey together. We watched bulletins from Dallas. We cursed the darkness. And then there was a film of Kennedy in life. Visiting Ireland for three days the previous June.

There he was, smiling in that curious way, at once genuine and detached, capable of fondness and irony. The wind was tossing his hair. He was playing with the top button of his jacket. He was standing next to Eamon de Valera, the aged and gravely formal president of Ireland. Jack Kennedy was laughing with the mayor of New Ross in County Wexford. He was being engulfed by vast crowds in Dublin. He seemed to be having a very good time. And then he was at the airport to say his farewell, and in the Rock Bar, we heard him speak:

"Last night, somebody sang a song, the words of which I'm sure you know, of 'Come back to Erin, mavourneen, mavourneen, come back aroun' to the land of thy birth. Come with the shamrock in the springtime, mavourneen...' " He paused, but did not laugh at the sentimentality of the words; he seemed rather to be feeling the sentiment itself, the truth beneath the words, the ineradicable tearing that goes with exile. "This is not the land of my birth, but it is the land for which I hold the greatest affection." Another pause and then a smile. "And I certainly will come back in the springtime."

Thirty-six springtimes have come and gone, and for those of us who were young then, those days live on in vivid detail. We remember where we were and how we lived and who we were in love with. We remember thc images on television screens, black and white and grainy: Lee Harvey Oswald dying over and over again as Jack Ruby steps out to blow him into eternity; Jacqueline Kennedy's extraordinary wounded grace; Caroline's baffled eyes and John-John saluting. We remember the drumrolls and the riderless horse.

Irish Americans of a certain age will carry those images to their graves. At the end of a century that began with much poverty and even more hope, the immigrants who are still alive and the children who are charged with remembering have much reason to rejoice. There are few doors any longer closed to Irish Americans. Irish Americans run vast corporations, control great wealth, have triumphed in every field in American life, from the great universities to the halls of Congress, from movies and television to journalism and literature. We have our scientists, our doctors, our athletes, our scholars. Irish Americans can say with confidence: we have won all the late rounds.

The turning point, it seems to me, was the election of John F. Kennedy. Or rather, the election and the assassination a thousand days later. The combination ended the last vestiges of the marginalizing of Irish Americans; the hyphen that so infuriated Kennedy's father was permanently removed (who refers to Mark McGwire as an Irish-American?) or altered into an identity card that suggests admission, not exclusion; welcome, not rejection. The traumatic shock of the assassination itself created subtle shifts in the ways that other Americans perceived Irish Americans: there was a sense of dues paid, of finality. Many glib assumptions were shot away with that Mannlicher Carcano rifle. Among them were the assumptions of the larger society, expressed in the shorthand of stereotypes. But Kennedy's moment also ended the more timid assumptions of too many Irish men and women who believed that a desire for personal excellence or worldly success was a surrender to the sin of pride. They had created for themselves and their children what I've called elsewhere the Green Ceiling; Jack Kennedy smashed that ceiling forever. After he was buried, the men and women he had inspired did not go away.

To be sure, across those thirty-six springtimes, there have been alterations made – some of them drastic – to the reputation of John Fitzgerald

JFK and family members in Ireland, 1963.

into the presidential palace in Saigon. Only a handful of addled right-wingers continue fighting over the Sixties. The revisionists have come forward; Kennedy's life and his presidency have been examined in detail, and for some, both have been found wanting. The Kennedy presidency, we have been told, was incomplete, a sad perhaps; the man himself was deeply flawed. Some of this analysis was a reaction to the overwrought mythologizing of the first few years after Dallas. The selling of "Camelot" was too insistent, too fevered, accompanied by too much sentimentality and too little rigorous thought. The Camelot metaphor was never used during Kennedy's 1,000 days (Jack himself might have dismissed the notion with a wry or obscene remark); it first appeared in an interview Theodore H. White did with Jacqueline after the assassination. But it pervaded many of the first memoirs about the man and his time.

Some of the altered vision of Kennedy came from the coarsening of the collective memory by the endless stream of books about the assassination itself. The murder was submerged to a welter of conspiracy theories. In the end, nothing has been resolved. If there was a conspiracy, the plotters got away with it. In a peculiar way, the details of Kennedy's death obliterated both the accomplishments and failures of his life.

Other tales have helped to debase the metal of the man: the smarmy memoirs of women who certainly slept with him and others who certainly didn't; the endless retailing of the gossip about his alleged affair with Marilyn Monroe, that other pole of American literary necrophilia; the detailed histories of the family and its sometimes arrogant ways. He was described in some gossip as a mere "wham, bam, thank you ma'am" character; other talk had him a hopeless romantic. By all accounts, he was attracted to beautiful and intelligent women, and many of them were attracted to him. And during the time he journeyed among us, this was hardly a secret.

Kennedy. Those who hated him on November 21, 1963 did not stop hating him on November 23; many carried their hatred to their own graves. Some who were once his partisans turned upon him with the icy retrospective contempt that is the specialty of the neoconservative faith. And time itself has altered his once-glittering presence in the national consciousness. An entire generation has come to maturity with no memory at all of the Kennedy years; for them, Kennedy is the name of an airport or a boulevard or a high school.

Certainly, the psychic wound of his sudden death triggered the Sixties, that era that did not end until Richard Nixon waved his awkward farewells and the North Vietnamese tanks rolled

When I was a young reporter for the *Post* in late 1960, I was once assigned to cover Jack Kennedy during one of his stays at the Carlyle hotel. He had been elected but had not yet taken office. "We hear he brings the broads in two at a time," the editor said. "See what you can see."

There was nothing to see that night, perhaps because of my own naive incompetence as a reporter, or because I was joined in my vigil by another dozen reporters and about a hundred fans who wanted a glimpse of John F. Kennedy. Most likely, Kennedy was asleep in his suite while we camped outside the hotel's doors. But I remember thinking this was the best news I'd ever heard about a president of the United States. A man who loved women would not blow up the world. Ah, youth.

Two other events helped eclipse the memory of Jack Kennedy. One was the rise of Robert Kennedy, and his assassination in 1968. The other was Chappaquiddick. Some who had been drawn to politics by Jack Kennedy at last began to retreat from the glamour of the myth. A few turned away in revulsion, seeing after Chappaquiddick only the selfish arrogance of privilege. Others faded into indifference or exhaustion. At some undefined point in the late 1970s, the country seemed to decide it wanted to be free of the endless tragedy of the Kennedys. Even the most fervent Kennedy partisans needed release from doom and death. They left politics, worked in the media or the stock market or the academy. A few politicians continued to chase the surface of the myth; Gary Hart was one of them; in a different way, so was Bill Clinton. They helped cheapen Jack Kennedy's image the way imitators often undercut the work of an original artist.

Out in the country, beyond the narrow parish of professional politics, the people began to look for other myths and settled for a counterfeit. It was no accident that if once they had been entranced by a president who looked like a movie star, then the next step would be to find a movie star who looked like a president. The accidental charisma of Jack Kennedy gave way to the superb professional performance of Ronald Reagan.

The mistakes and flaws of the Kennedy presidency are now obvious. Domestically, he often moved too slowly, afraid of challenging Congress, somewhat late to recognize the urgency of the civil rights movement, which had matured on his watch. He understood the fragility of the New Deal coalition of northern liberals and southern conservatives; he had been schooled in the traditional ways of compromise in the House and Senate and was always uneasy with the moral certainties of "professional liberals." When faced with escalating hatred and violence in the South, Kennedy did respond; he showed a moral toughness that surprised his detractors and helped change the region. But he was often bored with life at home.

Foreign policy more easily captured his passions. He was one of the few American presidents to have traveled widely, to have experienced other cultures. His style was urban and cosmopolitan, and he understood that developments in technology were swiftly creating what Marshall McLuhan was to call the "global village." But since Kennedy had come to political maturity in the Fifties, he at first accepted the premises of the Cold War and the system of alliances and priorities that had been shaped by John Foster Dulles.

Even today, revisionists of the left seem unable to forgive the role that Kennedy the Cold Warrior played in setting the stage for the catastrophe of Vietnam. He had inherited from Eisenhower a commitment to the Diem regime, and as he honored that commitment, the number of U.S. "advisers" grew from 200 to 16,000. By most accounts, Kennedy intended to end the American commitment to South Vietnam after the 1964 election. But since he'd won in 1960 by only 118,000 votes, he didn't feel he could risk

charges by the American right that he had "lost" Vietnam. The quagmire beckoned, and at his death, Kennedy still hadn't moved to prevent the United States from trudging onward into the disaster.

For most of Kennedy's two years and ten months as president, Vietnam was a distant problem, simmering away at the back of the stove. Kennedy's obsession was Cuba. It remains unclear how much he knew about the various CIA plots to assassinate Fidel Castro. But the two major foreign policy events of his presidency were the Bay of Pigs invasion of April 1961, and the missile crisis of October 1962. One was a dreadful defeat, the other a triumph.

According to Richard Goodwin and others (I remember discussing this with Robert Kennedy), Jack Kennedy had begun the quiet process of normalizing relations with Castro before his death. Although this, too, was to be postponed until after the 1964 elections, Kennedy had come to believe that Cuba was not worth the

destruction of the planet. He waited, a prisoner of caution, and Fidel Castro – seven presidents later – is still the ruler of Cuba.

Today, it's hard to recall the intensity of the Cuban fever that so often rose in the Kennedy years. I remember being in Union Square when the Brigade was going ashore. A week earlier, I'd actually applied for press credentials for the invasion from some anti-Castro agent in midtown; with great silken confidence, he told me I could go into Cuba after the provisional government was set up, a matter of a few days after the invasion. But from the moment it landed, the quixotic Brigade was doomed. And in Union Square on the second night, when it still seemed possible that the Marines would hurry to the rescue, there was a demonstration against Kennedy, sponsored by a group that called itself the Fair Play for Cuba Committee. Its members chanted slogans against the president. A year later, a much larger group demonstrated during the missile crisis. In a strange, muted way, these were the first tentative signals that the Sixties were coming. And later, after Dallas, when the world was trying to learn something about Lee Harvey Oswald, we all saw film of him on a New Orleans street corner, handing out leaflets. They were, of course, from the Fair Play for Cuba Committee.

During his years in power, as far as I can tell, John Fitzgerald Kennedy never uttered a word about Northern Ireland.

And yet. . .

And yet, across the years, learning all of these things from the memoirs and biographies and histories, understanding that Camelot did not exist and that Jack Kennedy was not a perfect man, why do I remain moved almost to tears when a glimpse of him appears on television or I hear his voice coming from a radio?

I can't explain in any rational way. I've tried. Hell, yes, I've tried. I've talked to my daughters about him, and to my wife Fukiko, after they've seen me turning away from some televised image of Jack. They've seen me swallow, or take a sudden breath of air, or flick away a half-formed tear. They know me as an aging skeptic about the perfectibility of man, a cynic about most politicians. I bore them with preachments about the need for reason and lucidity in all things. And then, suddenly, Jack Kennedy is speaking from the past about how the torch has passed to a new generation of Americans, born in this century, tempered by war, disciplined by a hard and bitter peace – and I'm gone.

There is more operating here for me (and for so many millions of others) than simple nostalgia for the years when I was young. Nothing similar happens when I see images of Harry Truman or Dwight Eisenhower. Jack Kennedy was different. He was at once a role model, a brilliant son or an older brother, someone who made us all feel better about being Americans. Not just those of us who are products of the Irish diaspora. All of us. Everywhere on the planet in those years, the

great nations were led by old men, prisoners of history, slaves to orthodoxy. Not us (we thought, in our youthful arrogance). Not now.

"Ask not what your country can do for you," Kennedy said. "Ask what you can do for your country."

The line was immediately cherished by cartoonists and comedians, and Kennedy's political opponents often threw it back at him with heavy sarcasm. But the truth was that thousands of young people responded to the call. The best and the brightest streamed into Washington, looking for places in this shiny new administration. They came to Kennedy's Justice Department and began to transform it, using the power of law to accelerate social change, particularly in the South. They were all over the regulatory agencies. And after Kennedy started the Peace Corps, they signed up by the tens of thousands to go to the desperate places of the world to help strangers. It's hard to explain to today's young Americans that not so long ago, many people their age believed that the world could be transformed through politics. Yes, they were naive. Yes, they were idealists. But we watched all this, and many of us thought, 'This is some goddamned country.'

Out there in the wider world, people were responding to him as we were. It wasn't just Ireland or Europe. I remember seeing the reports of his 1962 trip to Mexico City, where a million people came out to greet him, the women weeping, the men applauding him as fellow men and not inferiors. I'd lived in Mexico and knew the depths of resentment so many Mexicans felt toward the Colossus of the North. In one day, Kennedy seemed to erase a century of dreadful history. The same thing happened in Bogotá and Caracas where four years earlier Richard Nixon had been spat upon and humiliated. This was after the Bay of Pigs. This was while the Alliance for Progress was still trying to get off the ground. I can't be certain today what there was about him that triggered so much emotion; surely it must

Brothers John and Robert.

have been some combination of his youth, naturalness, machismo, and grace. I do know this: in those years, when we went abroad, we were not often forced to defend the president of the United States.

We didn't have to defend him at home, either. He did a very good job of that himself. We hurried off to watch his televised press conferences because they were such splendid displays of intelligence, humor, and style. We might disagree with Kennedy's policies, and often did; but he expressed them on such a high level that disagreement was itself part of an intelligent process instead of the more conventional exchange of iron certitudes. He held 64 press conferences in his brief time in office (Reagan held 47) and obviously understood how important they were to the furthering of his policies. But he also enjoyed them as ritual and performance. He was a genuinely witty man, with a very Irish love of the English language, the play on words, the surprising twist. But there was an odd measure of shyness in the man, too, and that must have been at the heart of his sense of irony, along with his detachment, his fatalism, his understanding of the absurd. He was often more Harvard than Irish, but he was more Irish than even he ever thought.

I loved that part of him. Loved, too, the way he honored artists and writers and musicians, inviting them to the White House for splendid dinners, insisting that Robert Frost read a poem at the inauguration. He said he enjoyed Ian Fleming's books about James Bond; but he also brought André Malraux to the White House, and James Baldwin, Gore Vidal and Saul Bellow, along with such musicians as Pablo Casals. Perhaps this was all a political ploy, a means of getting writers and artists on his side; if so, it worked. Not many writers have felt comfortable in the White House in all the years since, not even with Bill Clinton, who truly did make the effort.

Part of Jack Kennedy's appeal was based on another fact: he was that rare American politician, a genuine war hero. Not a general, not someone who had spent the war ordering other men to fight and die, but a man who had been out on the line himself. When he first surfaced as a national figure, at the 1956 Democratic Convention, reporters rushed to find copies of John Hersey's *New Yorker* account of the PT-109 incident in the South Pacific. They read: "Kennedy took McMahon in tow again. He cut loose one end in his teeth. He swam breaststroke, pulling the helpless McMahon along on his back. It took over five hours to reach the island. . . ."

Reading the story years after the event, some of us were stunned. Kennedy was the real article. There had been so many fakers, so many pols who were tough with their mouths and avoided the consequences of their belligerence. The type never vanishes. Over the past 20 years, the most fervent flagwavers, particularly among the Republicans, have been men who ducked service in Vietnam, their war. I think of them, and think of Kennedy, and they all seem to be frauds. Kennedy had been there, not simply as a victim but as a hero, a man who'd saved other men's lives. When he was president, that experience gave his words about war and peace a special authority. We also knew that his back had been terribly injured in the Solomons and had tormented him ever since. He had almost died after a 1954 operation, and he wore a brace until the day he died. But he bore his pain well; he never used it as an excuse; he didn't retail it in exchange for votes. Hemingway, another hero of that time, had defined courage as grace under pressure. By that definition, Jack Kennedy certainly had courage.

Years later, long after the murder in Dallas and after Vietnam had first escalated into tragedy and then disintegrated into defeat; long after a generation had taken to the streets before retreating into the Big Chill; long after the ghettos of Watts and Newark and Detroit and so many other cities had exploded into nihilistic violence; after Rohert Kennedy had been killed and Martin Luther King and Malcolm X; after Woodstock and Watergate; after the Beatles had arrived, triumphed, and broken up, and after John Lennon had been murdered; after Johnson, Nixon, Ford, and Carter had given way to Ronald Reagan; after passionate liberalism faded; after the horrors of Cambodia and the anarchy of Beirut; after cocaine and AIDS had become the new plagues – after all had changed from the world we knew in 1963, I was driving alone in a rented car late one afternoon through the state of Guerrero in Mexico.

I was moving through vast, empty stretches of parched mountainous land when the right rear tire went flat. I pulled over and quickly discovered that the rental car had neither a spare nor tools. I was alone in the emptiness of Mexico, on a road in its most dangerous state. Trucks roared by, and some cars, heading for Acapulco, but nobody stopped.

Off in the distance I saw a plume of smoke coming from a small house. I started walking to the house, feeling uneasy and vulnerable. A rutted dirt road led to the front of the house. A dusty car was parked to the side. It was almost dark, and for a tense moment, I considered turning back.

And then the door opened. A beefy man stood there, looking at me in a blank way. I came closer, and he squinted and then asked me in Spanish what I wanted. I told him I had a flat tire and needed help. He considered that for a moment and then asked me if I first needed something to drink.

I glanced past him into the house. On the wall there were two pictures. One was of the Virgin of Guadalupe. The other was of Jack Kennedy. Yes, I said. Some water would be fine.

Robert Kennedy
Moral Leader

"Moral courage is a rarer commodity than bravery in battle or great intelligence. Yet it is the one essential, vital quality for those who seek to change a world that yields most painfully to change . . . and those with the courage to enter the moral conflict will find themselves with companions in every corner of the world."

The seventh of the nine children born to Joseph and Rose Kennedy, Robert F. Kennedy was a graduate of Harvard College and the University of Virginia Law School. He began his political career as an attorney with the Justice Department, prosecuting cases involving corrupt business practices. He later served as counsel to a Senate committee investigating labor racketeering.

As attorney general for his brother, President John Kennedy, RFK was an indispensable partner. He threw his weight behind the Civil Rights Act of 1964 and prosecuted school desegregation cases. A passionate speaker who encouraged individual responsibility, personal courage, and compassion for those less fortunate,

Time, Inc.

Kennedy had "that rarest of qualities – a clear-eyed conviction in what he knew to be right", recalls Senator Christopher Dodd (D-CT), a former Peace Corps volunteer.

Kennedy had a passionate intensity about the issues of the day, whether it was the tragedy of racial hatred or the wretched conditions of the American Indian, the despair of homelessness or the blight of the urban poor. He portrayed an America where justice and fairness always prevailed, and he challenged us to create that place for ourselves.

One of Kennedy's most memorable of speeches came after the assassination of Martin Luther King, Jr. Still struggling to comprehend the death of his own brother, Kennedy – though warned against it by the Indianapolis Chief of Police – grimly decided to proceed as planned with a rally in the heart of that city's ghetto. When the Senator's car entered the black neighborhood, the police escort dropped behind, leaving Kennedy unprotected. Undaunted, he climbed on to a flatbed truck that was serving as a platform and addressed the crowd of about 1,000 people who still hadn't heard the news of King's death.

"He was up there," said television correspondent Charles Quinn, "hunched in his black overcoat, his face gaunt and distressed and full of anguish. Speaking extemporaneously, in a sorrowful voice, Kennedy told the crowd: 'I have bad news for you, for all our fellow citizens, and people who love peace all over the world, and that is that Martin Luther King was shot and killed tonight.'"

Kennedy, probably the only white person in America who could have broken the news of King's death to the largely black crowd that tragic night and not have encountered violence, continued: "For those of you who are black and tempted to be filled with hatred and distrust against all white people, I can only say that I feel in my own heart the same kind of feeling. I had a member of my family killed, but he was killed by a white man. But we have to make an effort in the United States, we have to make an effort to understand, to look beyond these rather difficult times." It was the first time Kennedy had publicly mentioned the death of his brother.

When asked to name his most important accomplishment, Robert Kennedy said: "Marrying Ethel." Together they had 11 children, the youngest, Rory, not yet born when he was killed by Sirhan Sirhan in Los Angeles on June 6, 1968, after claiming victory in California's 1968 presidential primary.

Peter King
The Ultimate Pol

"In my mind I had no doubt I was doing the right thing. What the president did was not an impeachable offense."

It is doubtful if there has been any Irish American politician this century who has dedicated more of his time in office to seeking a peaceful resolution of the Northern Ireland problem,

Representative Peter King (R-NY) has long been an ardent supporter of Irish causes, and has traveled to Northern Ireland over 20 times. He accompanied President Clinton on his trip in 1995 and again in 1998. King is an outspoken advocate of human rights and justice for the people of the North and was hugely instrumental in creating a platform for Sinn Féin in the United States.

King also made history by being one of only five Republicans who voted against the impeachment of President Clinton in the House of Representatives. His close relationship with the President on Irish issues undoubtedly helped him make his choice.

In January 1999, King was named chairman of the Investigation and Oversight Committee, a subcommittee of the Banking Committee in the House. The able politician has also turned his hand to writing fiction and his first novel,

Terrible Beauty, was published in 1999 by Roberts Rinehart. President Clinton was spotted leaving Air Force One with a copy of the book shortly after its publication.

King was elected Grand Marshal of the 1985 New York City St. Patrick's Day Parade, and has been honored by numerous organizations, including the Ancient Order of Hibernians, the Irish National Caucus and the Irish Northern Aid Committee.

First elected to represent New York's Third District in Nassau County on Long Island in 1992, King currently serves on the Committee on International Relations and is co-chairman of the Congressional Ad Hoc Committee for Irish Affairs. He also serves on the Committee on Banking, Finance and Urban Affairs.

Prior to serving in county government, King had extensive experience as a practicing attorney and civic leader. He began his political career in November 1977 by winning election to the Hempstead Town Council. He was also elected Nassau County Comptroller in 1981, and reelected to the position in 1985 and 1989.

A graduate of St. Francis College in Brooklyn, King earned his J.D. degree at Notre Dame. He traces his Irish ancestors to Counties Limerick and Galway. King and his wife have two children.

Eugene McCarthy
The Poetic Pol

"The only thing that saves us from bureaucracy is its inefficiency. An efficient bureaucracy is the greatest threat to freedom."

He is best remembered for his courageous stance against the Vietnam War, when all around him were denouncing those who opposed the military action as traitors and cowards. But millions of others soon came to realize that Eugene McCarthy, politician and poet, had been right all along.

Born in Watkins, Minnesota on March 29, 1916, McCarthy was once described by fellow Democrat Hubert Humphrey as "the son of a Minnesota farmer, handsome, witty, teacher, poet, Irish mystic, and a clever politician, cleverer for denying it."

He taught at both high school and college level before entering the U.S. House of Representatives in 1948. Ten years later, he was elected to the Senate. McCarthy's book *The Year of the People* documents his throwing down of the gauntlet in 1968 to then President Lyndon Johnson on the issue of ongoing U.S. involvement in Vietnam. He also sought the Democratic presidential nomination in that year, and although he lost, he led the way for Robert Kennedy to enter the race. McCarthy retired

from the Senate in 1971, and resumed teaching two years later.

A staunch supporter of Irish causes, McCarthy appeared before the Senate Foreign Relations Committee in 1985 during hearings on the Supplementary Extradition Treaty between the U.S. and the U.K. He made it quite clear, via a brief history lesson to the Committee, that he could under no circumstances support any agreement that returned IRA fugitives to Ireland or Britain.

Family, politics and history all play their part in McCarthy's many works of poetry, for which he is almost as well known as his politics. He is also a political essayist of some note. Married to Abigail Quigley, McCarthy has three daughters and one son.

George Mitchell
The Diplomat

"The people of Ireland are sick of war. They're sick of sectarian killings and random bombings. They're sick of the sad elegance of funerals, especially those involving the small white coffins of children, prematurely laid into the rolling green fields of the Irish countryside. They want peace, and I believe they now have it."

Among both Unionists and Nationalists in Northern Ireland, it is widely agreed that without George Mitchell, there would never have been a peace agreement on that Good Friday, 1998. The combination of his statesmanship, Job-like patience and willingness to make himself equally present to both sides won the respect and trust of all parties involved.

Of Irish and Lebanese descent, Mitchell was born in Waterville, Maine in 1933. His grandfather, named Kilroy, emigrated to the United States from Ireland with his wife at the end of the 19th century. The family history is sketchy, but Mitchell believes that his grandmother died, and his grandfather, unable to look after the children, put them in an orphanage. Mitchell's father was adopted and his name was changed from Joseph Kilroy to George Mitchell. He married a Lebanese woman, and worked as a college janitor while his wife worked the midnight shift in the woolen mills for nearly 30 years.

Young Mitchell graduated from Bowdoin College in 1954 and served two years as an officer with the U.S. Army Counter-Intelligence Corps in West Berlin. He went on to earn a law degree from Georgetown University. He became an executive assistant to Senator Edmund Muskie in Washington, D.C. but later returned to Maine to take a partnership in a law firm. After an unsuccessful run for governor of Maine in 1974, he served as U.S. Attorney and U.S. District Court Judge in his home state. When Muskie resigned from the U.S. Senate in 1980, Mitchell was appointed in his place. He easily won reelection in 1982 and 1988. In 1988 he was also elected Senate majority leader.

During his years in the Senate he established a reputation for supporting Irish American causes. In 1994, he supported the move to obtain a U.S. visa for Sinn Féin leader Gerry Adams. When he retired from the Senate after 14 years of service, he declined an offer to sit on the Supreme Court, but interestingly enough, agreed to become the President's special adviser for economic initiatives in Ireland, which ultimately led to his being selected to chair the peace talks in Northern Ireland.

In 1997, Mitchell's wife, Heather, gave birth to a baby boy, Andrew, while Mitchell was still chairing the talks. One can only imagine how difficult it must have been for him to face the intractable problem of the conflict in Northern Ireland when he was an ocean away from his new son. Still, as frustrating as it often was, his commitment to the process never waned.

When the talks threatened to become bogged down in the obstinacy of both sides, Mitchell took a step that made all the difference: he set a deadline for an agreement. This worked beautifully in getting the parties to focus on making progress. As the deadline drew nigh he summoned Taoiseach (Prime Minister) Bertie Ahern and British leader Tony Blair to Northern Ireland to coax the process along, keeping President Clinton regularly updated by telephone.

After the implementation of the Good Friday Agreement and the establishment of the Northern Ireland Assembly became bogged down over the issue of decommissioning, Mitchell returned to Northern Ireland to try to prevent the Agreement from falling apart. While he made it no secret that he was disappointed to have to return to Northern Ireland for this purpose, no one doubted his commitment to winning peace for Northern Ireland. If anyone can do the job, he can.

Daniel Moynihan and his wife Elizabeth.

Daniel Patrick Moynihan
The Intellectual

"Irish Americans are fast becoming an invisible ethnic group, not because they are quieter or fewer in number these days, but because they have met with extraordinary success here."

In his 24 years of service to the U.S. Senate, Daniel Patrick Moynihan has distinguished himself with an intellectual integrity that is increasingly rare in today's poll-driven politics. The outspoken champion of social welfare, it was Moynihan who, during the Reagan era, provided eloquent if unwelcome reminders of the people who Reaganomics had left behind.

Moynihan is widely regarded as the nation's leading expert on social welfare, which may seem surprising given his rather patrician bearing. But his bow-tie and suspenders belie his upbringing.

The grandson of a Kerryman, Moynihan was born in Tulsa, Oklahoma and raised in Hell's Kitchen on Manhattan's West Side, spending vacations in the Irish American enclave of Rockaway Beach, Queens. He was educated at Benjamin Franklin High School in East Harlem and in New York's public college system. After serving in the Navy during World War II, he earned a B.A. from Tufts University in 1948. He was a Fulbright Scholar at the London School of Economics and was awarded a Ph.D. from the Fletcher School of Law and Diplomacy.

He has since taught government at Harvard and served under the Kennedy, Johnson, Nixon and Ford administrations. But it is his continued involvement in social issues that reveals his loyalty to his roots. Moynihan's background helps explain his fascination with this country's multi-ethnic makeup, a topic about which he has written extensively, in publications including his book *Beyond the Melting Pot*.

After serving as Ambassador to the United Nations, Moynihan was elected to the U.S. Senate in 1976. He retired in 2000, leaving a void in national politics that will be hard to fill.

Not without his detractors, Moynihan is unusual in his ability to remain unswayed by them, continuing to work for what he genuinely believes is right. An ally of constitutional nationalism in Northern Ireland, he is completely intolerant of paramilitary violence, a fact that has earned him some criticism among Irish Americans. Still, the Irish consulate in New York has hailed him as "exceptionally helpful on every aspect of Irish-related issues in the Congress. He has had a profound and significant impact."

Bruce Morrison
Visa Savior

Bruce Morrison won the loyalty of thousands of Irish citizens when he authored and enacted the Immigration Act of 1990, the most comprehensive revision of the U.S. immigration law in the country's history. This legislation included the Morrison visas, which provided

chemistry from the University of Illinois. He is a 1973 graduate of Yale Law School and resides with his wife and son in Bethesda, Maryland.

Thomas P. "Tip" O'Neil
Master of the House
"All politics is local."

At the relatively tender age of 22, Thomas "Tip" O'Neill learned a lesson which was to resonate with him for the rest of his political career. After losing his bid for a seat on the Cambridge City Council, he discovered that he hadn't worked hard enough to secure the support of his own neighborhood. Another famous O'Neill story involves a supporter by the name of Mrs. O'Brien who voted without fail for him in every election, except the one where he forgot to call and ask for her vote. Her response to his surprised query after the election? "People always like to be asked, Mr. O'Neill." These anecdotes and others were used by O'Neill to highlight his deep-seated belief that "all politics is local", a motto he clung to throughout a long and successful political career.

Born December 9, 1912 in North Cambridge, Massachusetts, O'Neill was descended from Cork and Donegal stock. His paternal grandfather, Patrick O'Neill, came to New England during the Famine era at the age of 13

immigration opportunities for at least 48,000 Irish men and women.

Less well known is Morrison's dedication to the Northern Ireland peace process. In 1994, he was one of the leaders of a delegation of Irish American business people who toured the troubled Six Counties. His perseverance, and the work of others like him, played a large part in the securing of the first IRA ceasefire.

From 1983 to 1991, Morrison represented the third district of Connecticut in the House of Representatives. It was in this role that he began his work on Irish issues, serving as co-chair of the Congressional Ad Hoc Committee on Irish Affairs. He also distinguished himself as a staunch defender of human rights throughout the world.

In 1992, Morrison was chairman of the Irish Americans for Clinton-Gore and helped develop the campaign's Irish agenda. That same year, he established the law firm Morrison and Swaine in Connecticut, specializing in immigration issues and international trade and investment. In 1993, he helped establish Americans for a New Agenda, which he also chaired.

In addition to chairing the Federal Housing Finance Board, he serves on the U.S. Commission on Immigration Reform.

Morrison holds a bachelor's degree in chemistry from the Massachusetts Institute of Technology and a master's degree in organic

with his three brothers, and all began work with the New England Brick Company. His mother's family, the Tolans, were from Belfast and Donegal. In an interview with *Irish America* in 1986, O'Neill proudly mentioned the fact that he owned a 65-acre farm near Lough Swilly in Donegal, a gift given to him and his wife by two of their sons.

O'Neill's father, like his father before him, was a bricklayer, but when it came to his own children he wanted better for them. Consequently, O'Neill ended up in politics, his brother became a judge, and his sister was extremely successful in the field of education.

Growing up in Boston, three things were clear to O'Neill: the terrible indignities suffered by the Irish who faced "No Irish Need Apply" signs on arrival in the States; the suffering of those who came over on the so-called coffin ships of the time; and the importance of a United Ireland.

O'Neill entered the Massachusetts House, a staunch bastion of Republicanism, in 1936. Slowly, the tide turned, and by the time World War II ended, the House was Democratic, with O'Neill elected Speaker in 1948. He entered Congress in 1953, filling the seat that had become vacant when John F. Kennedy entered the Senate. From 1971-73, O'Neill served as Majority Whip; he was also Majority Leader from 1973-77; and Speaker from 1977-87. He resigned from Congress in 1987. "One of the things I got right was to get out when I did," he said later. "I left before I got pushed." He died in Boston on January 5, 1994, less than a month after his 81st birthday.

Ronald Reagan
The Great Communicator

"Heroes may not be braver than anyone else. They're just braver five minutes longer."

Ronald Reagan was hardly the first Irish American to make it to the White House, but he is perhaps the only President who could match JFK for charisma.

A staunch conservative, he quickly became the kind of Commander-in-Chief that people either loved or hated and is still remembered as one of the most persuasive leaders this country has seen.

Born February 6, 1911 in Tampico, Illinois, to John Edward Reagan and Nelle Wilson, Reagan was raised in the faith of the Christian Church, a Presbyterian outfit, like his older brother John. His brother, however, was christened, unlike Reagan, and later returned to Catholicism. Reagan's father was an alcoholic, which led to some tough times for the family when he found it hard to hold down a steady job. His grandfather, Michael Reogan (he later changed the name to Reagan), had left his native Tipperary in the early 1880s. He originally made his way to England where he met and married Katherine Mulcahy, and the couple emigrated to the States.

After graduating from college, Reagan began work as a radio sportscaster. During a trip to California in 1937 with the Chicago Cubs baseball team, he played hooky long enough to secure himself a screen test, which quickly led to a 30-year career in movies and television.

Originally a Democrat, like many of his fellow actors, Reagan gave his first political speech in 1945 at Hollywood Legion Stadium. It was to be the first of many, and Reagan quickly became known as "The Great Communicator." He spent several years as president and board member of the Screen Actors Guild, which heightened his political standing.

By the time he hit the state and national scene, however, he had changed colors and was supporting the Republican ethos. From 1967 to '74 he was Governor of California, and finally gained the nomination for the presidency in 1980, defeating Democrat Jimmy Carter by a landslide. His second term followed at the expense of Walter Mondale.

Reagan's time in office is defined by tax cuts, cutbacks in government programs, and increased spending on the nation's military. In 1981, he survived an assassination attempt by John Hinckley, who claimed he had tried to kill the President out of love for actress Jodie Foster. After retiring from politics he returned to ranching, a life-long passion. Married to former actress Nancy Davis, Reagan now suffers from Alzheimer's disease.

Al Smith
Big Apple Hero

"Law, in a democracy, means the protection of the rights and liberties of the minority."

He was the first Irish American Catholic Governor of New York, and a Democratic nominee for President in 1928. Regarded as the quintessential Irish urban politician, the product of generations of Tammany Hall artistry, he was named for his Italian-German father, Alfred Emanuel Smith. Young Al Smith nonetheless felt far closer to his mother's Irish roots, and chose to identify himself as Irish American for the rest of his life. His future as a politician was perhaps indicated well in advance when, at the age of 11, he won an oratory contest held in New York City for his oration on Robespierre.

Library of Congress

Born December 30, 1873 to Alfred Smith and Catherine Mulvihill, the daughter of an Irish father and an English mother, young Al was forced to leave school early and help support his family when his father died.

Smith learned the ropes politically from local Democrat Tom Foley, who introduced him to Tammany Hall. Foley helped Smith get a job as a process server for the commissioner of jurors, and later had the younger man picked as a Democratic candidate for the State Assembly of New York. Two years later, Smith was chosen as Speaker of the Assembly, and he went on to become widely known for his championing of various humanitarian issues.

After a devastating fire in a Manhattan clothing factory which killed 146 people, Smith sponsored legislation for the establishment of a commission to investigate working conditions in New York State factories. The commission's findings led him to usher in much-needed legislation on health, sanitation, fire laws and working conditions in general, especially for women and children.

In 1915, Smith was elected sheriff of New York City, and he went on to bypass a run for mayor, instead focusing on the office of the governor. He won handily, and ended up serving four terms. During this time, Smith was responsible for many far-seeing acts of social reform. He sponsored low-cost housing, extended rent controls, opposed legislation which aimed to reduce the civil liberties of socialists, and fought hard to outlaw the Ku Klux Klan.

In 1920, Smith's name was first mentioned in connection with a bid for the Democratic presidential nomination, but it would be four years before he got a bite at the apple. Failing to garner the coveted nomination that year, he tried again in 1928 and triumphed. It was a short-lived victory, however, as he lost the presidential election to Herbert Hoover. One of the reasons for Hoover's win was his enthusiastic support for Prohibition, an action Smith strongly opposed. Smith had a couple of other strikes against him: he was Catholic and a New Yorker.

In 1932, Smith committed what many saw as the unpardonable sin: he attempted to oust Franklin D. Roosevelt, the man who had twice nominated him as the Democratic candidate, from Roosevelt's race for the nomination. In 1936, he left many of his old friends and supporters feeling even more betrayed when he voted for a Republican. Smith died in October 1944. He was married to Irish immigrant Catherine Dunn, and they had five children: Alfred Emanuel, Emily, Catherine, Arthur and Walter.

Song & Dance

The Paddy Clancy Call

Frank McCourt mourns the passing of a friend and an era
BY FRANK MCCOURT

We're heading towards the end of 1999 and there are some, including myself, who may not see another year with a 9 in it.

And isn't that the gloomiest opening sentence you ever read in your life?

Still, it had to be written because they're going, my generation, the silent generation, slipping gently, one by one, into that good night, going with grace – unlike the bleating baby boomers behind us who seem to think they're exempt from mutability.

This has to be written because now The Call comes more often: "How are you, Frank? Do you know who died?" When couched like that I know it's one of my brothers, Alphie, Michael, Malachy, and we sense the old joke shimmering in the background.

"Hello there, Pat. Do you know who died?"
"No. Who?"
"Eamonn Lynch from Carey's Road."
"Aw, God rest him, and what did he die of?"
"Oh, nothin' serious."
"Well, thank God for that."

The Call came last year when Paddy Clancy died after months of struggling with a brain tumor. At first there was some satisfaction in the sweetness of Paddy's going: in his own bed, surrounded by his family, grandchildren crawling over him, his mind wandering when he asked if his own parents would come to his funeral. Of course it was a sad call, though it sent me back over the 40 years of our friendship, back to our early days in Greenwich Village, back to the White Horse Tavern, back to the San Remo, the Limelight on Sheridan Square and, above all, back to the Lion's Head on Christopher Street.

In the 1950s you could stand at the bar of the White Horse Tavern and listen to the talk. You might hear Daniel Patrick Moynihan on history, Delmore Schwartz on poetry, Michael Harrington on the poor, Kevin Sullivan on Irish literature. A "regular", cadging a drink, might be telling a tourist how Dylan Thomas drank himself to death at this very bar and often the tourist would say, "Who's Dylan Thomas?"

With all this talking and drinking there was background music – the Clancy Brothers and Tommy Makem singing away in a small room up a couple of steps. Makem came from a musical family in the North but the Clancys, I think, were discovering the power of traditional Irish song. Paddy and Tom Clancy had knocked around the world till they came to rest in Greenwich Village, where they acted and produced plays at the Cherry Lane Theater. Then, when brother Liam arrived from Ireland, they began to sing for their own label, Tradition Records. They sang at small venues all over the country till Ed Sullivan invited them on his show and that was the big time.

They were the first. Before them there were dance bands and show bands and céilidhe bands on both sides of the Atlantic. There were individual performers like Delia Murphy, Ruthie Morrissey, Mickey Carton, but not since John McCormack had Irish singers captured international attention like the Clancy Brothers and Tommy Makem. They opened the gates to the likes of the Dubliners and the Wolfe Tones and every Irish group thereafter. Their straight-forward, good-humored delivery restored life to many an Irish song that had suffocated for years under layers of syrup. They simply cut the sentiment and allowed each song its own dignity. They sang their songs. They didn't preach. And they were loved everywhere.

111

James Mullin

Frank McCourt and Paddy Clancy on an Irish Festival Cruise in January 1998.

When Paddy died he was referred to as the "strong man" of the group. He often laughed and told me he didn't think much of himself as a singer, that Tommy Makem was the real musician in the group, that Liam was the Voice. (Bob Dylan once said Liam had a better voice than anyone in the business.)

Despite all the traveling and singing, all the adulation and glamour, Paddy knew what he wanted – that 150-acre farm in Carrick-on-Suir in Tipperary, and when he married Mary Flannery from Mayo they stocked the place with prize French cows. When he wasn't all over the world singing, Paddy, gentleman farmer always dressed in suit, shirt, tie, would wander the farm puffing on his pipe, discussing the ways of cows with his hired man, Gus, who knew everything about every farm animal in Tipperary, their seed, breed and generation. Gus could look at a cow from a hundred yards away and tell you if she was ready for the bull or beyond the bull. Gus could stick his nose in the air and tell you when

the rain might come or if the sun had a notion of appearing today, and it was this man, Gus, I think, that Paddy admired most in the world because Gus was a genius out of the earth itself, the element Paddy loved most.

Whatever Paddy knew he discovered for himself and, because he read constantly, he wasn't shy about his lack of formal education. Someone told him in the Lion's Head one night he was an erudite man and he laughed. "I'm as erudite as shit," he said, though his head was crammed with poetry and history and whatever he learned from Gus. Poets and writers would pass through the Lion's Head and Paddy was always ready to talk – or to listen. He would puff on his pipe – and listen. He and Kevin Sullivan were powerful listeners and when I began to write I thought of them as the ideal audience, the perfect readers.

I am writing about Paddy Clancy because I loved him and because his death in 1998 stirred up sweet memories of other ghosts from the Lion's Head Bar: Joe Flaherty, Joel Oppenheimer, Kevin Sullivan, Archie Mulligan, Tommy Butler, Wes Joice, Mike Reardon, Nick Brown.

After 30 years the Lion's Head closed in 1996. It had become my home away from home, the place where we mumbled into our pints over troubled romances, crumbling marriages, wayward children, and careers gone astray. There was drink, of course, and there were long nights and hideous hangovers, but there were friendships and I am blessed for having known the likes of Paul Schiffman, Jack Deacy, Sheila McKenna, Dennis Duggan, Bill Flanagan, Barry Murphy, Pete Hamill, Jack Meehan.

Oh, the times I've had at the Head, and it was Paddy Clancy who invited me there on opening night.

The Clancy Brothers
& Tommy Makem
The Music Makers

"It's only in the last number of years that I realize how deep down into the soil of Ireland my roots really go. I had such a tremendous amount to draw on, and didn't realize it."
– Tommy Makem

The image is indelible – four Irishmen, clad in Aran sweaters, chests out, singing songs of Irish humor, history, and freedom. The Clancy Brothers, along with Tommy Makem, blazed a trail for Irish folk music in America in the 1960s. America is the richer for it.

Brothers Paddy and Tom Clancy emigrated to Canada in the late forties, eventually finding work in the States as house painters, singing on the side. By 1959, they were joined by youngest brother Liam, and Makem. New York became home to the Clancys, where they found a vibrant folk scene in Greenwich Village. Any given night could find them trading songs with the likes of Peter Paul & Mary, Pete Seeger, or Bob Dylan. They were invited to play at the prestigious Newport Folk Festival alongside Judy Collins

and Joan Baez; that led to a national television audience on *The Ed Sullivan Show*. The Clancys toured with a vengeance and topped charts all throughout the Sixties.

A Clancy Brothers show was legendary for its exuberance. Whoops, hollers, and foot-stomping punctuated the affair, and rare was the audience that didn't sing along. Songs like "The Wild Rover," "The Parting Glass," "Isn't It Grand, Boys," and "The Mermaid" delighted audiences worldwide.

By the end of the sixties, the original Clancy Brothers lineup disbanded amicably. Tommy Makem left to pursue a solo career, and was often joined by Liam. Various Clancy sons and nephews joined with their fathers and uncles to perform under the Clancy moniker.

Tom Clancy died of cancer in 1990; Paddy died in 1998 following a long illness.

No less than Bob Dylan invited the surviving Clancy Brothers and Makem to sing at his 30th anniversary concert in 1992. The Clancy Brothers' songs of joy, struggle, and hope made America take notice of Ireland – if you looked closely, you could even see Lady Liberty tapping her toe . . .

George M. Cohan
Yankee Doodle Dandy

"I'm a Yankee Doodle Dandy / A Yankee Doodle do or die / A real live nephew of my Uncle Sam's / Born on the Fourth of July."

Songwriter, actor, playwright, and producer, George M. Cohan is most remembered as the Yankee Doodle Dandy, whose spirited music reflected and shaped the American mindset in the early years of this century.

His father, Michael Keohane, was born in County Cork and changed the spelling to Cohan when he came to America. Born July 3, 1878 in Providence, Rhode Island, George Cohan left school early and joined his parents' vaudeville act, along with his sister. By age 11, he was writing sketches and, later, songs for the act known as "The Four Cohans."

In his twenties, he started writing musical comedies for Broadway. *Little Johnny Jones*, performed in 1904, was his first success, and introduced the popular song "The Yankee Doodle Boy." Two years later George had a hit with "George Washington, Jr." and the debut of the routine he is most identified with – parading around stage while singing praise to an American flag he carries.

Cohan went on to produce more than 50 plays, revues, and comedies with partner Sam Harris. His songs include "You're a Grand Old Flag" and "Give My Regards to Broadway." Of his starring roles on Broadway, Cohan won particular acclaim for his role in Eugene O'Neill's *Ah, Wilderness!*

Cohan's biggest single song was written in 1917 as a patriotic tribute when the United States entered World War I. "Over There" earned him a Congressional Medal of Honor from President Franklin D. Roosevelt in 1940.

Married twice, Cohan died in New York City on November 5, 1942. His career was made into the film *Yankee Doodle Dandy*, starring James Cagney.

Bing Crosby
Crooner

"When Irish eyes are smiling . . ."

Gilbert Seldes, the famous arts critic, once pointed out, "There was a time, not so long ago, when it was truthfully said that no hour of the day or night, year after year, passed without the voice of Bing Crosby being heard somewhere on this earth."

Bing Crosby was the consummate crooner. His smooth voice and relaxed, amiable manner easily beat all comers. And his eyes just seemed to ooze sincerity and romance – is it any wonder that he remains one of the best loved entertainers of the century?

Born Harry Lillis Crosby in Tacoma, Washington, Crosby descended from a long line of Irish immigrant stock. Nicknamed "Bing" after a character in the comic strip "The Bingsville Bugle", he began singing as early as 1921, and in 1931 he won immediate fame with his own radio show. His inimitable style and appealing songs made him an international star, and he won several gold records throughout his career. His hit song "White Christmas" from the 1942 movie *Holiday Inn* remains the all-time best-selling single record.

He also made several Irish recordings, dedicating the song "Harrigan, That's Me" to his maternal grandparents, Dennis and Katherine Harrigan, Irish immigrants both.

Crosby's film career began with Max Sennett shorts, and as one of the Rhythm Boys in Paul Whiteman's Orchestra in the 1930 *King of Jazz*. His Hollywood career was launched in 1932 with his starring role in *The Big Broadcast*.

Crosby's characters were never great stretches from his own personality, and they were all the more appealing for that. As Seldes pointed out, he had "a sort of gentlemanly ease . . . an indifference to effect." His natural style made him a delight to watch and his contribution to the musical and light comedy genre of films popular at the time was immeasurable. In 1936, he starred in the musicals *Anything Goes* (with Ethel Merman) and *Pennies from Heaven* (with Louis Armstrong). *The Road to Singapore*, starring that fabulous comic trio of Crosby, Bob Hope and Dorothy Lamour, was the most popular movie of 1940, and the series of "Road" films that followed became a part of the cinematic landscape of the Forties. Two of Crosby's most memorable roles were playing

men of the cloth. In *Going My Way* (1944) he won an Oscar for his portrayal of an easygoing, singing priest who solved the problems of a poor parish. The following year, he starred with Ingrid Bergman in the film's sequel The *Bells of St. Mary's*.

Crosby's pleasing, family-oriented movies continued to be huge successes into the 1950s, but after that, interest in this genre of films declined. After his last film, *Stagecoach* (1966), he turned his attention to television and personal appearances. He died in 1978 in perfect Crosby style – playing a relaxed game of golf.

The Dorsey Brothers
Sultans of Swing

To fans of jazz and swing, the Dorsey brothers need no introduction. As musicians, composers and dance band leaders, they are inextricably linked with the swing craze during the big-band era of the 1930s and 1940s. Their numerous hits include "I'm Getting Sentimental Over You", "I'll Never Smile Again" and "Boogie-Woogie." In all they sold a combined total of 110 million records in their 40 year careers.

Born to Thomas Dorsey and Theresa Langton, the two brothers grew up in an Irish mining community in Pennsylvania. A self-taught musician himself, Thomas Dorsey resolved to keep his boys out of the mines, and instead ignited in them his own love of music. He even formed a band with them, the Way Back When Dorsey Brothers Orchestra. After Thomas Sr. quit the band, they became Dorsey's Novelty Six, later to be renamed Dorsey's Wild Canaries. The band performed throughout Shenandoah until they broke up in 1922 and Tommy and Jimmy joined the Scranton Sirens.

As boys, Tommy and Jimmy started out playing the cornet. Later they branched out to include other instruments.

After two years with the Scranton Sirens, the

brothers moved to the Jean Goldkette jazz band in Detroit, Michigan where they performed with jazz talents Bix Beiderbecke, Joe Venuti and Eddie Lang. Jimmy began playing the saxophone and clarinet, becoming one of the finest players of his day, while Tommy took up the trombone, coaxing from it a velvety tone that would become hie trademark.

The Dorseys' big break came in 1927 when the entire Goldkette band was hired by the Paul Whiteman Orchestra of New York City, bringing the Dorseys radio and recording jobs and performances with singers like Bing Crosby and the Boswell Sisters. In 1934, Tommy and Jimmy formed their own band, the Dorsey Brothers Orchestra, with Glenn Miller on second trombone. However, the band broke up only one year later, after a dispute broke out between the two brothers during a Memorial Day weekend performance. The more exacting and temperamental of the two, Tommy is generally blamed for the band's demise. Over the next 18 years, the two went their separate ways. Jimmy led the original Dorsey Brothers Band, renamed the Jimmy Dorsey Orchestra, while Tommy took over a band from Joe Haymes, turning it into the Tommy Dorsey Band, a more jazz-oriented band that featured Frank Sinatra from 1940-42.

Over the next 18 years, Tommy and Jimmy enjoyed tremendous success with their respective bands. Both brothers compiled a healthy list of film and television appearances, and they reunited temporarily for the making of the 1947 film bio *The Fabulous Dorseys*.

In 1953, Jimmy's band fell apart and the brothers were reconciled. Jimmy joined Tommy's orchestra and they performed as Tommy Dorsey Orchestra featuring Jimmy Dorsey. The brothers performed together for the next three years, and in 1955-56, they enjoyed wide national coverage with their own show on CBS called *Stage Show*. The two brothers died within six months of each other, Tommy on November 26, 1956 and Jimmy on June 12, 1957. Two days before Jimmy died, he received a gold record for his greatest instrumental, "So Rare."

Movie Star News

Left to right, Tommy, Janet Blair and Jimmy.

Michael Flatley
Lord of the Dance

"You only have to look around you to see what Irishmen are accomplishing all over the world. I grew up very proud of that and I'm still very proud of that."

Critics struggle to outdo each other when it comes to superlatives to describe the dance maestro. "Truly great," says one critic, "A master," boldly proclaims another, while a third can only gasp, "[Flatley is] the centerpiece [of the show]."

And there's more. Some years ago, *National Geographic* magazine described Flatley as a "national treasure." These days, the description is likely to be more of a global treasure, as Flatley's *Lord of the Dance* continues to circumnavigate the world, playing to packed houses everywhere it stops.

One only has to look around at a Flatley show to see jaws drop as uncomprehending spectators wonder how two human feet can move so fast. How fast? Flatley has been recorded doing an astounding 28 taps per second, managing in the process to set a world record.

Formerly involved with *Riverdance*, until a dispute caused a parting of ways, Flatley's decision to set up *Lord of the Dance* was mocked by people who felt there was no room for a second stage show based on Irish dancing. In the first 18 months after *Lord of the Dance* debuted in Dublin's Point Theatre, the critics were noticeably silenced, and it is Flatley, by now a multi-millionaire, who is having the last laugh.

Two months after the show had opened, selling out night after night in Liverpool, Manchester and London, Flatley finally had the vindication he sought, and he described his brainchild enthusiastically to London's *Midweek Magazine*. "*Lord of the Dance* is a big step forward for Irish dancing and music because for the first time it means that 50 or so Irish artists can make a living doing what they're doing.

And it's completely different to anything that's gone before," he said.

The son of a Sligo-born construction worker, Flatley was born in Chicago in 1958. His mother is a native of County Carlow. He was comparatively old when he took up Irish dancing, and a teacher told him that 11 was really too late to start. His determination propelled him forward, however, and his perseverance paid off when he became the first American to win the All-World Championships in Irish Dancing.

Flatley has numerous other awards to his credit – he was the youngest ever recipient of a National Heritage Fellowship from President Ronald Reagan, and the American National Endowment for the Arts recognized him as one of his country's greatest performers.

Dancing is not the only art form Flatley has mastered. He is also an accomplished flautist and a superb chess player. Swiftly sure-footed, he was also a Golden Gloves boxing champion in Chicago.

Gene Kelly
Song and Dance Man

"I got started dancing because I knew that was one way to meet girls."

The name Gene Kelly conjures up the memorable image immediately: the rain-soaked young man with the smile as bright as a sunbeam, the twirling umbrella, the exuberant refrain. Along with fellow Irish American toe-tapper Donald O'Connor and Debbie Reynolds, Kelly made *Singin' in the Rain* a musical movie to treasure.

Born August 23, 1913 in Pittsburgh, Eugene Curran Kelly was one of five kids, all of whom were sent to music and dance lessons. During the Depression, he and his siblings teamed up to form The Five Kellys, and he and his mother started a dancing school in Pittsburgh.

During a 1990 interview with *Irish America*, Kelly said he treasured his Irish roots (he had immigrant ancestors on both sides, with his mother's father having come from County Clare) and had named his own two daughters Kerry and Bridget. He also referred to the Irish domination of popular dance as "a phenomenon of the time," and added, "I think it came from the fact that the dancing in Ireland for centuries had been clog dancing and reels and these dances certainly influenced the American people in the late 19th and 20th centuries so that it actually became part of American tap dancing."

Having put himself through university by means of his dancing, Kelly decided that this was how he wanted to make his living. He got his first break on Broadway in the Rodgers and Hart musical *Pal Joey*. From there Hollywood beckoned and he made a total of 43 movies, playing alongside such stars as Judy Garland, Rita Hayworth, Leslie Caron and Cyd Charisse. As well as singing and dancing, he choreographed his own movies and directed some of them. In 1969, he directed Barbra Streisand and Walter Matthau in *Hello Dolly*. His work on *An American in Paris* won him a special Academy Award for choreography. In 1980, Kelly won the Cecil B. DeMille Award. He died in 1996.

Irish Traditional Music Archive

Francis O'Neill
Musical Cop

"To illustrate the wealth of graces, turns and trills which adorn the performance of capable Irish pipers and fiddlers, skilful both in execution and improvisation, is beyond the scope of musical notation."

The survival of many of the old Irish dance tunes is thanks in large part to Cork native Francis O'Neill's tireless work as a collector and publisher of Irish music.

In 1918, O'Neill, a police chief in Chicago, wrote anxiously to a friend in Ireland, expressing his fear for the future of Irish music in America. "Few of our people care a snap for Irish music," he wrote. "The poor scrub who graduated from the pick and shovel and the mother who toiled for many years in some Yankee kitchen will have nothing less for Katie and Gladis or Jimmy and Raymond but the very latest." It was all part of a new desire to shed the old and take up the newest trends of their adopted land, but thankfully O'Neill's fears turned out to be unfounded and Irish music is more popular than ever in this country.

Born near Bantry, County Cork in 1849, O'Neill was raised with a love of music and he was an accomplished traditional flute player. Visiting musicians dropped into the family home regularly, and O'Neill once remarked that he never forgot a tune or song he heard.

Leaving home at the age of 16, O'Neill worked on the ships, and ended up in San Francisco. He later moved to Chicago, where he joined the police force, rising to Chief of Police in 1901. His passion for Irish music never deserted him, however, and he often helped traditional musicians find work as cops.

Along with his friend and fellow officer James O'Neill, he set about collecting tunes. His namesake was able to write music, and transcribed the tunes that Francis played for him. Other musicians then came on board, and their tunes were also recorded. When the collection reached almost 2,000 pieces, the decision was made to publish the material, and it appeared in 1903 as *The Music of Ireland*. Four years later, a second collection appeared, *The Dance Music of Ireland: 1001 Gems*. That volume soon became known as *O'Neill's 1001*.

An active member of the Chicago Music Club, O'Neill was also a staunch supporter of the Gaelic League, which he saw as a means to keep traditional Irish music and culture alive in America.

Sport

Maureen Connolly
Little Mo

She was the first woman and the youngest tennis player ever to win the Grand Slam – the four-in-a-row Australian Open, the French Open, Wimbledon and the U.S. Open – and one of only five players to do so. Her name was Maureen Connolly, but to adoring fans she was "Little Mo."

Born in San Diego on September 14, 1934, Connolly was just 18 years old when she captured the elusive Grand Slam in 1953. After this amazing feat, a horseback riding accident in the summer of 1954 ended her tennis career prematurely.

After her marriage to Norman Brinker, she moved to Dallas, Texas, where the couple lived with their children. According to her daughter, Cindy Brinker, Connolly was "a devout Irish woman", who treasured her Catholic beliefs and had an audience with the Pope.

In 1968, anxious to promote her beloved tennis to the best of her ability, Connolly co-founded the Maureen Connolly Brinker Tennis Foundation, an association which continues to be active today in the provision of a myriad of programs and activities for children throughout the U.S. and the world.

Connolly succumbed to cancer six months after the Foundation was established. Ever the tennis devotee, her death occurred on the eve of Wimbledon.

James "Gentleman Jim" Corbett
Fists of Fire

James John Corbett may have swapped a career as a bank teller for that of a prize pugilist, but he never fully shook the gentle manners and business style of dress that earned him the nickname by which he would become known throughout the States.

The son of a San Francisco stablehand, Corbett was a first-generation Irish American on both his mother's and father's side, but that didn't stop boxing fans from taking the side of John L. Sullivan, also Irish American, in the fight which was to catapult Corbett to sporting fame. Held in 1892, it was also the first U.S. World Heavyweight Boxing Championship to be fought with gloves, and the first to be governed by the Marquess of Queensberry Rules.

When Corbett beat Sullivan, he stunned the

Library of Congress

spectators into silence. The younger man had applied a scientific logic to his craft, making up for his weak "heavy punch" with a lightning-fast defensive punch. In over an hour of fighting, Sullivan landed only one punch on his opponent, and the match was to mark the Boston fighter's last time in the ring.

Corbett went on to defeat British champion Charley Mitchell in 1894, and became famous all over the world as heavyweight champion. He also became the first boxer to make his debut on the silver screen when he was filmed at Thomas Edison's studios, taking just six rounds to knock out Peter Courney. Corbett lost the heavyweight title in 1897 to Robert Fitzsimmons.

His distinctive attire and mild-mannered personality also earned Corbett leading parts in several plays, including *Cashel Byron's Profession* by George Bernard Shaw. When it came to immortalizing his life on film, the task fell to another Irish American – actor Errol Flynn. Corbett died on February 18, 1933 in New York City.

Jack Dempsey
The Manassa Mauler

Probably the most memorable fight of Jack Dempsey's career was his last. Having lost his heavyweight title to Gene Tunney in 1926 in a decision match, Dempsey's indomitable fighting spirit resurfaced the next year in a series of blows to Tunney's jaw. Tunney went down, but the referee didn't start the count until Dempsey moved to a neutral corner a few seconds later.

That few-seconds mistake cost Dempsey the title. Tunney didn't rise until the "official" count of nine, and went on to win by decision.

The match not only marked the end of Dempsey's career, but also the dominance of the Irish in boxing. The great fighters of Dempsey's childhood had names like O'Brien, Dillon, Ryan, and O'Dowd. So "green" was the boxing ring

that the Ancient Order of Hibernians remarked on the degrading effect it was having on the Irish image in America.

William Harrison Dempsey was born in 1895 in Manassa, Colorado, one of 11 children from a long line of Dempseys from County Kildare. He learned to fight as a way to survive after leaving home at 16 to aimlessly travel west. It was Jack "Doc" Kearns who first noticed Dempsey's remarkable strength, and quickly arranged fights for him. Dempsey won the heavyweight title in 1919 from Jess Willard, and successfully defended it for seven years.

One sports historian sums up the "Manassa Mauler's" greatness with this: "Dempsey may certainly rank among the great heavyweights of the past. He was not so fine a boxer as Corbett, or so wily a strategist as Fitzsimmons. He had not Jeffries' immense strength, and certainly none of Johnson's defensive genius. But he had more fighting spirit than was in all four of them rolled together."

Dempsey was inducted into the Boxing Hall of Fame seven years after his death on May 31, 1983.

Library of Congress

Frank Leahy
Leader of Lads

One of the most successful coaches in the history of college football, Frank Leahy rose from humble beginnings to put himself and his "lads" firmly on the sporting grid. His legacy lives on today at the University of Notre Dame, a testament to his hard work and burning desire to succeed.

Born in McNeal, South Dakota in 1908 of Irish parents, Frank Leahy was a serious young man who worked diligently at every task assigned to him, whether at home or in school. In high school, he excelled in sports, particularly. football, basketball, baseball and amateur boxing. He caught the eye of the legendary Knute Rockne, who offered the young Leahy an athletic scholarship to attend the University of Notre Dame. Leahy played for Rockne at Notre Dame and then embarked on a coaching career with assistant coaching stints at Georgetown, Michigan State and Fordham before landing his first head coaching job at Boston College. After two successful seasons at Boston College, he accepted the offer to be head coach at his alma mater, the University of Notre Dame, at age 33.

During Leahy's 11 years as the head football coach at Notre Dame (1941-53), his record was nothing short of phenomenal. With two years out of coaching because of the war, Leahy's teams won four undisputed National Championships in 1943, 1946, 1947, and 1949 and a split Championship in 1953. His teams were undefeated in six of the seasons and had an undefeated string of 38 consecutive games. His overall record (including two years as head football coach at Boston College) of 107 wins, 11 defeats and 9 ties for a .864 percentage makes Leahy the number two ranked coach in all of college football, second only to Knute Rockne. During that period four of his players won the Heisman Trophy, two the Outland Trophy and 12 have been inducted into the College Football Hall of Fame, as was he. No college football coach can match this achievement.

Leahy was known as much more than a great coach, he was known as a molder of men. He taught his players, or "lads" as he liked to call them, more than winning football, he taught them lessons of life. In recognition of their respect and gratitude for their coach, The Leahy Lads formed the Frank Leahy Memorial Fund in 1994 to raise money to honor their coach with a visible reminder of the coach and a scholarship fund in his name. The first goal was achieved in September 1997 when a ten-foot-high bronze sculpture of Coach Frank Leahy was dedicated outside the Notre Dame stadium. In addition, the Lads formed the Frank Leahy Scholarship Fund, an endowed fund administered by the university that allows deserving young students, both male and female, to further their education at the school Frank Leahy loved so much. There are currently four students, a Freshman, a Sophomore, a Junior and a Senior, being educated because of the Frank Leahy Scholarship Fund.

The legacy of Frank Leahy is more than that of a successful football coach, it is an inspirational story of an Irish American man who has influenced countless numbers of young men who played for him. And the story is ongoing. So long as the University of Notre Dame exists, Frank Leahy will continue to inspire young students and all who visit the sculpture. This is truly the mark of an influential man.

Connie Mack
Baseball Supremo

"Play ball . . ."

One of the pioneering greats of baseball, Connie Mack played a huge role in popularizing the new sport. Born Cornelius McGillicuddy in 1862 to Irish immigrants Michael McGillicuddy and Mary McKillop, Mack ("Connie Mack" was a nickname bestowed on him in childhood, and he stuck with it as he grew into adulthood) left school at age 13 and became a factory laborer. His free time was consumed with baseball, which he played on weekends.

After a number of years as a player, Mack joined the Pittsburgh Pirates of the National League, eventually becoming manager in 1894. He later joined the Philadelphia Athletics, leading them to the 1905 World Series. The Athletics lost to the New York Giants that year, but came back in 1910 to win the league pennant and the World Series. In the four years that followed, Philadelphia gained three league titles and two more World Series wins.

Trouble started in 1914 with the onset of World War I, and the Athletics ran into financial difficulties that led Mack to make the difficult decision of letting some team members go. The move did untold harm to his reputation and the team's performance, and it was not until 1929 that he and the Athletics recovered, with another league pennant and a fourth World Series title.

Under Mack's leadership the Athletics established one of the most remarkable records in baseball history, winning a total of nine American League championships and five World Series. He received the Edward Bok Philadelphia Award for his positive influence on the sport of baseball.

Elected to the Baseball Hall of Fame in 1938, Mack saw Philadelphia's Shibe Park renamed Connie Mack Stadium in 1953, three years before his death in 1956 at the age of 93. Most of today's baseball managers follow his scientific style of keeping detailed notes on hitters and pitchers.

John McEnroe
Tennis Titan

"Everybody loves success, but they hate successful people."

Wimbledon was always so much more interesting when John McEnroe was around. From his fiery ball-bashing to his inevitable temper tantrums,

Movie Star News

the curly headed court champion dominated the scene in a way that today's milder players can never hope to emulate.

The statistics are awesome. The youngest player to advance to the men's semifinals in Wimbledon history, McEnroe has a total of 77 singles titles, including seven Grand Slams, under his belt. He joined the circuit in 1978 at the age of 19, and within three short years he had reached the number one spot. Defeated by Bjorn Borg in the 1980 Wimbledon finals, after a thrilling five sets, the tenacious "Mac" returned the following year to claim his first Wimbledon title in just four sets.

"Superbrat", as he became known on (and off) the court, is also hailed as one of the greatest doubles players of all time, and at one point he ranked number one for almost five consecutive years. He has 74 doubles titles, including eight Grand Slams. In 1984, McEnroe became a tennis commentator, and he was one of the professional observers at the 1999 Wimbledon champion-ships. He made no secret of the fact that he was rooting for Andre Agassi, who was defeated in the final by Pete Sampras.

Born in West Germany to John and Kay McEnroe and raised in Queens, New York, McEnroe is descended from Irish Catholic immigrants. He was recently inducted into the Tennis Hall of Fame.

It was a magical year for baseball fans who kept a close eye on proceedings as the 6-foot, 5-inch red-haired California native surpassed records previously set by Babe Ruth (60 home runs in 154 major-league games) and Roger Maris (61 homers in 161 games) and made it look somehow *easy*.

Born October 1, 1963 in Pomona, California to John and Ginger McGwire, the genial athlete joined the ranks of the greats with his record-making feat. McGwire started with the Oakland A's as a pitcher, and was moved to first base because of his powerful hitting skills. He was traded to the St. Louis Cardinals in 1997.

In an interview with *Irish America* in 1998, McGwire said he hadn't made much of an effort to trace his Irish ancestry, but added: "Maybe I'll go back some day when I'm retired."

Off the field he is admired for his passionate dedication to children's causes. The father of an 11-year-old son, Matthew, McGwire has started a foundation which funds child abuse centers in St. Louis and Los Angeles. He has also recorded a public service announcement to publicize the cause, and plans to work on a documentary on the issue.

"You have to like Mark McGwire, ballplayer," concluded sportswriter John Kernaghan after interviewing him for *Irish America*. "But you like the man better."

Mark McGwire
Slugger

"It still blows me away. It really does. Considering when I was a kid and all I ever wanted to do was pitch . . . then the next thing you know, they're talking about my name along with Babe Ruth, Maris, Mantle, down the line. It's overwhelming."

With Chicago's Sammy Sosa nipping at his heels all the way, the Cardinals' Mark McGwire set an astonishing new 70-home run record 1998.

Mark O'Meara
Golfer

The dream of winning one of golf's most prestigious events is enough to sustain most pros through all those fallow years. But it is rare for a golfer to grind it out for 18 years on the tour and then win two glamour tournaments in one season.

Mark O'Meara did it in 1998 at the advanced age, at least for golf, of 46. He won the Masters and slipped comfortably into the green jacket of the winner, then a few months later held firm during a four-hole playoff to capture the British Open and hug the claret jug that is traditionally awarded.

O'Meara became the oldest man to win two major titles in one year and he came awfully close to matching the legendary Ben Hogan's three majors in a year when he came up short in the final round of the PGA Championship.

And after the shortest off-season in the history of professional sport, just 24 days, the Orlando-based veteran feels grateful for his dream season. "It was a lot of fun," he said on the PGA Tour's website of his remarkable year. "I knew that '99 would come around fast and there wasn't a whole lot of time off, but I don't feel tired. Even at the end of the year when I traveled around the world, I felt mentally fresh." He said he cherished his wins in the majors more because

of that 18-year test of patience, and his experience means, now that he's successful, that he can handle the inevitable dry spell better.

O'Meara is no stranger to Ireland. He took time out before winning the British Open to play a few practice rounds with Tiger Woods and Payne Stewart at Ballybunion Golf Club in County Kerry. O'Meara's father, also an avid golfer who has played the Irish greens with his famous son on more than one occasion, once said, "Every time we go to Ireland, before we leave, we always start to plan our next trip."

Nolan Ryan
Pitcher Perfect

"I like being known as just a regular guy. I'm not perfect. I have my likes and dislikes, my pet peeves, and . . . my opinions. I'd rather have you not like me for who I am than like me for who I'm not."

Winning all but six votes of the 497 cast in January 1999, Texas native Nolan Ryan swept into baseball's Hall of Fame in the very first year he was eligible. Ryan threw his final pitch on September 22, 1993 after 27 dazzling seasons – the longest by any major league player in history. During that time he had 5,714 strikeouts and seven no-hitters, both of which are record-making tallies. He won a total of 324 games.

Born Lynn Nolan Ryan, Jr. in Refugio, Texas on January 31, 1947, Ryan now lives in Alvin with his wife Ruth. The couple has two sons, Reid and Reese, and a daughter, Wendy. In a past interview with *Irish America*, he described his off-the-field devotion to ranching, describing the work as "a very big part of my year-round activities." He owns three cattle ranches in Texas, and serves as chairman of The Express Bank, which he also owns. In 1995, he was appointed to a six-year term as a commissioner with the Texas Parks and Wildlife Commission.

In his 1992 book *Miracle Man*, co-written with Jerry Jenkins, Nolan remarked: "My basic philosophy of life came from my parents: Treat people the way you want to be treated, with honesty and integrity."

Back in 1991, after interviewing Ryan for *Irish America*, Mary Pat Kelly concluded, "Like so many Americans of Irish descent in this country a long time, only Nolan Ryan's name indicates a connection to Ireland . . . but talking about his pride in his family animated him, and if that doesn't make him an Irish American, nothing does."

John L. Sullivan
Boston Strong Boy

"My name's John L. Sullivan, and I can lick any man in the world!"

He was known to drink almost as hard as he fought, but John L. Sullivan – "the Great John L." – was much loved by the legions of fans who loved to see him win in the ring, which he invariably did for much of his career.

Born in Boston in 1856 to Michael Sullivan from Kerry and Roscommon immigrant Catherine Kelly, John Lawrence Sullivan was much more interested in sports than his school studies, and he immersed himself in baseball, a game he loved. As he grew bigger, however, Sullivan developed an interest in boxing, and

fought his first exhibition match at the age of 22, after the fighter in the ring challenged members of the audience to a sparring bout. He won that contest, and then sensibly took a year out to further study various boxing techniques.

His return to the ring in 1879 was marked with another victory, but it took three years of exhibition fights before Sullivan finally got his chance. On February 7, 1882, he faced off against Tipperary native Paddy Ryan, commonly regarded as the American champion of boxing. Sullivan knocked Ryan out in the ninth round and became the new champ. Ryan later said: "When Sullivan struck me, I thought a telegraph pole had been shoved against me sideways."

At the time, boxing was still fought bare-knuckled, and Sullivan went on to fight a wide range of opponents, winning all his matches.

In 1887, shortly after beating English fighter Charlie Mitchell in France, he was rapturously welcomed in Dublin City, where fans were proud to call out the Boston greeting, "Shake the hand that shook the hand of John L. Sullivan." In 1889, Sullivan lasted an incredible 75 rounds against fighter Jake Kilrane, and the fight ended after doctors warned that Kilrane would die if he stayed in the ring.

On September 7, 1892, Sullivan entered the ring against a fellow Irish American, "Gentleman Jim" Corbett, for a gloved fight. The match went 21 rounds, but the younger Corbett emerged victorious. It was to be Sullivan's last fight.

In later years he turned to acting, and also appeared on the vaudeville circuit. He opened bars in New York and Boston but never really managed to make a successful living as a saloon-keeper. Sullivan died on February 2, 1918, never having fully recovered from the death of his beloved second wife, Kate Harkins, the previous year.

Gene Tunney
The Fighting Marine

One of the great heavyweight boxers of the century, Gene Tunney will always be remembered for the "Long Count" fight. With just one professional defeat in a 76-fight, 11-year boxing career he quickly joined the ranks of great champions.

Born James Joseph Tunney in New York City on May 25, 1898 to parents from Kiltimagh, County Mayo, he worked for the Ocean Steamship Company as a clerk, and began boxing at the age of 17. His father had given him his first pair of boxing gloves when he was ten years old. An early ambition to join the priesthood was abandoned, and Tunney worked for awhile as a stenographer.

In 1917, Tunney joined the U.S. Marine Corps and served in France during World War I. While in Paris he won the light heavyweight championship of the American Expeditionary Force, which earned him the nickname "The Fighting Marine."

After returning home, Tunney pursued a career in prize-fighting, and he fought against Harry Greb in the 1922 U.S. light heavyweight championship. He lost that year, but returned the next year to take the title from Greb.

By 1924, Tunney was fighting as a heavyweight, and in 1926 he challenged fellow Irish American Jack Dempsey to a match in Philadelphia. Dempsey was the favorite to win, but Tunney triumphed after ten rounds.

The two met again the next year in a rematch which gave rise to the controversial "long count," occurring when Dempsey knocked Tunney to the floor but failed to return to his corner immediately, thus giving the fallen man a precious few extra seconds to recover. Tunney went on to defeat Dempsey in ten rounds. In 1928, Tunney successfully defended his title against Tom Henney, after which he announced his retirement from boxing.

He went on to a very successful career as a businessman in the varied fields of banking, manufacturing, insurance and newspapers. He authored two books – *A Man Must Fight* and the autobiographical *Arms for Living*. He had four children, one of whom became a U.S. Senator. Tunney died November 7, 1978 in Greenwich, Connecticut.

Library of Congress

Stage &
Screen

Movie Star News

James Cagney
Screen Giant

"If you listen to all the clowns around you're just dead. Go do what you have to do."

Little James Cagney had two dreams as a kid – to be an artist and live on a farm – and with talent and hard work, he made it happen.

Born July 17, 1899 on New York City's Lower East Side, James Francis Cagney was the second of five children. After high school, he attended Columbia University, and began appearing in plays put on by Lenox Hill Settlement House.

Cagney gradually worked his way up to bigger and better roles. He worked as a Broadway chorus boy, toured in vaudeville, and received small parts in dramas and musicals. A stand-out performance in *Penny Arcade* (released by Warner Bros. as *Sinners' Holiday*) led to a contract with Warner Bros. His fifth film, *The Public Enemy* (1931), secured his spot as one of the studio's top stars, where he stayed for over 20 years.

Cagney's command of his characters was unparalleled. His quiet, modest demeanor off screen seemed the antithesis of his explosive, fast-talking, tough-guy roles. On his performance in *Torrid Zone* (1940) *Time* magazine wrote, "Cagney . . . can express a complete characterization with one little gesture." On preparing a character, Cagney said, "I try to fully realize the man I am playing . . . I draw upon everything I've ever known, seen, heard, or remember." Some of Cagney's most memorable films are *Angels With Dirty Faces* (1938), *White Heat* (1949) and *Yankee Doodle Dandy* (1942), for which his performance as song-and-dance man George M. Cohan won him an Oscar.

Married 65 years to Billie Vernon, whom he met while a chorus boy, James Cagney lived on a farm, staying close to the land from the 1930s to his death on March 30, 1986.

Walt Disney
Mouseketeer

"If you can dream it, you can do it. Always remember, this whole thing was started by a mouse."

Disney is a household name to millions of families throughout the world thanks to Walter Elias Disney, whose creative genius has been providing children and their families endless hours of entertainment since the 1920s. Along with giving us the endearing icons Mickey Mouse, Donald Duck and their cohorts, he was responsible for technical innovations in sound, color and photography in the movies and television. And of course, he was responsible for

Movie Star News

two of the world's most famous amusement parks, Disneyland and Disney World.

Disney was born on December 5, 1901 in Chicago. His family name is a corruption of the French Huguenot name d'Isigny, many of whom, including members of his family, fled to Ireland to avoid religious persecution.

His father, a Canadian of Irish descent – the family roots go back to County Carlow – moved the family to a farm in Marceline, Missouri when Walt was quite young. It was on this farm that he developed the deep love and respect for animals that would become apparent in his films. After Marceline, the family moved to Kansas City.

Walt never finished high school, but worked at several jobs while studying in the evenings at the Chicago Academy of Fine Arts. When he was 15, young Walt resolved to join the Army, creating documents falsifying his age so he could enlist. After working for three years as a driver for the Red Cross Ambulance Corps in France, Disney returned to Kansas City and turned his attention to filmed cartooning.

In 1923, Disney decided to take his chances in Hollywood, and in partnership with his brother Roy, set up a small studio to develop short cartoons. This was the beginning of what would become the Walt Disney empire.

Disney's best known character, Mickey Mouse, was an instant success when he made his debut in 1928 in the cartoon *Steamboat Willie*. Disney Studios began churning out Mickey Mouse cartoons as fast as it could, and the adorable mouse won a huge fan base that included King George VI of England, Arturo Toscanini and Cole Porter.

Disney's creativity was inexhaustible. He first introduced the Technicolor process in film in *Flowers and Trees* (1932). Five years later he produced the first feature-length cartoon in history, *Snow White and the Seven Dwarfs* (1937).

Snow White was followed in rapid succession by *Fantasia* (1940), a tour de force in animation, *The Reluctant Dragon* (1941), *Dumbo*, and *Bambi* (1942), Disney's most successful cartoon ever. Throughout the Forties and Fifties, Disney Studios produced both cartoon and live-action short and long films, including *So Dear to My Heart* (1948) and *Cinderella* (1950). In the Fifties, Disney branched out into television, producing the *Davy Crockett* series and launching *The Mickey Mouse Club*.

Disney's next venture was a huge risk that was greeted with strong opposition by executives at the Walt Disney Company. As he had done with film, Disney now resolved to create something wonderful in amusement parks. Disneyland opened in California in 1955, followed by Walt Disney World in Florida. The lasting success of these amusement parks is a testament to Disney's vision.

The success of *Mary Poppins* in 1965 proved that the aging Disney had not lost touch with his childlike creativity and sense of fantasy. Walt Disney succumbed to lung cancer in 1966, but his spirit lives on in the imaginations of children touched by his legacy.

John Ford The Quiet Man

"If there is any single thing that explains either of us,"
John Ford once said to Eugene O'Neill, "it's that we're Irish."

BY JOSEPH MCBRIDE

"If there is any single thing that explains either of us," John Ford once said to Eugene O'Neill, "it's that we're Irish."

Their worlds intersected in 1940, when Ford directed his film version of O'Neill's sea trilogy, *The Long Voyage Home.* That dark and moody film about men on a tramp steamer perfectly captured O'Neill's Irish fatalism, and it was the playwright's favorite among the films made from his work.

John Ford (1894-1973) was a man of many varied and often conflicting moods, themes, and obsessions. Although Ford usually is identified with the Western genre, in which he made such masterpieces as *Stagecoach* and *The Searchers,* his vast body of work encompasses a wide range of subject matter. He made many films about small town and rural America, about men at sea, and about America's wars from the Revolution through Vietnam. But perhaps closest to his heart were his films about his beloved Ireland, such as *The Quiet Man* and *The Rising of the Moon.*

At a time when it was not fashionable to do so, Ford took defiant pride in his ethnic origins. Born John Martin Feeney – not Sean O'Feeney, O'Fearna, or O'Fienne, as he variously liked to claim – he was the son of Irish immigrants who left their native County Galway and settled in Portland, Maine. His father was a saloonkeeper and Democratic Party ward boss. Contrary to Ford's romantic claims of poverty, he grew up in a comfortable lace-curtain environment, but he was always conscious of the struggles and slights that Irish Americans had to endure in Yankee-dominated New England. In the words of Orson Welles, Ford had "chips on his shoulders like epaulets." Following the lead of his older brother Francis, Jack Feeney changed his name to Ford and went into the movies. But legally he always kept the name of his birth.

Ford's sense of having a dual identity as an Irish American was a source of many tensions in his life and career, and he turned it to fruitful artistic advantage. Like many children of immigrants, he felt the need to prove his patriotic sense of belonging. This led Ford to a side career in the Navy that eventually, because of his exploits as a U.S. government filmmaker in World War II and Korea, brought him the rank of rear admiral. Ford's classic films about the U.S. Cavalry, such as *Fort Apache* and *She Wore a Yellow Ribbon,* are filled with Irish immigrants moving up the ladder to achieve full social acceptance, often at the cost of their own self-sacrifice for the sake of future generations.

There was a subversive, anarchic side in Ford as well, enabling him to probe deeply into America's failings and injustices as well as to mock the gunfighting heroics he sometimes celebrated. No other American director of his era was so attentive to the challenging roles played by minority groups in the national psyche. Not only the Irish, but also such groups as Native Americans and African Americans are strongly represented in his films, although sometimes problematically. Standing apart from his era in believing in assertive ethnic identity rather than melting-pot assimilation, Ford always hoped that the rich and diverse strains in the American experience would result in a greater national harmony.

Whatever his subject matter, a Ford film typically revolves around some very Irish preoccupations – the importance of family and community, the sense of exile, the tension between compulsive wandering and the need for home, and the melancholy sense of the transient nature of human existence and worldly institutions. His films often show the breakup of families and the collapse of entire societies; the intermittent periods of optimism in Ford's work, as seen in such postwar films as *My Darling Clementine* and *Wagon Master*, eventually gave way to a deep pessimism about the future of American society. Underlying everything in Ford are the typically Irish traits that make his work so moving and entertaining: a willingness to express powerful emotions without embarrassment and a tragicomic view of existence. Although shortsighted critics often fault Ford's use of comedy, it is the

Shakespearean virtuosity with which he interweaves the serious and the ridiculous aspects of life that gives his films such vitality and truth.

Ford's films about Ireland tend to be filmed from an exile's perspective, seeing the land of his ancestors through a sentimental romantic haze, like Eden before the Fall, as the lavish Technicolor landscapes of *The Quiet Man* so strikingly demonstrate. Even Ford's films about the struggle of the Irish against the British and the Irish Civil War – such as *The Informer, The Plough and the Stars*, and the 1921 segment of *The Rising of the Moon* – are filtered through an extravagant visual expressionism. The same aestheticizing tendencies can be seen in his silent films about Ireland, including *The Shamrock Handicap, Mother Machree*, and *Hangman's House*.

And yet, if Ford is not particularly attuned to capturing the mundane realities of life in Ireland, his Ireland has great mythic appeal and perhaps conveys more poetic truth than a strictly realistic treatment could ever hope to achieve. The dark and tragic side of Irish life and politics is never absent from Ford's films, even from such a joyous romance as *The Quiet Man*, which centers on a man's attempt to put his violent past behind him and includes several characters (including the village priest) who belong to the IRA. *The Quiet Man* is the film in which Barry Fitzgerald utters one of the most memorable lines in Ford's body of work, a line improvised by the director himself: "Well, it's a nice soft night, so I think I'll go and join me comrades and talk a little treason."

Ford's ineradicable Irishness perhaps shows up most clearly not in his films set in Ireland, but in those set in the multicultural society of the United States, for if his Irish Americans suffer from a "shamrock handicap," they never turn their backs on their cultural identities in order to be accepted as Americans. In the very first film he directed, a 1917 two-reel Western called *The Tornado*, Ford himself plays a cowboy who wins a $5,000 reward and sends it to his mother in Ireland so she can keep their ancestral home. Ford films as diverse as *The Iron Horse, Riley the Cop, The Long Gray Line, The Last Hurrah*, and *Donovan's Reef* pay tribute to the pervasive and life-enhancing influence of Irish Americans on their adopted homeland.

Even a classic Ford film about non-Irish people, *The Grapes of Wrath*, is suffused with the director's ethnic memories of poverty and injustice. Ford said he was drawn to the John Steinbeck novel about dispossessed Okies in the Dust Bowl of the 1930s because it reminded him of the Great Famine that drove so many of the Irish to America. By finding such universal qualities in the particularities of his own background, Ford was able to speak to people of all countries, all economic classes, all ethnic groups, and all levels of sophistication. It is that far-reaching quality of empathy and understanding that makes John Ford one of America's greatest popular artists, perhaps the closest we have come since Walt Whitman to having a national poet.

Jackie Gleason
Funnyman

"To the moon, Alice! One more time and it's to the moon!"

Born in Brooklyn on February 26, 1916, Herbert John Gleason was raised by his mother (who affectionately called him Jackie) after his father abandoned the family when Jackie was eight years old. Young Jackie never stopped to wonder what he would be when he grew up. He wanted to be on stage, to entertain, and after winning an amateur-night competition at 15, Gleason was on his way. When he wasn't emceeing stage shows all over New York, he worked as a Master of Ceremonies for carnivals, a radio disc jockey, a daredevil driver, and an exhibition diver in the water follies.

Gleason built his career slowly, making five Hollywood films before returning to New York to work in Broadway musicals. He began his television career on Ed Sullivan's *Toast of the Town* and with the series *The Life of Riley*, but it was his brief appearance on DuMont's *Cavalcade*

of *Stars* in 1950 that made him an overnight TV sensation. After *Cavalcade of Stars* and several big contracts with major TV networks, Jackie returned to Broadway in 1959 and won a Tony Award for *Take Me Along*, and an Academy Award nomination in 1962 for the film *The Hustler*.

Although Jackie could neither read nor write music, he released over 20 albums between 1953 and 1969 and wrote the themes for *The Jackie Gleason Show* and *The Honeymooners*. Despite 50 years of a wide array of creative achievements, Gleason is best known for a character he created during his two years with *Cavalcade of Stars* – Brooklyn bus driver Ralph Kramden. When his sidekick Art Carney asked why *The Honeymooners* lasted only one season, Gleason said, "The excellence of the material could not be maintained, and I had too much fondness for the show to cheapen it." Maybe that's why those shows have become classics, in constant reruns. He died in Miami, Florida on June 25, 1987.

Helen Hayes
First Lady of the Theater

"I have Ireland in my blood and every exciting actor or actress that I've known has an Irish background. It's a strange thing but we are performers, we are actors by heritage."

One might think that Helen Hayes was genetically predisposed to the theater. Her great-great-aunt was the famous Irish singer Catherine Hayes, known as "The Swan of Erin," and Helen's own mother dreamt of making a career on the stage.

So it may come as a surprise that the most famous stage actress of the century did not want to become an actress. Instead she was pushed into acting by her mother, Catherine.

Born in Washington, D.C. in 1900, Helen first began appearing in amateur productions at the age of five. One production was seen by the comedian Lew Fields, who was so impressed with the child's talent, he told Helen's parents that he would help her if she wanted to become an actress. Neither Helen's father, Francis, nor

Helen herself had much say in the matter. Catherine promptly left her husband and moved herself and her child to New York, where Helen was cast in Fields' Broadway production *Old Dutch* in 1909.

In many ways, Hayes was robbed of her childhood. A working actress at the age of nine, she also assumed the responsibility of bread-winner for herself and her alcoholic mother. Afraid of losing work, Hayes allowed her producer George Tyler, who made her an adult star in ingenue roles, to exercise an almost tyrannical control over her professional activities.

Her life changed with her marriage to the playwright Charles MacArthur (*The Front Page*). Though they were complete opposites, the two complemented each other well, and Hayes credited him with her growth as an artist. She and Charles had two children, Mary, born in 1930, and James, whom they adopted in 1938.

After her marriage, Hayes finally discarded the ingenue and paper-thin movie roles and entered her greatest period as an actress, beginning in 1933 with *Mary of Scotland*. In 1935, she created her masterful portrayal of Queen Victoria in *Victoria Regina*, a role that required her to age 60 years before an audience. She would go on to perform in the plays of Tennessee Williams, George Bernard Shaw, Eugene O'Neill, Thornton Wilder and William Shakespeare. She was underrated by some critics because her seamless acting emphasized the basic humanity and simplicity of her characters, and lacked any of the posturing of stardom.

Hayes' move to Hollywood sprang not out of any ambition to further her fame or career, but to stay with her husband, who had become one of the highest-paid screenwriters. She received an Oscar for her very first film, *The Sin of Madelon Claudet* (1931). While she went on to be cast in major productions, she realized these movies were second-rate in story quality to the work she had been doing in the theater.

She decided to quit Hollywood in 1934 after

MGM butchered the film version of her favorite stage play, *What Every Woman Knows*. As she told one reporter, "I don't think I'm much good in pictures, and I have a beautiful dream that I'm elegant on stage." Her departure from Hollywood did not prove permanent, however. During the 1950s she appeared in three movies and from the late '60s to the late '80s she regularly appeared in movies and in television films. She was awarded her second Oscar for her role as the stowaway grandmother in *Airport* (1970).

Along with her extraordinary achievements, Hayes also experienced intense personal loss. In 1949, her daughter Mary, herself a promising actress, died of polio at the age of 19. Unable to cope with his sorrow, Charles spent the remaining seven years of his life sinking into alcoholism before dying in 1956.

Hayes turned her grief toward a positive end, helping to create the Mary MacArthur Memorial Fund which raised millions to eradicate polio, as well as becoming the spokesperson for many other charities. Over the years she has garnered such awards as the Presidential Medal of Freedom, the Kennedy Center Honors, two Tonys, an Emmy, a Grammy, the Fred Allen Humanitarian Award from the Catholic Actors Guild, the USO Woman of the Year Award and the Drama League Medal.

In Washington, D.C., the Helen Hayes Awards are given annually for distinguished achievement in the nation's capital, and several Broadway and regional theaters have been named for her.

A friend of Hayes once said, "One of Helen's favorite expressions about other people is that he or she 'rose above the situation,'" an observation that could easily be made about Hayes at several points in her remarkable life. She died on St. Patrick's Day in 1993.

Anjelica Huston
Screen Siren

"I don't feel anywhere in the world the way I feel in Ireland. I feel at home [there] and I still miss it."

She brought James Joyce's Gretta to life in her father's screen adaptation of Joyce's short story *The Dead*, and created the unforgettable Maerose in the 1985 film *Prizzi's Honor*, which also starred her then lover Jack Nicholson. Anjelica Huston has lit up our screens in many guises through the years, but a part of her is indelibly Irish, thanks to the many childhood years she spent growing up on her father's Galway estate.

In various interviews with *Irish America* through the years, Huston has stressed how important her time in Ireland has been to her and how much those years shaped her life. She attributes her early interest in imaginative pursuits to the decidedly less glamorous Irish country upbringing, where television and Toys 'R' Us didn't feature to any extent.

Speaking to *Irish America* in 1995, she said: "I'm completely proud of my Irish background. It's a nation of poets, a nation of speakers, a

nation of communicators. I root for the Irish on any possible occasion. Instantly."

Having lived in Ireland since she was 18 months old, Huston found it very difficult to leave Galway to attend school in London. Then her Italian American mother died suddenly in a car accident and she and brother Tony moved back to the U.S. In later years, she and her brother worked with their father on *The Dead*, an experience she thoroughly enjoyed.

Her many films have included *The Addams Family*, *The Grifters*, *The Postman Always Rings Twice* and *The Witches*. One of her most recent projects, *Agnes Browne*, saw her back in Ireland at the start of 1999. Adapted from *The Mammy*, a book by Irish comedian Brendan O'Carroll, the film was directed by Huston, who also played the title role. O'Carroll had nothing but praise for her handling of his work, and Huston explained her interest in the story of a young Dublin widow raising seven children alone by remarking that she was constantly "drawn to survival stories."

Huston is married to Mexican American sculptor Robert Graham.

Movie Star News

John Huston
The Director

"Nostalgia for Ireland sweeps over me often, not just when I'm working with an Irish cast. I love Ireland and I miss it very much."

He was a lightweight professional boxer, a stage actor, a member of the Mexican cavalry and a writer, but it is for his unparalleled directing skills that John Huston is best remembered today. He won an Oscar in 1948 for *The Treasure of Sierra Madre*, and in a career spanning over four decades he made a total of 30 pictures.

Born in 1906 to actor Walter Huston and Rhea Gore, Huston was raised in Nevada and Missouri where his father worked in engineering. When Huston senior returned to acting on the

vaudeville circuit, his son's education suffered somewhat, and young John left high school early to become a boxer. By the age of 18 he had followed his father into the theater.

A period of two years in the Mexican cavalry followed, after which Huston became a writer, dabbling in short stories and eventually working as a reporter for the same newspaper that employed his mother. He was next hired by Samuel Goldwyn as a writer, and his first script was for *A House Divided*.

Stints in England and Paris followed, but in 1938 Huston succumbed to his destiny and returned to Hollywood, where he wrote for Warner Bros. He directed his first film, *A Passenger to Bali*, in 1939. Two years later, he was assigned to work on *The Maltese Falcon*, which was to become just one high point in a career full of them. Other notable films included *Quo Vadis* and *We Were Strangers*.

Throughout the 1950s and '60s, Huston's was a familiar face in County Galway, where he lived in St. Clerans with his children and regularly attended local hunting functions. The estate was recently bought and restored by American TV personality Merv Griffin, who named various suites in the impressive house after the Huston family. Huston held Irish and U.S. citizenship during his life, and traveled on an Irish passport.

In a 1987 interview with *Irish America*, Huston traced his long-time passion for the work of James Joyce back to his youth, when his mother smuggled a copy of *Ulysses* into the

Movie Star News

States in 1928. The book was banned at the time, but it was to have a profound influence on young Huston. "I'll never forget reading it," he told *Irish America*. "It's probably what motivated me to become a writer and filmmaker."

Almost 50 years later, his love for Joyce's words was immortalized into a remarkable celluloid tribute to the Irish writer with the highly acclaimed film *The Dead*. In a bid to "preserve the integrity" of Joyce's work, Huston insisted on an all-Irish cast, and would have filmed in Ireland if ill health had not prevented him from traveling that far. Huston died in 1987, not long after completing work on *The Dead*.

Grace Kelly
Princess

"Because I am pessimistic, I always expect the worst. When it doesn't happen, I have a nice surprise."

She was known for her icy cool blond poise and her ladylike charm, and when she married Prince Rainier III of Monaco in 1956, it was seen the world over as a fairytale match – the prince had found his beautiful princess.

Born in Philadelphia to Margaret and John Kelly on November 12, 1929, Grace Patricia Kelly was a leading lady long before she met Prince Rainier. Discovered while modeling in

New York, she went on to act in almost a dozen feature films. She won an Academy Award in 1954 for her portrayal of Georgie in *The Country Girl*.

As the star of such notable movies as *High Noon* and *High Society*, she was the epitome of glamour and grace. Director Alfred Hitchcock chose her to star in three of his best-known works: *Dial M for Murder*, *Rear Window* and *To Catch a Thief*.

Kelly retired from acting upon her marriage to Prince Rainier, and the couple had three children: Caroline, Albert and Stephanie. Her sudden death on September 14, 1982 in a car accident shook her legions of fans who had not stopped hoping for her eventual return to the screen.

During her lifetime, Kelly made several trips to Ireland, and bought her ancestral home in Louisburgh, County Mayo. Her grandfather, John Henry Kelly, had left his native Mayo in the 1860s, landing in Vermont, where he met and married fellow Irish immigrant Mary Costello. They eventually settled in Philadelphia and had ten children, one of whom was John Brendan, the father of Princess Grace and a champion oarsman. "John Kelly, grandson of an Irish pig farmer . . . won the Olympic singles gold medal," his proud daughter is recorded as saying years later.

Maureen O'Hara
Screen Colleen

"You [have to] stay with what you believe in and what you feel. You cannot sway and swing with the opinion of the few who have big mouths. You have to stick with your own values."

As Mary Kate Danaher in John Ford's classic film *The Quiet Man*, Maureen O'Hara has engaged the hearts of viewers the world over for over four decades.

Born Maureen Fitzsimons on August 17, 1921 in Ranelagh, County Dublin, O'Hara was one of several actors and singers in the family. Her mother was an actress and singer who performed on stage in Dublin, while her father, a clothing retailer, founded Dublin's Shamrock Rovers soccer team.

O'Hara started her career, as have many other notable Irish actors, with the Abbey Theatre in Dublin. Her 1939 performance in *Jamaica Inn*, a film shot in London, so impressed her co-star Charles Laughton that he cast her as Esmeralda in *The Hunchback of Notre Dame*. As well as giving the budding actress her first big break, Laughton renamed her, telling her that the name Fitzsimons was too complicated for Hollywood.

O'Hara's versatility saw her cast as everything from a Castilian to a French adventuress in a series of costume epics. She made a total of five films with John Ford, including *How Green Was My Valley* and *Rio Grande*. She and *Quiet Man* co-star John Wayne teamed up for a further four pictures. She also gave sterling performances in such timeless classics as *Miracle on 34th Street*. She made a total of 58 pictures in a career which has spanned almost 50 years. Her most recent film was *Only the Lonely*, in which she starred as the feisty mother of the late John Candy.

In 1998, O'Hara realized a long-held ambition when she became the third woman to lead the New York St. Patrick's Day Parade up Fifth Avenue. Adoring crowds shouted greetings as she marched along proudly, her trademark red locks shining in the bright sun.

Movie Star News

Kit DeFever

Gregory Peck

Actor

"The Irish influence has been a big thing in my life – kind of an anchor – it means a lot to me."

While studying for pre-med, Gregory Peck was bitten by the acting bug and decided to change his direction in life. He enrolled in the Sanford Meisner Neighborhood Playhouse in New York, and upon graduating debuted on Broadway in Emlyn Williams' play *The Morning Star*. One year and three plays later, in 1943, he was in Hollywood, starring in *Days of Glory*, a war movie.

A glorious screen career followed, and in 1962, less than 20 years after that fresh young face had arrived in L.A., Peck won an Academy Award for his riveting performance as Atticus Finch in *To Kill a Mockingbird*. He had previously received four Oscar nominations. In January 1999, he stepped up to a podium yet again, this time to accept a Golden Globe award for Best Supporting Actor in *Moby Dick*. Peck was greeted with laughter when he deadpanned, "I think I won one of these in 1947 and it was very encouraging. It's very encouraging now."

Among his other notable movies are *The Yearling*, *Gentleman's Agreement*, *Beloved*

Infidel, *Roman Holiday* and *The Gunfighter*. He also starred in one of the most successful horror films of the 1970s, *The Omen*.

Peck's grandmother Katherine Ashe, a native of Dingle, County Kerry, raised her son – Peck's father – partly in her native county. The young Eldred Gregory Peck, who later dropped his first name, was born in La Jolla, California on April 5, 1916, and grew up hearing stories of his father's Irish childhood.

Peck is still very active on behalf of a number of worthy charities and organizations. He has helped the American Cancer Society to raise over $50 million, and has established a number of film scholarships at University College Dublin. He lives in Beverly Hills with his second wife Veronique. The couple has a son and a daughter, and Peck also has three sons from his first marriage to Greta Rice.

He has been the recipient of numerous awards, including the Medal of Freedom (1969), Lifetime Achievement Awards from the American Film Institute (1989) and the Lincoln Center Film Society (1992), and the Marian Anderson Award (1999), bestowed annually on individuals who exemplify humanitarian efforts during the course of their life and professional career.

Movie Star News

Spencer Tracy
Chieftain of the Screen

"I wouldn't have gone to school at all if there had been any other way of learning to read the subtitles in the silent films"

His kind eyes, hard face and gruff honesty map a Celtic landscape. One can easily imagine Spencer Tracy serving as a pagan chieftain and (in true Irish style) making it look easy. There is a sublime offhandedness in every Tracy performance.

Born on April 5, 1900 in Milwaukee, Wisconsin to John Edward Tracy and Carrie Brown, Tracy was educated by Jesuits. Family legend has it that Tracy senior ("a devout, hard-driving, Irish Catholic businessman," according to Bill Davidson's book *Spencer Tracy: A Tragic Idol*) spent the night of his son's birth getting drunk in all of Milwaukee's Irish bars.

Tracy came to acting after serving with the navy in World War I. His performance in a 1929 Broadway drama called *The Last Mile* so impressed film director and fellow Irishman John Ford that the actor was given the lead in Ford's

next feature, a prison comedy called *Up the River* (1931), which co-starred Humphrey Bogart.

There were handsomer men on screen, but none with Tracy's solid, fatherly warmth. He won two Academy Awards in a row: one for *Captains Courageous* (1937), the next for playing a priest in *Boys Town* (1938). A devout Catholic throughout his life (he'd almost entered the priesthood as a young man), Tracy married former actress Louise Treadwell in 1923 and was the proud father of two children, but he suffered terrible pangs of guilt over his numerous extramarital affairs.

When he and Katharine Hepburn were teamed to star in *Woman of the Year* (1939) it was love on sight, and something like emotional stability entered Tracy's life. Their on-and off-screen romance through such gems as *Adam's Rib* (1949), *Pat and Mike* (1955) and *Guess Who's Coming to Dinner* (1968) lasted until his death. His ability to puncture her ballooning pretensions with a silent, impish look was a classic trademark of their comic chemistry.

Whether playing a disabled veteran trying to mete out justice in a seedy western town in *Bad Day at Black Rock* (1955), or a dying political leader in John Ford's great drama of Irish America, *The Last Hurrah* (1958), or holding courtrooms in thrall in *Inherit the Wind* (1960) and *Judgement at Nuremberg* (1962), Tracy positively embodied the hard wisdom of life.

John Wayne
The Duke

"Talk low, talk slow, and don't say too much."

"How many times do I gotta tell ya," he'd say. "I don't act – I react." This is as close as John Wayne ever came to a soul-baring confession, and there was no need for him to elaborate. His whole being was invested in his reactions. He could defeat an attacker with a quick gunshot, a right to the jaw or a silent, contemp-tuous look. He was equally capable in any circumstance – and the camera loved him for it.

Audiences adored him too, and in the decades since his death, John Wayne is not only cherished as an icon of masculine beauty and power, he is celebrated as the greatest reactor the movies have yet produced. Born Marion Michael Morrison, of Irish descent, in Iowa, he won the nickname "Duke" as a teenager after his family moved to Los Angeles. He excelled at football and won a scholarship to USC. His good looks won him bit parts in westerns, at first under the name Duke Morrison.

Directors took a shine to him. One early admirer, John Ford, introduced him to Raoul Walsh and, under the name "John Wayne," he made his debut as the star of the spectacular epic *The Big Trail* (1930).

What Wayne did over the next eight years remains forgettable, but when Ford starred him in *Stagecoach* (1939), Wayne became a top star.

War films, cop films, costume dramas all followed. In *The Conqueror* (1956), he drawls unforgettably, "This Tartar woman is for me, and my blood says take her."

And yet, that same year, he gave one of the great performances of his life in John Ford's *The Searchers* (1956), playing an obsessed and quite frightening Indian hunter. His best work is with John Ford: *They Were Expendable* (1945*); She Wore a Yellow Ribbon* (1949); *The Man Who Shot Liberty Valance* (1962) and, of course, that epic Irish movie, *The Quiet Man* (1952). He won an Oscar for *True Grit* (1968), directed by Henry Hathaway.

After years of battling cancer, his final film, *The Shootist* (1978), about a dying gunfighter, constitutes a heartfelt personal statement – offered not so much in words but in deeds. Wayne was a particularly great reactor when looking death in the eye. He made his strength and courage seem like natural reactions to the mysterious fact of his having been born at all.

Movie Star News

My Wild Irish Mother

BY MARY HIGGINS CLARK

In 1967 when she was 80, I tossed a birthday party for Mother. There were over 70 people present: my generation and hers; friends and cousins; our children; cronies from way-back years. The party started at three in the afternoon because I was sure that Mother and the other old girls would get tired early. I should have known better. Twelve hours later, I and my contemporaries sat limply in the den while Mother and her peers stood around the piano lustily singing "Sweet Molly Malone."

That night I marveled at Mother. Wearing her best beige lace dress, her silver hair framing her almost unlined face and bright blue eyes, she was obviously having the time of her life. Before that party finally ended, she had cast her cane aside, locked arms with the remaining "Bungalow Girls"– Rockaway Beach circa 1912 – and led a spirited rendition of an Irish polka.

My mother, Nora, the first generation of her family to be American born, was the second child of Bridget Kennedy Durkin and Thomas Durkin, a pair of youngsters newly arrived from County Sligo. All her life she was to personify the best of her Irish heritage – a warm and generous heart, undauntable faith in her God, unswerving allegiance to the Democratic Party, heroic resiliency in trouble and always, always, an unquenchable sense of humor.

By the time Nora was 13, seven more children had arrived to fill the parlor-floor-and-basement apartment on East 79th Street and she went off to work. Her first job at McCreery's paid three dollars for a 48-hour week. She walked the two miles back and forth each day to save the nickel carfare and at nights went to high school and Hunter College. She worked her way up from messenger girl at McCreery's to buyer at Altman's.

She was determined that when she married she would be able to give her children everything and would have enough money saved for lifelong security. Hers was a typical Irish courtship. She and my father "kept company" for seven years and were nearly 40 when they exchanged vows.

She promptly produced three children. The firstborn was Joseph. I, Mary, was next. When my younger brother arrived a few years later the doctor came into her room, looked at the baby nestled in her arms and the rosary entwined in her fingers and sighed, "I assume this one is Jesus."

He was half-serious. Mother was a devout Catholic with a pipeline to heaven. For 70 years she received Holy Communion every First Friday. The one break in the chain occurred when she went to the hospital to have her third child. Forever after she fretted that she really had had time to make Church. After all, she'd been in the hospital a good 20 minutes before John was born. She was then 45 years old.

All her life, Mother had dreamt of owning a home of her own and she and my father bought one a few years after they were married. To Mother, Buckingham Palace, the Taj Mahal and Shangri-La were all wrapped up in that six-room, brick, semi-detached dwelling in the Pelham Parkway section of the Bronx. But then the Depression years set in. My father's once-flourishing Irish pub began to lose money. Their stocks were lost in the crash; their savings dwindled to nothing. My father let one of the bartenders go and began working 20-hour days. One morning he didn't wake up and at age 51 Mother was left with the three of us and a mortgaged house.

It was impossible to get a job. So she put her "thinking cap" on and came up with a solution.

Left to right: (back) Warren, Mary, Marilyn, Warren. (front) David, Carol and Patty.

A sign, "Furnished Rooms, Kitchen Privileges" was bought and tacked over the doorbell. The neighbors demurred. They didn't mind "furnished rooms" but "kitchen privileges" stuck in their craw. Always agreeable, Mother snipped off the bottom half, thanking the Lord she hadn't wasted money on a metal sign that would have been impossible to alter.

And then began the parade of people who were to be woven into the fabric of our lives for the next five years.

There was Miss Mills, the grammar school teacher who tried valiantly to teach me the piano. I never got past "Drifting."

There were Mr. and Mrs. Fields who took the big, front bedroom for five dollars a week with the garage thrown in. They asked Mother if they could bring their dog, Buck. No dog lover, Mother asked doubtfully how big he was. Mrs. Fields made a little cupping move with her hands, a motion suitable to describe a toy poodle, and reluctantly Mother agreed that their pet could join our establishment.

Buck was a wild-eyed boxer. He had the instincts of an attack dog and we huddled behind closed doors in the dining room when Eddy Fields brought him down for his airing. Eddy was a slight man and his feet never seemed to touch the floor as he came hurtling down the stairs behind Buck, who by then was frenzied to relieve himself.

A 21 year-old Phi Beta Kappa student in the WPA took over my room. He was so thin that Mother worried about him and often invited him to have dinner with us. This meant that Joseph, John and I had to endure the dirge-like music he favored and played on the phonograph which he thoughtfully brought to the dining room table.

Before any new tenant came in, Mother gave what we called her "palace guard" speech. "Yes," she would say, "we're blessed with excellent police protection here. There's Officer Potters to the left and Officer Ahlis on the right. There's Sergeant Garrigan across the street and

directly opposite him . . . ", here she paused so the full weight of her pièce de résistance could sink in . . . "directly opposite him we have Inspector Whelan."

Mother had been going steady with a moving man when she was in her 20s and had somehow caught the virus that is the sine qua non of his profession. She loved to move furniture. We all got to recognize that speculative look in her eyes. "I was thinking if we put the piano at the window and the couch on the stair wall and . . ." No matter how loud and heartfelt our protests, Joe, John and I would find ourselves on the lighter end of the piece to be moved, lifting and hauling as she admonished, "Now don't strain yourself."

Her peccadillo led to the entrapment of her one and only paying-guest failure who was two weeks behind in his rent and was trying to tiptoe out at dawn. Unfortunately for his scheme, we'd moved the furniture the night before and he tripped over a lamp that had been freshly placed on the landing at the bottom of the staircase.

Mother rushed out from the dining room-turned-bedroom to find him sprawled on the floor, his feet entangled in the lamp cord.

She sighed. "If you didn't have the money to pay, all you had to do was to tell me," she said. "God knows I can understand that." When he left, he had two dollars pressed in his hand. He'd claimed he'd been promised a job in New Jersey. It would be nice to say that our departing roomer never forgot the kindness and returned the gift a thousandfold but unfortunately that was not the case. He was a deadbeat.

In spite of all our concerted efforts, the roomers who came and went, our babysitting jobs and Joe's newspaper route, Mother couldn't keep up the mortgage payments and lost the house. She was urged to take Joseph out of school and put him to work but she refused. "Education is more important than any house," she said firmly. "Joseph will get his diploma." Our next stop was a three-room apartment near the trolley line and into it she moved the full contents of the six rooms, sure that someday our fortunes would change and we'd get the house back. We never did, and whenever she returned from visiting the old neighborhood, her eyes would shine with unshed tears as she remarked how beautifully her roses had grown.

As the only girl, she guarded me with the vigor of a dragon-slaying St. George. She felt it was her duty to my dead father to see that I came unscathed through the dating years. I called her Barbara Fritchie because whenever I came up the block with a date, no matter what the hour, she would be at the window. Shoot if you must this old gray head, I'd groan inwardly and wait for the familiar call, "Is that you, Mary?" I'd want to reply "No, it's Gunga Din." But her methods were effective. No date ever got "fresh" with that alert sentry dangling 20 feet above his head.

Her prayer was that I'd marry an Irish Catholic with a government job so that someday I'd have a pension. She had a mortal fear that I'd marry outside the faith, and if I ever went out with a non-believer, she began a flying novena to St. Jude that the romance would cool.

When at 21 I began dating Warren Clark, she was delighted. So good-looking, so bright, half the girls in the parish had set their caps for him. How had he ever stayed single for 29 years? And a more respected family could not be found. His mother, Alma Claire Clark, was the national head of the Companions of the Forest of America. For the first time Mother withdrew from her window perch and went to bed early because I was safe with Mrs. Clark's son. When I remarked that dating Mrs. Clark's son was not precisely the same as dating Mrs. Clark, the insinuation sailed completely over her head and she continued to slumber blissfully away while in between kissing him goodnight, I would hiss, "Warren, you know better than that!"

Mother was a Democrat to the marrow of her bones. A captain in her district, she took her duties seriously and no matter how insignificant the election, she'd ring the bell of every voter in her area and urge one and all to go to the polls. To her the Democratic Party understood the needs of the working man and took care of its own. The one thing she couldn't forgive Warren was that he took me to register for my first vote and "turned me into a Republican."

The two of them relished many a political discussion and Warren spent the remainder of his life trying to wring from her the admission that just maybe, occasionally, the Republican candidate was better qualified than his Democratic opponent.

Finally he thought he had her. "Mrs. Higgins," he inquired, "if the Party put up Joseph Stalin for President, would you vote for him?"

It was a lady or tiger question . . . her Catholicism and her devotion to the Democrats were on the line but Mother skirted the issue neatly. She replied that if the Party put up Stalin she'd surely vote for him, because they'd have a good reason for putting him up. "Warren, mark my words, they always know what they are doing."

Her occupation and hobby, vocation and avocation was Motherhood. A Jewish mother looks into the cradle and sees a possible Messiah. It's equally true that an Irish mother gazes at her firstborn son and sees the Christ-child. Joseph was a premature baby weighing only four pounds when he was born. She fed him with an eyedropper that first year and never left him for an instant. I found a diary she kept and in it she wrote, "I was so afraid he'd slip away. He was such a beautiful baby. The other two had allergies."

Growing up, Joseph justified her pride in him. He won the General Excellence medal all eight years of grammar school. He won a scholarship to Fordham Prep. He was the captain of every team, the lead in the school play. He had the newspaper route and every penny he earned he brought home to her, turning his pockets inside out to make sure he didn't forget a dime. Then they shared their own special treat, a half-pint of ice cream.

At 13, Joe contracted osteomyelitis. Mother was told that an operation to remove the hipbone was necessary to save his life. Widowed only a few months, she made the stunning decision not to operate. She wouldn't make a cripple of Joseph and she knew God wouldn't take him from her. It was Christmas. He was on the critical list and the doctors held no hope for his recovery. Mother and John and I carried all his presents to the hospital. His main gift was a hockey stick. "You'll use it next year," she promised him. He did.

Joe graduated from high school in 1944. Mother could have claimed him as her sole support and kept him out of service. Instead she let him enlist in the navy with his friends. Six months later she took the only long trip of her life, a plane ride to California to be at Joe's deathbed in the Long Beach Naval Hospital. To the people who fumbled for words of sympathy she said, "It is God's will. I couldn't let Joseph go when he was sick the other time but now God wants him even more than I do."

That June when I graduated from Villa Maria Academy Mother threw a party for me that held no hint of sadness. It was my day and nothing was going to spoil it. Johnny graduated from grammar school a few weeks later and he too had all the aunts and uncles and cousins and friends there to celebrate.

She bought a black and white print dress to wear to both occasions. She felt her black mourning dress was out of place on those two days.

Her pride in all of us was enormous. We were never simply doing well in school. We were "taking all the honors." I never had a job. I had "a big job." When John went to Notre Dame she must have written a dozen letters to long-forgotten cousins. The letters began, "My, what a busy summer, what with getting John ready for Notre Dame . . ." This kick-off would be followed by a careful explanation of why Notre Dame was the finest college in the world and therefore eminently qualified to educate her son.

After Warren and I were married, she never quite forgave us for moving to New Jersey. Warren urged her to live with us and avoid the endless bus trips back and forth, but even given carte blanche to come with all her beloved furniture, there was never the faintest chance she'd move. You only had to drive her halfway across the George Washington Bridge to have her start sniffing the air and remarking on the heavenly breezes that originated in the Bronx.

She delighted in being a grandmother. She had a deep horror of my leaving the children with a young babysitter and thought nothing of taking the two-hour, three-bus trip to New Jersey to mind them.

From the time they could toddle half a block alone, Mother was whisking them on the Circle Line Tour, to the Central Park Zoo, to the Statue of Liberty, to parades and to beaches. She especially adored amusement parks. In 1939 she took my brothers and me to the World's Fair.

It was the summer Daddy died and I can still see her, the long mourning veil trailing wraith-like behind her as we plunged down on the parachute jump. A quarter of a century later, when she was 76, she was taking my five offspring on the steeplechase at Coney Island.

Long years of making one dollar do the work of ten couldn't be unlearned and if the kids had any complaint, it was that Nanny made them share a soda or divide a sandwich in the Automat. She once promised my then five-year-old that she'd take him up to the top of the Empire State Building. Upon realizing that she had to pay for the tickets to the Observation Tower, she whisked him up on the business elevator to the 86th floor, stood him at a window and said brightly, "Here we are at the top. Isn't this fun?"

Her caring for the children encompassed Warren and me. She adored Warren, and to her "himself" was the grandest husband any girl could have. "The disposition of a saint," she'd sigh. "I hope you know how lucky you are, Mary." The only time she wavered in her devotion to him was during my pregnancies when, totally unconsciously, and to our huge amusement, Mother would speak of Warren as "that fellow."

But even then she'd be fussing over him, making his tea just the way he liked it, worrying over his habit of never wearing a hat even in the coldest weather. One night I awoke to find Mother tucking the covers around him. "Mother, in God's name, what are you doing in here?" I groaned. "Mary, he'll catch his death of cold," she sighed.

After that whenever she stayed over, I locked the door of the master bedroom and she darkly murmured something to the effect of "you two barricading yourselves in there when your children might need you."

We'd been married ten years when Warren began having chest pains and we learned that, incredibly, this handsome, vibrant man who excelled in every sport had the arteries of an 80 year-old. In the next four years he had two heart attacks. He'd just come home from the hospital when a third attack took him from us.

"God's will, but oh it is so hard sometimes," Mother said and I made myself remember that she'd never taken her grief out on us and I wouldn't take mine out on my children. It was because of Mother that I was able to go out to work, but of course she didn't think she was minding only five youngsters. She immediately resumed her role as guardian of a young girl . . . me.

A week after Warren's death, the funeral director came in with some papers for me to sign. Mother herded the boys upstairs. In five minutes my visitor was gone and Marilyn, my high school freshman, turned on her French language records. For the next 30 minutes, a suave masculine voice asked such questions as "Voulez vous aller au bibliotheque avec moi?" When the record was finished, Mother rushed down the stairs, indignation etched in every line of her face. "Mary, what was that fellow doing talking French to you?" she demanded.

Another evening I came home at midnight to find her waiting in the living room. "Mary, what will the neighbors think of a girl your age coming home at this hour of the night?" she demanded. I was then 36.

Mother began having arthritis when she was 20. It was in keeping with her whole approach to life that she caught it dancing barefoot in the snow in Central Park. As she aged, it spread into her knees and legs, her feet and hands and back. Her feet were the worst and she literally walked to heaven on those painful appendages, so swollen and sore she could hardly endure her weight on them. She probably would have been confined to a wheelchair except that her need to do for other people was so great that she kept pushing herself, forcing activity on those tired limbs, literally willing them to function.

Paradoxically she may have sped her own end by electing to go into a nursing home for a few weeks' rest. After all, she pointed out, she was spending three dollars a month for Medicare and getting nothing out of it. As soon as she began to take it easy, everything in her body slowed up. Her heartbeat became more and more uncertain. I knew it would soon be over when one day, just coming out of a sleep, she said drowsily, "Mary, I had the children down to the beach and Carol wandered off. I couldn't find her. I just don't think I really can take care of them anymore." She could no longer take care of others and didn't want anyone to take care of her.

She had a total of $1700 in insurance from nickel and dime policies she'd paid on for years. They were tied together in an old brown envelope. There was a note to Johnny and me with them. It said, "Don't waste more than a thousand dollars on the funeral. Give one hundred dollars to each of my grandchildren." She didn't realize that she'd already given us all

a priceless legacy, her ceaseless devotion and unfailing love.

And Mother is still part of us. "Remember when Nanny . . ." is heard frequently in my home and after the story is told, there's bound to be laughter. Last fall, Patty, my youngest, was in the attic, apprehensively getting out suitcases to pack for her freshman year in college. She began rummaging and came down, wrapped in a pale pink terrycloth robe. "It still smells like Nanny," she said happily and surely it did. The faint scent of her talcum was there and the robe went off to college with Pat.

I have Mother's old black felt hat with the brief edging of black veiling in my closet. It's battered now and out of shape but over the years when things weren't going well, when the bills were piling up or one of the children was sick, I'd give it a quick rub and say, "Come on, Nora, do your stuff." I had no doubt that my first novel would be successful because it was dedicated to her. "I can just see Nora," a friend said laughing. "'Dear Lord, not to bother you . . . the paperback sale on the book was excellent but how about the movie rights?'"

Time is slipping by so quickly. Months and seasons become years. My contemporaries and I ruefully discuss the fact that now we are the older generation. But when dawns the day that shall be my last I have no fear. Because I am very sure that the first sound I hear when I enter eternity will be that well-loved voice anxiously asking, "Is that you, Mary?"

Mary Higgins Clark is a best-selling author of books including Where Are the Children? *and* A Stranger Is Watching. *Her new novel,* On the Street Where You Live, *will be published in April 2001.*

The Services

James and Sarah Brady.

James Brady
Crusader

Since the Brady Law went into effect on February 28, 1994, it has stopped an estimated 100,000 convicted felons and other prohibited purchasers from buying a handgun. Every day the law keeps guns out of the hands of dozens of felons. It took seven years to bring this law into being, and the driving force behind this effort was Jim Brady.

We might never have heard of Brady if he hadn't been in the wrong place at the wrong time. In 1981, he took a bullet meant for President Ronald Reagan. Lodged in his skull, the bullet left Brady permanently disabled – he has difficulty walking and lives in constant pain.

But instead of becoming bitter, he and his wife, Sarah, focused their energy on handgun control. Because of their tireless efforts and in spite of a huge, well-organized gun lobby, the Brady Law now imposes a seven-day waiting period for anyone who wishes to buy a gun. In a country where the threat of handgun violence continues to grow, Irish Americans, and indeed all Americans, owe their thanks to James Brady for his efforts to protect the American family.

Reverend Francis Duffy
Fighting Father

"If I've helped anyone become a better man and he loves me for it, that's my Distinguished Service Cross."

Beloved pastor and battlefield legend, the Reverend Francis Patrick Duffy, known as "Fighting Father Duffy," was truly a man of the people. From the rarefied world of academia to the trenches of World War I France to the mean streets of New York, Father Duffy moved effortlessly, earning the love and respect of all he encountered along the way.

Canadian by birth, Duffy moved to New York at the age of 22 to teach at St. Francis Xavier College, quitting shortly thereafter to join a Catholic seminary. He was ordained in 1896 and was assigned by his superiors to Catholic University for more graduate study. Two years later he was sent to Dunwoodie, the seminary in Yonkers, to teach psychology and logic.

While teaching, he also worked as founding editor for the *New York Review*, designed to acquaint readers with the new work of European and American theological and biblical scholars.

He was sent to the Bronx in 1912 to develop a new parish, the Church of Our Savior. In the meantime, he also became chaplain for the "Fighting" 69th, the famed New York National Guard unit, part of the 165th Infantry. When the United States entered World War I in 1917, the 165th was sent to France and Father Duffy went with them. He was 46 years old.

During 180 days of combat that claimed the lives of 900 men, Father Duffy was on every battlefield. After every battle, he would walk the fields, collecting metal identification tags from bodies, hearing the last words of the dying, giving absolution and helping to bury the dead. One officer recalled seeing Duffy burst into tears as he bent over a dead soldier. When asked why, he replied, "I baptized him as a baby."

Duffy's bravery under fire prompted General Douglas MacArthur, the U.S. Chief of Staff, to consider promoting the chaplain to colonel and placing him in command of the division. His bravery during the particularly bloody battle at the Oureq River won him a decoration, and his citation read, "Despite constant and severe bombardment with shells and aerial bombs, he continued to circulate in and about two aid stations and hospitals, creating an atmosphere of cheerfulness and confidence by his courageous and inspiring example." He was also proposed for the Medal of Honor, the nation's highest award for bravery, but he declined the honor.

When he returned to New York in 1919, Duffy was assigned as pastor of Holy Cross parish in Times Square, where he became deeply involved in educational issues and fostering ecumenical dialogue and the discussion of church and state relations. Living in the heart of the theater district, he befriended such theater luminaries as Spencer Tracy, John Barrymore, Gene Tunney and George M. Cohan.

When Father Duffy died in the summer of 1932, thousands of New Yorkers, both Protestant and Catholic, went to pray on the steps of Holy Cross Church. More than 20,000

filed past his coffin to pay their last respects. He was given a military funeral and the Mass was held at St. Patrick's Cathedral instead of Holy Cross because the diocese believed he belonged to the whole city, not just Holy Cross parish.

Five years later, New York honored his memory by erecting his statue at 43rd Street and Broadway in a square bearing his name.

William "Wild Bill" Donovan
Fighting Irish

At one time he had the intention of studying for the priesthood, but William Joseph Donovan ended up having a far more colorful and varied life. A lawyer, a diplomat, a military man and a public representative, he lived his 76 years to the fullest limits.

Born in Buffalo, New York on January 1, 1883 to Timothy Patrick Donovan and Anna Lennon, "Wild Bill" graduated from Columbia University in 1907 with a law degree, and subsequently opened his own firm in his native city.

During World War I he served in the National Guard and was stationed on the Mexican border. As a colonel in the New York 69th Regiment (he was commander of the "Fighting Irish") he was posted overseas to France, quickly emerging as a heroic officer, for which he received the

Library of Congress

Distinguished Service Cross, the Distinguished Service Medal, and the Congressional Medal of Honor.

In the postwar years, Donovan turned to politics, and in 1922 he was appointed U.S. Attorney for western New York. Two years later, he became U.S. Assistant Attorney General. A long and successful career as a diplomat was to follow, and Donovan spent time in Libya, Spain and England, all at the behest of the U.S. government.

Following a request from President Franklin D. Roosevelt, he became deeply involved in the running of the Office of Strategic Services (OSS), the forerunner of the Central Intelligence Agency. His OSS involvement led to Donovan's becoming known as a principal "spymaster" in the U.S.

Six years before his death, Donovan served as U.S. Ambassador to Thailand. Failing health forced his retirement from public service. He died in Virginia on February 8, 1959.

Steven McDonald
Hero Cop

When Steven McDonald appeared at the Irish memorial Mass in New York City for John F. Kennedy, Jr. and the Bessette sisters, there was a prolonged round of applause for the young cop, wheelchair bound since a tragic shooting in 1986. In the years that followed the shooting, McDonald has proven that physical limitations do not have to be perceived as psychological restrictions, and he has transcended the confines of his wheelchair in ways an able-bodied person can only watch and envy.

McDonald made the headlines in the summer of 1986 when he was shot and paralyzed during an attempt to break up a robbery in Central Park. He was the sixth member of his family to join the ranks of New York's Finest, and he is still on the force as a detective.

His wife, Patti Ann, who was pregnant at the time of the shooting, is a familiar face alongside McDonald's at various Irish events and charity functions, and the two work tirelessly to educate others about the work that police officers do, and about the importance of forgiveness. McDonald had long since publicly forgiven his attacker, who was killed in a motorcycle accident three days after being released from prison.

McDonald's ancestors hail from Counties Laois and Leitrim, and he is deeply committed to a number of Irish causes. He and his wife have one son, Conor. They live on Long Island.

Audie Murphy
Soldier/Actor

"We have been so intent on death that we have forgotten life."

For the most decorated U.S. soldier in history, Audie Murphy certainly had a hard time getting into the army. When he tried to join at the age of 17, he was rejected as being too small. Undaunted, he tried again and was accepted in the summer of 1942. Murphy proved to be a fierce warrior: when he left the army in 1945 he had been awarded an astounding 37 medals: 11 for valor, including the Distinguished Service Cross, two Silver Stars, four Purple Hearts and the Congressional Medal of Honor.

His later fame and glory belied his difficult upbringing. Murphy was born in Texas, the son of Irish American sharecroppers. By the age of five, he was out working in the cotton fields under the broiling Texas sun. The Murphy family lived on the brink of impoverishment and sometimes lived in boxcars provided by social service organizations. There were 12 Murphy children, but three died young.

Matters were made worse by Audie's father, Emmet, or Pat, an alcoholic who would periodically leave the family for months at a time. He finally left the family for good in 1940, when Audie was 16. One year later, Audie's mother died. She was only 49. Years later, Audie would say of his childhood, "I never had just 'fun.' It was a full-time job just existing."

Once in the infantry, Murphy quickly distinguished himself as an exemplary soldier. He earned his first decoration, a bronze star, in February, 1943, after destroying a German tank during night patrol. He received the majority of his decorations during the Allied invasion of southern France in August 1944.

But the climax of his military career occurred on January 26, 1945. Murphy's company, down to only 18 men and supported by two tanks, encountered six German tanks supported by 250 German infantrymen. One Allied tank got stuck in a ditch, while the other took a direct hit and burst into flames. Murphy ordered his men back under cover, then jumped on the burning tank and trained the machine gun onto the Germans. At the same time, he directed American artillery fire over his field telephone. After half an hour, Murphy had killed 50 Germans and had repulsed the German attack. For this incredible act of bravery and daring, Murphy was awarded the Congressional Medal of Honor, the highest military honor.

After Murphy returned to the States in 1945, it was only a matter of time before Hollywood called and he launched a career in the movies that lasted into the 1960s. Still, haunted by ghosts of his childhood and wartime trauma, happiness eluded him. He suffered nightmares, gambled compulsively, and his emotional volatility sometimes made him difficult to work with. He died in 1971, at the age of 47, when the small plane he was flying in crashed on a flight between Georgia and Virginia. He was buried in Arlington National Cemetery, and to this day, only John F. Kennedy's grave is visited by more people.

Movie Star News

The Archives of The Grout Museum

The Sullivan Brothers
Patriots

In kinder circumstances we might never have heard of the Sullivan brothers. The five fun-loving, hard-working Irish American brothers from Iowa would have settled down, married, raised families and died at ripe old ages in peaceful anonymity. However, their intense loyalty to their friends and to one another proved to be their undoing. As a result, The Fighting Sullivans will be remembered for generations as having made the ultimate sacrifice in the name of patriotism.

The five boys were born to Thomas Sullivan, a second-generation Irish American, and Alleta Abel, also descended from Irish stock. None of the brothers finished high school, which was not uncommon at the time, and they all found work in the local meat packing company.

When the five brothers – George, Francis, Joseph, Madison (Matt) and Albert – heard of the death of a friend in the attack on the U.S.S. *Arizona* at Pearl Harbor, they all determined to enlist, even though the two older brothers, George and Frank, had already completed tours of duty with the Navy.

The brothers had one condition on enlisting – that they be allowed to stick together. The Navy agreed and the Sullivan brothers were sworn in on January 3, 1942. Not one was over the age of 30 – George, the eldest, was 27 and Albert, the youngest, was only 19.

All five brothers were stationed on the U.S.S. *Juneau,* which was sent in late 1942 to reinforce Guadalcanal, an island the Marines were trying to wrest from the Japanese.

In a battle with the Japanese, the *Juneau* was destroyed by a torpedo, killing nearly everyone on board. A handful of survivors remained clinging to life rafts, including the last Sullivan brother, George. One night George decided to take a dip in the water. While swimming away from his raft, he was pulled under by a shark. The brothers were reunited in death.

The boys' deaths rocked the nation, and there was a huge outpouring of publicity and sympathy for the Sullivan family. Their parents, accompanied by their only surviving child, Genevieve, mustered their courage, giving radio broadcasts, and making public appearances at ship yards and war plants urging more production to help other sons still fighting.

In April 1943, Mrs. Sullivan christened a new destroyer, U.S.S. *The Sullivans,* at the Bethlehem Steel Shipbuilding Yard in San Francisco.

Two months later, Genevieve Sullivan, the last Sullivan child, joined the WAVES. While as a woman she would never see combat, she remains a symbol of one family's undying patriotism in spite of unimaginable loss.

The memory of the five Sullivan brothers lives today in the Sullivan Law, which prohibits siblings from serving on the same ship. Their story also provided part inspiration for 1998's blockbuster movie from Steven Spielberg, *Saving Private Ryan.*

Writers
& Media

Nellie Bly
Newspaperwoman

"Energy rightly applied can accomplish anything."

Nellie Bly's biographer, Brooke Kroeger, captured the essence of his admirable subject when he wrote: "In the 1880s, she pioneered the development of 'detective' or 'stunt' journalism, the acknowledged forerunner to full-scale investigative reporting."

Born Elizabeth Jane Cochran on May 5, 1864 to Michael Cochran and Mary Jane Cummings, both of whom were of Irish descent, Bly had the distinction of being born into a town renamed Cochran Mills in honor of her father, a local judge. She was called "Pink" as a child, that being the color her mother usually dressed her in.

One of 14 children, Bly and her family were thrown into disarray after her father died suddenly when she was just six years old. Her mother's subsequent marriage ended in divorce after her husband turned out to be an alcoholic and wifebeater. When she was 15, determined to be a teacher, Bly enrolled at the Indiana Normal School in Western Pennsylvania. After only one term, however, her money ran out.

At the age of 22, Bly had a letter published in the *Pittsburgh Dispatch* which impressed the editors and earned her a job with the publication.

As a prospective journalist for Joseph Pulitzer's *New York World*, she later posed as a mental patient in a New York institution, publishing her experiences in an explosive story which led to reform in mental health care.

"People in the world can never imagine the length of days to those in asylums," she wrote poignantly. "They seem never ending, and we welcomed any event that might give us something to think about as well as talk of."

Bly's article provided good insight into the logic of her thinking. "Take a perfectly sane and healthy woman," she wrote, "shut her up and make her sit up straight from 6 a.m. to 8 p.m. Do not allow her to talk or move during these hours, give her nothing to read, let her know nothing of the world or its doings, and see how long it will take to make her insane."

She added: "The insane asylum on Blackwell's Island is a human rat-trap. It is easy to get in, but once there it is impossible to get out . . . I had looked forward so eagerly to leaving the horrible place, yet when my release came and I knew that God's sunlight was to be free for me again, there was a certain pain in leaving. For ten days I had been one of them. Foolishly enough it seemed intensely selfish to leave them to their sufferings. I felt a quixotic desire to help them by my sympathy and presence. But only for a moment. The bars were down and freedom was sweeter to me than ever." Pulitzer's response to her story? "Obviously this girl is very suited for this profession," he told a friend, "and of course I have given her a very large bonus."

One of the forerunners of modern investigative journalism, Bly was reputed to be a fearless character who would go anywhere and do anything for a good story. Add to that her excellent writing skills and you end up with a world-class reporter.

In 1889, Bly had her 15 minutes of fame worldwide when she set out to beat the record set by Phileas Fogg in the Jules Verne novel *Around the World in Eighty Days*. Setting out from Hoboken, New Jersey on November 14, and garbed in a checkered coat, she journeyed by boat, train, rickshaw and horse, and managed to beat the 80-day record by just under eight days. Despite the perils of her journey, she said she "would rather go back to New York dead than not a winner."

The diary of her trip records her impressions of the many cities she visited. She describes London as a city of "dim lights and a gray, dusty shade . . . [with] some fine buildings [and] beautifully paved streets." Amiens, France, meanwhile, provided her with the opportunity to meet Jules Verne, the inspiration for her journey. Egypt struck her as an unappealing place, with its hordes of beggars, while in Hong Kong it seemed to her as though "one seems to be suspended between two heavens."

But it was her arrival back in New Jersey that really struck a chord with Bly, as is obvious from her recollections. "The station was packed with thousands of people," she wrote, "and the moment I landed on the platform, one yell went up from them . . . I took off my cap and wanted to yell with the crowd, not because I had gone around the world in seventy-two days, but because I was home again."

In the aftermath of her record travels, completed when she was just 25, Bly saw a hotel, a train and a racehorse named in her honor.

After her marriage to billionaire businessman Robert Seaman in 1895, Bly retired from journalism. After he died, she lost a lot of her fortune to swindlers. Three years after an unsuccessful attempt to restart her career, she died of pneumonia on January 27, 1922. Fellow journalist Arthur Brisbane, a prominent and much-admired newspaperman, described her as "the best reporter in America."

Jimmy Breslin
Newspaperman

"Rage is the only quality which has kept me, or anybody I have ever studied, writing columns for newspapers."

A New Yorker to his core, Jimmy Breslin has chronicled the lives and injustices of his fellow city folk for over 40 years now, and has distinguished himself from dozens of other writers in the process. Like many other columnists of his generation, he has spread his wings in many directions, and is also the author of several novels, screenplays and stage plays.

Born and reared in Queens, he got his start in journalism at the now defunct *Long Island Press*, and went on to work for such publications as the *Journal-American*, the *New York Herald Tribune*, the *Daily News* and (his current posting) the Long Island-based *Newsday*. His earlier assignments were mostly sporting ones, but Breslin got his start in column writing in 1963 with the *Herald Tribune*. Some of the world-changing events he has covered include the assassination of President Kennedy, the civil rights movement of the '60s and the Vietnam War.

Breslin's immigrant grandparents hailed from Counties Clare and Donegal, and *Village Voice* columnist Jack Newfield described him as "classic black Irish. He loves conflict and he acts like each day is the worst day of his life."

After Breslin's first wife, Rosemary, died, leaving him to raise six children, he married New Yorker Ronnie Eldridge, a widow with three children. The couple's hectic family life, and their merging of the Catholic and Jewish traditions, ended up as material for some amusing columns. In 1986, he won a Pulitzer Prize for commentary.

Thomas Cahill
Scholar

"In the 15th century, Edmund Campion described the Irish as 'religious, frank, amorous, irefull, sufferable of paines infinite . . . delighted with warres, great almesgivers, passing in hospitalitie . . . sharp-witted, lovers of learning . . .' – and they haven't changed a bit."

The title alone – *How the Irish Saved Civilization: The Untold Story of Ireland's Heroic Role from the Fall of Rome to the Rise of Medieval Europe* – galvanized the Irish and Irish American community. In a century in which the

Irish are just beginning to emerge from the national inferiority complex resulting from hundreds of years of oppression, Thomas Cahill's book gave us further reason to celebrate our own rich heritage. Reading his book, in which he distills centuries of complex history, is as easy and entertaining as sitting around the dining room table after the plates have been cleared and listening to the stories of a dear old uncle.

The best-selling *How the Irish Saved Civilization* is the first in a prospective seven-volume series entitled *The Hinges of History*, in which Cahill recounts formative moments in Western civilization. It was followed in 1998 by the second volume in the series, *The Gifts of the Jews: How a Tribe of Desert Nomads Changed the Way Everyone Thinks and Feels*. His third volume, released in the fall of 1999, is called *Desire of the Everlasting Hills: The World Before and After Jesus.*

One of six children born to a middle-class Irish family in the Bronx, New York, Cahill grew up in Queens and attended a Jesuit high school on Long Island. He later became a Jesuit seminarian earning a pontifical degree and becoming proficient in Latin and Greek. He went on to complete his M.F.A. in film and dramatic literature at Columbia University. He also studied scripture at New York's Union Theological Seminary, and most recently spent two years as a Visiting Scholar at the Jewish Theological Seminary of America. He has taught at Queens College, Fordham University and Seton Hall University. He has also served as the North American education correspondent for the *Times* of London. Prior to retiring recently to write full-time, he was director of religious publishing at Doubleday for six years. He and his wife, Susan, also an author, divide their time between New York and Rome.

Rachel Carson
Earth Mother

"It is a wholesome and necessary thing for us to turn again to the earth and in the contemplations of her beauties to know the sense of wonder and humility."

Hailed as the mother of the modern environmental movement, Rachel Carson's contribution to our current environmental awareness is immeasurable. Her book *Silent Spring*, published in 1962, revealed to the public the dangers of indiscriminate pesticide use and its hazardous effect on the land and the creatures that live on it. The book prompted President Kennedy to call for the testing of the chemicals mentioned in the book. As a marine biologist, Carson was well aware of the interdependence of all living things and the threat posed by humanity's lack of awareness.

Carson was born in 1907 in a farmhouse in Springdale, Pennsylvania. It was here that her Irish American mother, Maria McLean Carson, taught her a love and respect for the land. A schoolteacher and musician, Maria also fostered in her young daughter a love of literature and encouraged her to consider a career in writing. When Carson enrolled in the Pennsylvania College for Women (later Chatham College) she planned to study English, but all that would change in Mary Scott Skinker's biology class. She found this science so fascinating, she abandoned her literary aspirations and decided to become a scientist.

In 1929, Carson received a fellowship to study at the Woods Hole Marine Biological Laboratory in Massachusetts. She found the study of the sea captivating. The fellowship was followed by one at Johns Hopkins University. She went on to earn an M.A. in Zoology in 1932 from the University of Maryland and began teaching there.

Carson's father, Robert, died suddenly in 1935 and she was left to find a way to support herself and her mother. She began to work for the U.S.

Corbis / Bettmann – UPI

Department of Fisheries in Washington on a part-time basis writing for a radio show about ocean life entitled *Romance Under the Sea*. One year later, she became the first woman to take and pass the civil service test and first full-time female employee of the bureau. Over the next 15 years she would rise from the position of full-time junior biologist to chief editor of all publications of the U.S. Department of Fisheries.

All the while, Carson continued with her own writing and scientific investigation. At the behest of her boss, Carson submitted one of her manuscripts as an article to *The Atlantic*. The article was entitled "Undersea," and when the magazine hit the newsstands, the article was so highly praised that Carson was encouraged to put it into a book. The result was the best-seller *Under the Sea-Wind*.

Carson continued to write government publications throughout the war, taking time off afterwards to write another book with the help of another fellowship. *The Sea Around Us* also hit the best-seller list, staying there for 86 weeks.

While the public was fascinated by Carson's scientific explanations and insights, readers were equally drawn to her beautiful writing, which seemed more like poetry than science. To Carson this was only natural. "No one could write truthfully about the sea," she said, "and leave out the poetry."

When *Silent Spring* was published, it was viciously attacked by chemical companies; however, her research was vindicated by subsequent government inquiries.

Carson developed cancer and heart disease when she was only 57, and she died in 1964. In 1980, President Carter posthumously awarded her the Presidential Medal of Freedom, saying of her, "Always concerned, always eloquent, she created a tide of environmental consciousness that has not ebbed."

Maureen Dowd
Columnist

No columnist in America has been as influential as Maureen Dowd over the past decade. She casts a cold eye on Washington affairs and has skillfully skewered president, senators and the high and mighty for so long that her *New York Times* column has become a fixation on the breakfast tables of the rich and powerful.

It is hard to overestimate her influence. As the eyes of the world zeroed in on the impeachment saga in Washington, D.C. for more than a year, it was Dowd whom people turned to for a no-nonsense view of the proceedings. Her acerbic "Liberties" column appears twice-weekly on the Op-Ed page of the *Times*. She is an equal-opportunities offender, who directs her caustic wit at both Republicans and Democrats on a regular basis.

Her efforts won her a Pulitzer Prize for Commentary in April 1999, for her "fresh and insightful" musings on the President Clinton impeachment scandal. Her reaction was pure Dowd: "To paraphrase Monica Lewinsky's favorite poet, T.S. Eliot, April is the coolest month."

The daughter of an Irish cop, Dowd began her journalism career in 1974 as an editorial assistant for the *Washington Star*. She went on to cover sports, features and metropolitan stories. In 1981 she moved to *Time* magazine, after the *Washington Star* closed.

In August 1986, she joined the *New York Times* as a correspondent in its Washington bureau. After covering two presidential campaigns, she was appointed a columnist of the paper's Op-Ed page in 1995. In 1991, Dowd received the Breakthrough Award from "Women, Men and Media" at Columbia University. She also received a Matrix Award from New York Women in Communications in 1994, and was named one of *Glamour* magazine's Women of the Year in 1996.

Finley Peter Dunne
Satirist
"Trust everybody, but cut the cards."

Out of the Chicago Irish community came one of the greatest satirists in American history. In the place where journalism, satire and humor meet, Finley Peter Dunne occupies a special place. As a journalist for the *Chicago Evening Post* he created the character Martin Dooley, a bachelor saloon-keeper and Roscommon native on Chicago's South Side as the central character of his weekly newspaper sketches.

These columns, which recounted in lengthy monologues the opinions of Mr. Dooley, went beyond Irish comic dialogue to focus on the

personalities and issues of the day. Created in 1893, the columns spanned more than 20 years and were published in book form.

Until Mr. Dooley, the Irish brogue had been used in 19th-century drama, fiction and journalism to portray the stereotypical "stage Irishman," a demeaning caricature that portrayed the Irish as alternately belligerent and garrulous and always ignorant. Mr. Dooley's brogue smashed the stereotypes for good. He provoked laughter not because he was ignorant, but because he was so perceptive.

The bright light of Dunne's satire was laceratingly funny and unforgiving in its exposure of the delusion and hypocrisy of Chicago's political and social leaders: "Jawn, niver steal a dure mat. If ye do ye'll be invistigated, hanged, an' maybe rayformed. Steal a bank, me boy, steal a bank."

Dunne was born in Chicago's near West Side in the shadow of Old Saint Patrick's Church on July 10, 1867. As a youth he was encouraged to read and develop intellectually by his mother, Ellen Finley Dunne, and his older sister, Amelia, a teacher in the Chicago public schools. He graduated from high school in 1884 and took a job as an office boy and cub reporter for the *Chicago Telegram*. Eight years and five jobs later, he was the editorial chairman at the *Chicago Evening Post*, where, at the age of 26, he created Martin Dooley.

In 1898, the popularity of Mr. Dooley's satiric perspective on the Spanish-American War led to national syndication and the publication of his first book of selected columns. Dunne moved to New York in 1900 and became one of the most popular humorists of his day. But it is widely agreed that the Chicago Dooley pieces remain his best work, where the Irish oral tradition and the written word come together to preserve the cultural memories and mores of the Chicago Irish at the end of the 19th century. Dunne died in New York City on April 24, 1936.

Jim Dwyer
Columnist

A trio of New York Irish journalists – Jimmy Breslin, Pete Hamill and Jim Dwyer – have profoundly changed the way newspaper columns are written. Where once columns were either think pieces or puffery of the rich and powerful, Breslin, Hamill, and Dwyer have pioneered a "man on the street on the side of the little guy"–style that has transformed modern journalism.

To New Yorkers the fact that Jim Dwyer is responsible for the first bus and subway fare reduction is reason enough for his inclusion as one of the top Irish Americans of the century. In October 1997, his front-page disclosure of a multi-million dollar surplus – initially denied by the government – forced state officials to roll back the fares.

To the rest of the world, he is simply one of the best journalists of the century, and his two Pulitzers prove it. He won the prize in 1995 for commentary and shared the prize in 1992 for metropolitan reporting. And the fare reductions are not the only way his writing has directly benefited the lives of Americans. He set off a national media stampede with columns exposing sweatshop conditions in a 38th Street garment factory where the Kathie Lee Gifford clothing line was manufactured. The ensuing uproar led to new legislation to protect the working poor.

To Irish Americans, he is even more. He is the

source of factual, compelling reports on the state of Northern Ireland. In 1997, he traveled to Northern Ireland and broke the word that a new IRA ceasefire was likely to be declared, while the rest of the international media was predicting a civil war. His commitment to balanced reporting has led him where few American journalists have gone before – he once turned up at a street beer-bash in a loyalist neighborhood in Belfast. The residents were astonished – they had never met an American journalist before.

In 1997, he presented a moving yet clear-eyed account of the life and death of Bernadette Martin, an 18 year-old Catholic who was murdered in her sleep for loving a Protestant.

Dwyer joined the *Daily News* in 1995. Before that he worked for more than 11 years at New York *Newsday* as an investigative reporter, courthouse reporter, subway columnist and general columnist. He has reported from England, Ireland, Israel, Italy, Spain and Sweden.

A first-generation Irish American – his mother and father are from Counties Galway and Kerry respectively – Dwyer attended Fordham College and Columbia University. He is the author of two acclaimed books, *Subway Lives* and *Two Seconds Under the World*, an account of the World Trade Center bombing.

He and his wife, Cathy, live in New York with their two daughters, Maura and Catherine.

James T. Farrell
Wordsmith

"For many of us Americans, there is a gap between our . . . childhood and our productive manhood. . . Our beginnings were naive, and we must still understand the difference between our present and our past."

In the obituary he penned for himself, James Thomas Farrell described himself as one who "wrote too much . . . fought too much [and] kissed too much." Born February 27, 1904 to

Corbis / Bettmann – UPI

James Francis Farrell and Mary Daly, Farrell was one of 15 children, and was raised by his maternal grandmother and an uncle.

Best known for his Studs Lonigan trilogy (*Young Lonigan, The Young Manhood of Studs Lonigan* and *Judgment Day*), Farrell was a prolific writer who penned some 250 short stories, collected in a variety of volumes. He also published almost 30 novels, and a body of critical essays on literature, politics and society.

Farrell's South Side Chicago Irish roots were rarely far from his writing, and he always remained very aware of his origins. "I am a second-generation Irish American," he once wrote. "The effects and scars of immigration are upon my life. The past was dragging through my boyhood and adolescence. Horatio Alger, Jr. died only seven years before I was born. The 'climate of opinion' (to use a phrase of Alfred North Whitehead) was one of hope. But for an Irish boy born in Chicago in 1904, the past was a tragedy of his people . . ."

The first volume of the Studs Lonigan trilogy was published by Vanguard Press in New York, who attached a warning that the book should only be sold to "physicians, surgeons, psychologists, psychiatrists, sociologists, social workers, teachers and other persons having a professional interest in the psychology of adolescence."

In 1931 Farrell married Dorothy Patricia Butler. They were later divorced and he married the actress Hortense Alden, with whom he had a son. After divorcing Alden, he remarried his first wife in 1955, but it was to last just three years. The writer died in New York, at the age of 75, on August 22, 1979, but not before seeing his Studs Lonigan creation dramatized as a six-hour miniseries on television.

William Faulkner
Voice of the South

"I believe that man will not merely endure: he will prevail. He is immortal, not because he alone among creatures has an inexhaustible voice, but because he has a soul, a spirit capable of compassion and sacrifice and endurance."

William Faulkner's is the voice of the South, capturing this region in all its decadence and decay in the years following the Civil War and the anguish surrounding the loss of traditional values as the Old South gave way to the New in all its brash recklessness. Centered around residents of the fictitious Yoknapatawpha County, Faulkner's novels broke new ground in literature in their use of stream of consciousness and established Faulkner as a master of rhetorical style.

Faulkner was born William Falkner in New Albany, Mississippi in 1897. His father, Murray Falkner, claimed that the Faulkners came to America from Ulster, and indeed, Faulkner was a popular name in Ulster, particularly County Derry. When William Faulkner published his first collection of poems, *The Marble Faun* (1924), he reverted to the original spelling of the family name, becoming Faulkner.

After the tenth grade Faulkner's education was sporadic. During World War I, he joined the Canadian Air Force, but the war ended before he finished training. He returned to Mississippi, where he studied rather fitfully at the University of Mississippi.

A writer since his adolescence, Faulkner published his first book of poetry in his early 20s. A period of travel followed, with Faulkner spending time in New Orleans (where he was encouraged by the writer Sherwood Anderson), and in Europe before returning to Oxford, Mississippi.

Aside from travel and short stints as a Hollywood scriptwriter to try and earn money, Faulkner remained in Oxford for the rest of his life writing, farming and hunting. And there was little reason for him to live elsewhere, for Oxford proved to be fertile soil for his imagination. In two years he published two novels, *Soldier's Pay* (1926) and *Mosquitoes* (1927). These were followed by *The Sound and the Fury* (1929), the first of the complex, stream-of-consciousness novels that were to become his trademark. That same year he married Estelle Oldham Franklin.

Over the years, he would continue to develop a saga around Yoknapatawpha County, delving into his characters' savage cruelty and dark redemption. One of the recurring themes in his

fiction was individual and societal damage incurred by white Southerners' treatment of African Americans. Other early novels include *As I Lay Dying* (1930), *Light in August* (1932), *Absalom, Absalom!* (1936), *The Hamlet* (1940) and *Go Down, Moses* (1942). During these years Faulkner also began to drink heavily.

The difficulty of the novels' subject matter and narrative style contributed to a decline in Faulkner's critical reputation during the early 1940s. However, the publication of *The Portable Faulkner* in 1946 sparked a renewal of interest in his work, and his career took off from there. In 1949, he was awarded the Nobel Prize in Literature, and his *Collected Stories* won the National Book Award the following year. In 1954, his novel *A Fable* won both the National Book Award and a Pulitzer Prize, and in 1957-58 he was writer in residence at the University of Virginia. He continued to publish novels until his death in 1962.

F. Scott Fitzgerald
Great Scott

"An author ought to write for the youth of his own generation, the critics of the next, and the schoolmasters of every afterwards."

Over 50 years after his death, F. Scott Fitzgerald would doubtless be gratified to learn that his writings are still taught in schools all over the United States. The son of a Procter & Gamble salesman and a slightly eccentric mother whose father, Philip F. McQuillan, immigrated to the U.S. from County Fermanagh, Fitzgerald was born and raised in the Irish enclave of St. Paul, Minnesota.

He got an early start to his writing career, selling his first short story at the tender age of 13. While never overtly referring to his Irishness in his work, it remains a strong undertone in many of his books, especially *Tender Is the Night* and *The Great Gatsby*.

The Princeton University Library

In a 1933 letter to friend and fellow writer John O'Hara (*Butterfield 8*), Fitzgerald provided a revealing glimpse at his heritage: "I am half black Irish and half old American stock with the usual exaggerated ancestral pretensions. The black Irish half of the family had the money and looked down upon the Maryland side of the family . . . So being born in that atmosphere of crack, wisecrack and countercrack I developed a two cylinder inferiority complex."

Fitzgerald left Princeton before graduating after a brush with tuberculosis, and joined the army in 1917. The following year, while stationed in Alabama, he first laid eyes on the woman who was to become his destiny: Zelda Sayre. On learning that he intended to pursue a career of writing, the single-minded young woman told him she had no intention of marrying a struggling writer, so he had better make money fast. By 1919, Fitzgerald had sold his first novel, *This Side of Paradise*, but not before amassing some 122 rejection slips and a broken engagement.

True to her word, however, Zelda returned to his side shortly before the publication of his first book, and the two were married a week after the book was released. Their only child, Frances Scott, known as Scottie, was born in 1921. The couple had a stormy relationship, and many of their problems were immortalized in Fitzgerald's writing. By the 1930s, his failing health left Fitzgerald struggling with his writing, a situation that improved when he moved to Hollywood in 1937 and took up screenwriting. He died on March 10, 1948.

Thomas Flanagan
The Bard

"I am American but when I write Ireland liberates me."

One day in 1974, Thomas Flanagan sat down to write his first novel. Five years and 502 pages later, the best-selling *The Year of the French* was published and Flanagan was established as a writer to be reckoned with.

The Year of the French, which recounted the ill-fated Irish rising of 1798, was followed by *The Tenants of Time* (1988), praised by *The New York Times* as a "wonderful new book. Every sentence seems to shine." *The End of the Hunt* followed in 1993, recounting Ireland's struggle for independence and the Anglo-Irish treaty that led to the creation of the Free State and civil war.

Meticulously researched and captivatingly told, Flanagan's novels breathe new life into Irish history and assuredly will keep it alive for

generations to come. Like the bards and poets of ancient Ireland, keepers of Ireland's history who handed it down from one generation to the next, Flanagan's writing promises to keep Irish history alive and vibrant for future generations.

The son of a physician, Flanagan grew up in a wealthy middle-class home in Connecticut. His grandparents were from County Fermanagh, and it is his grandmother whom Flanagan credits for his early interest in Irish literature and history.

Flanagan's first samples of creative writing were a far cry from the historical fiction for which he is now famous. From 1948 to 1957, he had several stories published in *Ellery Queen's Mystery Magazine*, even winning the magazine's best story of the year award in 1957.

Flanagan made his first trip to Ireland in 1962, and in an interview with *Irish America* he described a feeling of homecoming. "I don't think I can recall any jolting surprise – just a thickening of the texture of experience. After I arrived in Dublin the taxi driver took me to the center of town. I told him to turn at the Custom House. He turned to me in surprise and said, 'I thought you said you had never been here before.' I hadn't, I just had an instinctive sense of place."

A professor of English at the State University of New York at Stony Brook, Flanagan now divides his time between Dublin and New York. He is currently working on a book about the Irish rebel Roger Casement.

News Hours

Doris Kearns Goodwin
Treasure Trove
"Once you start reading, you can never stop."

Her unrivaled contribution to the body of work on U.S. presidents marks Doris Kearns Goodwin as a writer and historian to treasure. Her book *The Fitzgeralds and the Kennedys* was on the *New York Times* best seller list for over six months. She attributes her interest in the dynamic Kennedy clan to "my lifelong absorption in American history and my special interest in the presidency."

Born in New York in 1943 to Michael Francis Aloysius Kearns and Helen Miller, Goodwin grew up in Rockville Center, Long Island where, as she wrote in her 1997 memoir *Wait Till Next Year*, her early years were "happily governed by the dual calendars of the Brooklyn Dodgers and the Catholic Church." Her maternal grandparents, Thomas Kearns and Ellen Higgins, had emigrated to the States from County Sligo, and his father worked as a firefighter in Brooklyn.

Goodwin worked as an assistant to President Lyndon Johnson during his last year in the White House and later assisted him in preparation of his memoirs. She has also written *No Ordinary Time: Franklin and Eleanor Roosevelt, The Home Front in World War II*, and *Lyndon Johnson and the American Dream*, which was described by one *New York Times* reviewer as "the most penetrating political biography" the reporter had ever read.

Goodwin is a consultant and on-air person for PBS documentaries on LBJ, the Kennedy family and FDR. She is as passionate about baseball as she is about politics and was the first woman journalist to enter the Boston Red Sox locker room. She is married with three children.

Pete Hamill
Writer

"Our parents, the immigrants, were the products of an interrupted narrative. The story of the American children was a much different narrative."

One of the great stylists who embodies New York writ large to many, Pete Hamill has a similar feel for his city that Studs Terkel had for Chicago. He is also an outstanding and perceptive commentator on the Irish American identity.

Throughout his lengthy career he has been, at various times, a journalist, essayist, columnist, short story scribe, novelist, commentator and editor, but there is one very simple word that perfectly describes Hamill – writer. In his 1995 introduction to a collection of his journalism, he said writing was "so entwined with my being that I can't imagine a life without it."

Born in Brooklyn in 1935 to immigrants from Belfast, Hamill joined the Navy in his youth. After his service he traveled to Mexico, a trip which was to herald a life-long love affair with that country.

As part of a Library of Contemporary Thought series of essays, Hamill's byline appeared last year on a work entitled *News Is a Verb: Journalism at the End of the Twentieth Century*. In the piece he detailed his own newspaper career, which began on June 1, 1960, when Hamill was hired to the night roster of reporters at the *New York Post*.

In the following years he covered the beat at three of the city's dailies, and has contributed to a dizzying array of major magazines, including *Esquire, Playboy, Conde Nast Traveler* and *Vanity Fair*. Hamill also served two brief editorial stints, in 1997 at the *New York Daily News* and a five-week term in 1993 as editor-in-chief of the *New York Post*.

His works include such novels as *Snow in August* and *Loving Women*; two short story collections; two collections of journalism and his memoir, *A Drinking Life*. Last year, his tribute to Ol' Blue Eyes, *Why Sinatra Matters*, was hailed by *Publishers Weekly* as "confident, smart and seamless."

Choosing him as one of its hall of famers in December 1997, *Vanity Fair* described Hamill as "a star and staple of New York tabloids and taprooms since the '60s."

Hamill has two daughters, Adriene and Deirdre. He lives in Manhattan with his wife, Japanese journalist Fukiko Aoki. The couple also spends long periods of time in Hamill's beloved Mexico.

Mary Higgins Clark
The Queen of Suspense

Known as the "Queen of Suspense," Mary Higgins Clark is one of America's premier "who-done-it" writers. Her books are worldwide best-sellers. Several of her novels have been made into television dramas and two, *Where Are the Children?* and *A Stranger Is Watching*, have been made into major movies.Her $10 million deal with Simon and Schuster a few years ago made publishing history, but as one book after another passes the million mark in sales, the arrangement looks like a bargain.

Higgins Clark always wrote, but the untimely death of her husband, Warren, made selling a necessity in order to support her five young children. Every morning she got up at five and wrote until seven, when she had to get the kids ready for school. Her first suspense novel, *Where Are the Children?* (1975), was a best-seller.

Her many honors include the 1997 Horatio Alger Award, being named a Dame of Malta, 13 honorary doctorates, and winning the Grand Prix de Literature of France.

All four of Higgins Clark's grandparents were born in Ireland. She considers her Irish heritage an important influence on her writing. Her father owned a pub in the Bronx, and as a young girl Mary listened to the yarns told by the Irish patrons. "The Irish are by nature storytellers," she says. Her daughter, Carol Higgins Clark, is also a mystery writer. A graduate of Fordham University, Higgins Clark now resides in New Jersey with her third husband, John Conheeney, a retired Merrill Lynch CEO. Her latest novel *On the Street Where You Live*, will be published in April 2001.

William Kennedy
The Albany Author

"I believe that I can't be anything other than Irish American. . . [It's] a psychological inheritance that's even more than psychological. There's just something in us that survives, and that's the result of being Irish."

His books have featured the Quinns, the Phelans, the McIlhennys and the Daughertys – Irish clans every one. He is known as the author who has captured Albany, New York in much the same way that Pat Conroy waxed so lyrical about the South. William Kennedy knows very well, however, that his books are less about place than they are about people.

Born in 1928 in Albany, Kennedy is descended on his mother's side from Monaghan immigrants and on his father's side from Tipperary stock. After a stint of military service, Kennedy

returned home in 1952 and began work with the *Albany Times-Union*. Four years later he moved to Puerto Rico where he worked on an English-language newspaper.

An eventual move back to Albany saw him back in place at the *Times-Union* as a freelancer and he took the opportunity to indulge his ambition to write fiction. His first novel, *The Ink Truck*, was published when he was 40. It was followed by the first two installments of the Albany Cycle, *Legs* and *Billy Phelan's Greatest Game*.

It was another novel, one about Depression-era down-and-outs, that would earn Kennedy his greatest acclaim and land him a coveted Pulitzer Prize in 1984. *Ironweed* was subsequently made into a film starring Jack Nicholson and Meryl Streep. Kennedy himself wrote the screenplay for the much lauded film, and for another screen hit, Francis Ford Coppola's *The Cotton Club*.

In a 1985 interview with Peter Quinn, Kennedy praised the writings of Edwin O'Connor and his portrayal of Irish America, but added that he felt the Irish America of his experience came down to more than just tension between Church and politics. "I felt I had to bring in the cat houses and the gambling and the violence," said Kennedy, "for if you left those out you had only a part of Albany.

"The idealized Irish life of the country club and the Catholic colleges was true enough, but that didn't have anything to do with what was going on down on Broadway among all those raffish Irishmen. They were tough sons of bitches, dirty-minded and foul-mouthed gamblers and bigots, and also wonderful, generous, funny, curiously honest and very complex people."

Kennedy is married to Dana Sosa, and the couple has two daughters and a son. He is a regular marcher in the Albany St. Patrick's Day Parade, and likes to gather with friends, play the banjo and sing Irish songs.

Dorothy Kilgallen
The Voice of Broadway
"I don't need a psychiatrist. I'm a Catholic."

Born July 3, 1913 in Chicago to James Lawrence Kilgallen and Mae Ahern, Dorothy Mae Kilgallen was so christened because her name meant 'gift from heaven.' Her paternal grandfather, John Kilgallen, had emigrated from Bohola, County Mayo, and her maternal grandmother, Delia Conlon, was also Irish born.

Although her mother wanted young Dorothy to be an English teacher – a "nice profession for a girl" – her daughter was far more interested in following Dad's example. His job as a newspaper reporter seemed infinitely more interesting to her than those of her friends' fathers, she recalled in later life. "He never suggested that I follow in his footsteps," she once remarked. "But the footsteps were there, and what other way could I have gone?"

A long-time employee of the Hearst organization, Jim Kilgallen moved his family numerous times, finally ending up in New York, and Dorothy's first published piece of writing appeared in the *Brooklyn Eagle* when she was 12. She started her first job, with the *Evening Journal*, just a couple of months shy of her 18th birthday. Cutting her teeth on various feature and human interest pieces, Kilgallen quickly moved on to write about murder, kidnapping and other such events.

Many reporters who worked the same beat as Kilgallen spoke admiringly of her to biographer Lee Israel, whose *Kilgallen: A Biography of Dorothy Kilgallen* was published in 1979. A highly talented writer, Kilgallen traded on her girlish looks to wangle her way into places no other woman would have been welcome. Wrote Israel: "Dorothy Kilgallen could out-write, out-wit and out-ruse anyone in yellow journalism."

Without a doubt one of the biggest stories Kilgallen covered was the 1935 trial of Richard Bruno Hauptmann, who was charged with and eventually convicted of the kidnapping and murder of the Lindbergh baby. In September 1936, she was invited by her paper to follow in the footsteps of fellow Irish American reporter Nellie Bly, and compete with two other newspaper reporters in a flight around the globe, traveling at one point on the *Hindenburg* on its final safe North Atlantic crossing. Even Amelia Earhart sent a telegram wishing her luck.

Although she didn't win the race, Kilgallen returned to a rapturous reception and a message of congratulations from Eleanor Roosevelt, who wrote, "I was rather pleased to have a woman go! It took a good deal of pluck and must have held a good many thrills!" The book *Girl Around the World* told her story, and a song was written about her called "Hats Off to Dorothy." *Fly Away Baby*, a thinly veiled movie about the race, with screenplay by Kilgallen, was released in 1937.

At the age of 23, Kilgallen changed direction somewhat and moved to California, from where

Corbis / Bettmann – UPI

she filed a daily column for the *Evening Journal* entitled "As Seen in Hollywood by Dorothy Kilgallen." Working this beat, she competed directly with Louella Parsons, one of the most famous gossip columnists of her time. She also found the time to appear in a movie called *Sinner Take All*.

On moving back to New York, Kilgallen wrote a Broadway column entitled "The Voice of Broadway," which soon became one of the most widely-read columns in the country. A radio show sponsored by Johnson & Johnson, and hosted by Kilgallen, had the same name. Reuben's, a restaurant favored by Broadway types, named a sandwich, their most expensive, after her. Among her beaux at the time were actor Tyrone Power and writer Paul Gallico.

In April 1940 she married stage actor Richard Kollmar and they had three children, Richard, Jill and Kerry. The couple teamed up to host "Breakfast With Dorothy and Dick," a live daily radio show broadcast from their living room. Kilgallen made her television debut in 1949 on "Leave It to the Girls," and she subsequently became a regular panelist on "What's My Line?," a show which served to make her "the most visible and celebrated journalist of her time," according to Lee Israel.

For her coverage of the coronation of Queen Elizabeth II, Kilgallen was nominated for a Pulitzer Prize and was cited for excellence in reporting by the Silurians. Her coverage of the Sam Sheppard murder trial earned her praise from none other than Ernest Hemingway, who said: "This Dorothy Kilgallen is a good girl."

In time, Kilgallen and her husband grew apart. He had never attempted to hide his many affairs, and at the age of 44 she began a dalliance with singer Johnnie Ray which was to last just over six years.

When President John F. Kennedy was assassinated in Dallas in 1963, Kilgallen was distraught, remembering a visit to the White House the previous year when the young President had been particularly kind to her son Kerry. After a jailhouse interview with Jack Ruby, she filed no story but began to gather a file on the Kennedy murder. There is speculation that she planned to include the Ruby interview as a chapter in a book she was preparing entitled *Murder One*. After Ruby's conviction, she wrote: "The point to be remembered in this historic case is that the whole truth has not been told." After the Warren Commission Report was released, she became even more determined to solve the mystery behind the assassination. She visited Ireland in the summer of 1965 and attended a ball in Dublin at which Princess Grace of Monaco was a guest.

Various sources who spoke to Lee Israel recalled Kilgallen's excitement that she had "the scoop of the century" with regard to the Kennedy assassination. She was found dead in the bedroom of her Manhattan apartment on Monday, November 8, 1965. A death certificate described the cause as "acute ethanol and barbiturate intoxication – circumstances undetermined," or an overdose of pills and alcohol. It was never determined whether she died by her own hand or by the hand of another, but biographer Lee Israel, after a lengthy investigation, is certain of one thing: there was a cover-up of some sort involved in her death. Her husband Richard Kollmar claimed after her death that he had destroyed the mysterious Kennedy folder.

Frank McCourt
Limerick Leader

"It is an honor to be included among a group of men and women who haven't yet produced a saint."

In *Angela's Ashes*, Frank McCourt has written one of the most popular memoirs of the century, and in the process has redefined the memoir in American literature.

Almost three years after the 1996 publication of the book, there was a slight slowdown in the excitement surrounding *Angela's Ashes*, but the release of Alan Parker's movie in 1999 livened things right back up. Then came the September 1999 publication of *'Tis*, which picks up where *Angela's Ashes* left off.

If the media hullabaloo over *Angela's Ashes* has died down somewhat, the fan base is still as strong as ever. The Irish newspapers carried stories in December 1998 about a Massachusetts woman so enamored of McCourt's Pulitzer Prize-winning memoir that she moved to Ireland for a month and a half to secure a spot as an extra in the movie. Ensconced in a Dublin hotel, she ran up a large bill, but had no regrets. "Absolutely, this is the craziest thing I've done in my life – and I'd do it again," said Maureen Quill, speaking to reporters about her long and costly stay.

Fans in Japan might not go to equally expensive lengths, but they certainly believe in paying tribute to their hero on the worldwide web. A website called "The Club of Angela's Ashes" is lovingly maintained by the Ireland-Japan Friendly Club, and features numerous pictures of McCourt in his native Limerick. Someone has also gone to great lengths to reference a map of the city with marker points for sites included in the McCourt story – and visitors to the site can see where the old Lyric Cinema, beloved of the young Frank and his boyhood pals, once stood. Leamy's National School, which closed in the 1950s, is also there in all its faded glory. Hundreds of visitors to the website have recorded their impressions of *Angela's Ashes*, with contributions ranging from long (and almost always glowing) reviews to eloquent pleas for a follow-up.

Born in Brooklyn in 1930 to Malachy and Agnes McCourt, McCourt was named for St. Francis of Assisi, and was the oldest of seven siblings, four of whom survived. When he was four years old, the family moved back to Ireland, to his mother's native Limerick. Years of

Kit DeFever

poverty followed, dotted with the frequent disappearances of Malachy Sr.

As soon as he was old enough, Frank hightailed it back to his native New York, and apart from a brief stint in Korea in the 1950s, he's never left since. To those who wonder whether he identifies himself as Irish, American or Irish American, he cheerfully replies that he's a true blue New Yorker. A recent move to Connecticut has done little to alter this mindset. His accent, meanwhile, marks him out as a son of Limerick City.

U.S. Education Secretary Richard Riley, who presented McCourt with *Irish America* magazine's Irish American of the Year award in 1998, said he was convinced that the Brooklyn-born writer had honed his skill throughout his years as "a wonderful teacher" in the New York City public school system. To date, the book has spent over 100 weeks on the *New York Times* best-seller list and there are over two-and-a-half million copies in print.

McCourt is married to Ellen Frey, and it was their honeymoon which inspired him to begin work on *Angela's Ashes*. He has a daughter, Maggie, from his first marriage and two grandchildren.

Alice McDermott
Novelist

"I knew that we were Irish and I knew that Irish was the best thing to be."

When Alice McDermott won the 1998 National Book Award for *Charming Billy*, no one was more surprised than she. In fact, she was so sure that she would not win that she did not prepare an acceptance speech, something all finalists are asked to do. Instead she improvised, joking, "I wouldn't be true to my Irish heritage if I thought this was entirely a good thing . . . I will clutch onto my Irish humility with great vigor."

McDermott was born in Brooklyn, New York, and spent her childhood on Long Island, where a sense of Irishness was instilled in her, she recalls. And it is from the Irish-American community of her childhood that she draws inspiration. Over the past 16 years, she has published three other novels: *A Bigamist's Daughter* (1982); *That Night* (1987), finalist for the National Book Award, and *At Weddings and Wakes* (1992). *Charming Billy* explores the nature of faith and family ties among Irish Americans in an attempt to individualize the stereotype of the Irish American alcoholic.

Writing always came naturally to McDermott – she wrote her first novel when she was ten years old – but it was one of her writing professors at the State University of New York at Oswego who really brought home to her that this should be her profession. On handing back her first writing assignment, he informed McDermott, "I've got bad news . . . you're a writer."

And the writing is beautiful – intensely visual, sensuous and evocative. Her novels are character rather than plot driven, and her characters are so finely drawn they remain in your memory like a distant relative. The worlds they inhabit are so detailed, you wonder if you haven't actually visited these places.

After graduating from Oswego, McDermott

enrolled in the graduate writing program at the University of New Hampshire. It was in graduate school that she met her husband-to-be, a graduate student at Cornell Medical School in New York City. They married a year later and eventually settled in Bethesda, Maryland, where McDermott successfully balances her writing with raising their three children.

And perhaps that is her greatest triumph – she has arranged her life on her own terms, choosing both career and family and refusing to sacrifice one to the other. She has developed the routine necessary to get it all done – she writes when the kids are at school, putting it away when they come home. She also teaches writing one day a week at Johns Hopkins University in Baltimore. Her lifestyle is a deliberate choice, not something she has fallen into. "This is a life I've arranged for myself," she points out. "For me, it's the best way for my children to be happy and for me to get writing done . . . It's something I've done consciously."

Eileen McNamara
Columnist

"Is there an Irishman alive who doesn't have a love affair with words?"

Despite years studying Irish step dancing, Eileen McNamara never won any awards, she says, because she smiled too much. All's changed now, and smiling is absolutely encouraged, but it's doubtful that McNamara would seriously consider an offer even from the Lord of the Dance himself to join him on stage.

That's because she won a far bigger award a few years ago – a Pulitzer Prize for a selection of her 1996 columns in *The Boston Globe*. A reporter for over 20 years, McNamara was installed as a columnist just 18 months before winning the prestigious award.

Her columns have won her much acclaim, focusing on such topics as battered women,

juvenile killers and infant mortality. As well as winning the Pulitzer, McNamara also took home the 1997 American Society of Newspaper Editors award for writing, and she was previously awarded a citation by the Robert F. Kennedy Foundation for her commitment to the disadvantaged.

Her first book, *Breakdown*, a non-fiction examination of the malpractice case against Harvard psychiatrist Dr. Margaret Bean-Bayog, was also published in 1997, to positive reviews from both *The New York Times* and *The Washington Post*.

When she's not writing or spending time with her husband and three children, McNamara teaches a course on media and public policy in the journalism program at Brandeis University.

Her grandparents were Irish, her mother's family from Malinhead, Donegal and her father's folks from Ennistymon, County Clare.

Margaret Mitchell
Southern Belle

"Death and taxes and childbirth. There's never any convenient time for any of them."

In creating one of the most famous heroines of all time – *Gone With the Wind*'s Scarlett O'Hara – writer Margaret Mitchell undoubtedly drew on her own Irish roots. She was Catholic on both sides of her family; her Irish ancestors were on her mother's side. Her maternal great-grandfather, Phillip Fitzgerald, was born in County Tipperary and moved with his family to France shortly after his birth. As a young man, he moved again, this time to the States, where he landed in Charleston. He eventually settled in Taliaferro County, Georgia. One of his daughters, Anne, married another Irishman, Offaly native John Stephens.

According to Mitchell's biographer, Darden Asbury Pyron, "These two Irishmen [Stephens and Fitzgerald] helped shape the most fundamental stuff of Margaret Mitchell's imagination." It is widely believed that Anne Fitzgerald Stephens served as the inspiration for Scarlett O'Hara, although Mitchell always denied any connection between her family and her fiction.

Of her grandfather and great-grandfather, Mitchell said: "They were both Irishmen born and proud of it and prouder still of being Southerners, and would have withered any relative who tried to put on the dog. I'm afraid they were so proud of what they were that they'd have thought putting on the dog was gilding the lily, and anyway, they left that to the post-war nouveaux riche who had to carry a lot of dog because they had nothing else to carry."

Mitchell endowed her feisty character with an Irish immigrant father, Gerald O'Hara, who named his homestead Tara, after the ancient stronghold in his native Meath. As a child, Mitchell made many visits to the Fitzgerald family homestead in Clayton County, where her mother's two maiden aunts still lived.

Mitchell will long be remembered for having

written the best-selling work of fiction ever produced in America, which was made into a beloved movie, starring Vivien Leigh and Clark Gable. Within six months of publication, the book sold a million copies, an incredible achievement during the Depression era. It's a feat all the more remarkable when you learn that Mitchell worked on her opus largely in secret, and was reluctant to show it to anybody.

After graduating from college, Mitchell worked for several years as a feature writer for the *Atlanta Journal*. She won a Pulitzer Prize for *Gone With the Wind*. She died on August 11, 1949, not long before her 48th birthday, after being struck by a taxi in downtown Atlanta.

John Montague
Versemaker

"At times I see it, present
As a bright day, or a hill,
The only way of saying something
Luminously as possible."

John Montague was born in Brooklyn, New York in 1929, the son of immigrants from County Tyrone. His family returned to Northern Ireland when John was still a child, and because of financial hardship, decided to foster young

John out to his father's two maiden aunts seven miles away.

Returning to a homeland he had never seen, being sent away by his family, and struggling with the shame of a childhood speech impediment created in the young boy a sense of displacement that would later figure in his poetry as he struggled to find his place within his own family and within Ireland. In his essay "The Complex Fate of Being American-Irish," he states, "My early poems were attempts to do justice to that world I had returned to, its Scotch-Irish speech patterns, its long history."

After earning his bachelor's and master's degrees from University College Dublin, he completed an M.F.A. degree at the University of Iowa. He was the Paris correspondent for *The Irish Times* before beginning his career as university professor teaching at universities in France, Ireland, Canada and the United States.

Currently, he is Distinguished Professor in the New York State Writer's Program at SUNY-Albany. He is the recipient of numerous prizes and awards, including the 1995 American Ireland Fund Literary Award and his nomination as Ireland's Professor of Poetry. He has edited two volumes of Irish poetry and published nine volumes of his own poetry. His collected poems were published in 1995.

Flannery O'Connor
Woman of Words

"I don't deserve any credit for turning the other cheek as my tongue is always in it."

Deserving of her reputation as one of America's most important Southern writers of fiction, Mary Flannery O'Connor was lost to the world at the age of 39. During her all-too-short life, she produced two collections of short stories and two novels, but many writers who've lived twice as long have not come close to the literary perfection that O'Connor attained.

Born on March 25, 1925 in Savannah, Georgia, Flannery O'Connor (she dropped the Mary after graduating from Georgia State

College in 1945) constantly returned to Christian and Catholic imagery in her work, hardly surprising given her devout Roman Catholic roots. Her maternal great-grandfather took part in the first Catholic Mass in Milledgeville, Georgia, while her paternal great-grandfather left Ireland in the 1830s and set up a wagon manufacturing business in Savannah.

O'Connor lost her father days before her 16th birthday to disseminated lupus erythematosus, the same disease that was to kill her some 23 years later. She honed her writing skills while editing her college's literary magazine, and was subsequently accepted to the University of Iowa's graduate journalism program. The director of the university's writing workshop recognized her talent and encouraged her to persist. At the age of 21, she sold her first short story, thus beginning an almost 20-year career in writing.

In later years, after extensive hospital treatment for her illness, O'Connor lived with her mother on a farm called Andalusia, a few miles outside Milledgeville. Her frail health made travel difficult, and she was largely house-bound, but continued to receive and enjoy visitors. She also continued to write, devoting her mornings to her craft.

O'Connor's first novel, *Wise Blood*, was published in 1952, followed by her short story collection, *A Good Man Is Hard to Find and Other Stories* (1955) and a second novel, *The Violent Bear It Away* (1960). Her final collection of stories, *Everything That Rises Must Converge*, was published after her death. Two of her stories were adapted for television, and noted director John Huston made a film version of *Wise Blood*. O'Connor's work also made it onto the stage. She and her writing became the focus of thousands of articles, books and dissertations. She died August 3, 1964, and is buried in her beloved Milledgeville, Georgia, alongside her parents.

John O'Hara
Novelist

"Socially, I never belonged to any class, rich or poor. To the rich I was poor, and to the poor I was poor pretending to be rich."

John O'Hara once described himself as "the hardest working author in the U.S." and his body of work remains a testament to that. In a career that spanned 35 years, O'Hara published over 30 novels and collections of short stories. Some of his more popular novels include *Appointment in Samarra*, *Butterfield 8*, and *Pal Joey*.

His extraordinary ability to tell a good story, capturing people and events realistically, especially in his short stories, have influenced such prominent writers as John Cheever, John Updike, Raymond Carver and Richard Ford.

O'Hara's artistic vision and his keen journalistic eye were indelibly shaped by the fact that he was Irish American. Born in Pottsville, Pennsylvania in 1905 to Dr. Patrick H. and Katherine Delaney, O'Hara never really gained acceptance into the WASP local aristocracy in spite of his respectable "nouveau riche" background. It was this lack of acceptance, the sense of being on the outside looking in, that developed in O'Hara an eye for people's behavior: the way they spoke, dressed, what cars they drove and how they lived. In fact, his career could be described as being dominated by a kind of social insecurity; like his contemporary F. Scott Fitzgerald, he longed for acceptance by the Ivy League elite, but unlike Fitzgerald, he never attained it.

Instead he wrote about their lives with a mixture of resentment and envy. Even though he would go on to gain fame and fortune as a writer and travel in the best literary circles, Pottsville, immortalized by O'Hara as the fictitious town Gibbsville, remained a major focus of his imaginative efforts.

O'Hara's educational history was less than stellar. While he dreamed of the Ivy League, he hardly conformed to anyone's standard of the model student. He was dismissed from Fordham Preparatory School in 1921, and from Keystone State Normal School the following year. After being chosen as class valedictorian at Niagara Preparatory School in 1924, he was not allowed to graduate. Still, his writing spoke for itself, and he went on to a successful career in journalism.

The course of O'Hara's personal life did not run smoothly either. In 1931, he married Helen Ritchie Petit. They were divorced two years later. In 1937, he married Belle Wylie. This union produced his only child, Wylie. Belle died in 1954, and one year later O'Hara married Katharine Barnes Bryan, with whom he remained until his death in 1970 in Princeton, New Jersey.

While O'Hara certainly has his detractors who write him off as a minor author, he is undergoing a vindication of sorts in a renewal of interest in his work. His more popular novels are back in print, three biographies have been published, and his short fiction is now the subject of scholarly study.

Library of Congress

Eugene O'Neill
Master of Words

"Man's loneliness is but his fear of life."

"You write like an Irishman, not an American" was the ultimate compliment that the great Sean O'Casey paid Eugene O'Neill. James Joyce concurred, once remarking that O'Neill was "thoroughly Irish." In a letter to his son, O'Neill himself said, "The critics have missed the important thing about me and my work. The fact that I am Irish."

Though Eugene O'Neill was born in New York, his father instilled in him a great pride in his pure Irish heritage. James O'Neill emigrated with his family from Kilkenny, and his wife's parents came from Tipperary.

O'Neill's first experience of the theater came when he accompanied his parents on tour and watched his father star in the play adaptation of *The Count of Monte Cristo*. O'Neill's own plays dealt with topics American theater-goers were not used to: racial discrimination, the mistreatment of workers, and characters whose dreams were lost, as in *The Iceman Cometh*.

That play, a daring experimental work which earned him one of his four Pulitzer Prizes, looked for meaning in modern life, and the power behind people and their actions. When it was revived in 1999 on Broadway, starring Kevin Spacey in the title role, the play proved O'Neill's worth as a playwright, being as relevant now as it was when it premiered over 50 years ago.

O'Neill is credited by some historians as single-handedly establishing serious American drama, and is the only American playwright to have won the Nobel Prize in Literature (1936).

His work turned autobiographical with *A Long Day's Journey into Night*, his final play, which allowed him to turn his tumultuous childhood around, and to finally approach his family, he said, with "deep pity, understanding, and forgiveness."

After a life filled with addiction, depression, sickness, divorce, and death, O'Neill died in Boston in 1953.

Anna Quindlen
Writer

"Familiarity breeds content."

Actress Meryl Streep received rave reviews in 1998 for her touching portrayal of a cancer-stricken mother in *One True Thing*, but in one interview she gave full kudos for the character to Anna Quindlen, the woman who wrote the book on which the movie was based.

Quindlen has long been praised for her writing skills, beginning with her "Life in the 30s" columns for *The New York Times* in the 1980s. Two years as an op-ed columnist for the *Times* followed, and many of Quindlen's avid readers were devastated when she quit in 1994 to become a full-time novelist. The column, which appeared twice weekly, won her a Pulitzer Prize for commentary in 1992.

Her first novel, *Object Lessons*, spent time on *The New York Times* best-seller list when it was published, and she followed up with two more best-selling novels, *One True Thing* in 1994 and

Black and Blue in 1998. Writer Alice Hoffman called Quindlen "a national treasure," while *New York* magazine once referred to her as "the laureate of real life."

Quindlen has three non-fiction books to her credit – two of them are collections of her columns, *Thinking Out Loud: On the Personal, the Political, the Public and the Private* and *Living Out Loud*. She is also the author of two children's books, *Happily Ever After* and *The Tree That Came to Stay.*

In a 1991 interview with *Irish America*, Quindlen spoke fondly of her Irish roots, saying; "In my family you can't just say, 'I'm Anna Quindlen.' It's very, very important to say, 'I'm Anna Quindlen. I'm Irish.'" Her paternal ancestors moved to this country in the early 1800s. She and her husband, attorney Jerry Curvatin, live in New Jersey with their three children.

Peter Quinn

Irish history, New York history and Civil War history are the three topics that most interest Peter Quinn. Put all three together, add a dollop of fiction, set the stage with a wide range of characters, hold them all together with writing reminiscent of William Faulkner and you have *Banished Children of Eve*, a novel set in New

York in 1863 before and during the draft riots, that is so powerful and colorful that it's considered one of the greatest Irish Americans novels of all time.

Quinn, whose day job is corporate editorial director for Time Warner, is a former speechwriter for New York governors Carey and Cuomo and was born in the Bronx. "I was brought up in the Bronx where no one was brought up to think of themselves as American. You were Irish, you were Jewish or Italian, and then I went to school, for three months, in Galway and they didn't think I was Irish at all. . . I was caught between two worlds – Ireland and America – both parts of me. And that's what this book is about, both parts." *Banished Children of Eve*, which took ten years to complete, won a 1995 American Book Award. Quinn, a fourth generation-New Yorker – his parental great-grandparents were Famine immigrants who arrived from Ireland in 1847 – also wrote the script for McSorley's *New York*, which was awarded a 1987 New York area Emmy for outstanding historical programming. He and his wife Kathleen reside in Hastings-on-Hudson. They have two children, Genevieve, age 13, and Daniel, 9.

John Steinbeck: The Voice of the Dispossessed

BY JIM DWYER

"Irish blood doesn't water down very well; the strain must be very strong."

All the great novels and stories of John Steinbeck slice into the American experience, clear to the bone. They are set in California, or along Route 66, where the Joads trekked across the southwest from the Dust Bowls. And Steinbeck himself, born with the century, was raised in Salinas, California, when it was still a small town on the last frontier of America.

Yet the voice of this all-American writer, he himself believed, rose from his Irish grandparents and their daughter, Olive, his mother. "I am half-Irish, the rest of my blood being watered down with German and Massachusetts English," Steinbeck once wrote. "But Irish blood doesn't water down very well; the strain must be very strong."

So, too, are Steinbeck's gifts. To this day, 31 years after his death, stories by John Steinbeck often are the first great works that school children discover and embrace. Sales of his books still number in the tens of thousands annually; he is published in a dozen languages; his stories continue to be produced on stage and screen. No halfway serious list of great American writers would be complete without the 1962 Nobel laureate in literature, the author of such American touchstones as *The Grapes of Wrath*, *Of Mice and Men*, *Cannery Row*, *Tortilla Flat*, *East of Eden*. And for that matter, no survey of the great Irish American writers can bypass Steinbeck. All his life, he claimed the Irish as his own.

"I guess the people of my family thought of Ireland as a green paradise, mother of heroes, where golden people sprang full-flowered from the sod," Steinbeck wrote in *Collier's Magazine*

in January 1953. "I don't remember my mother actually telling me these things, but she must have given me such an impression of delight. Only kings and heroes came from this Holy Island, and at the very top of the glittering pyramid was our family, the Hamiltons."

Steinbeck's grandfather, Samuel Hamilton, left a farm near the Derry village of Ballykelly, around 1848 or 1849. "He was the son of small farmers, neither rich nor poor, who had lived on one landhold and in one stone house for many hundreds of years," Steinbeck wrote in *East of Eden*. The reason for Samuel's emigration was a mystery. "There was a whisper – not even a rumor but rather an unsaid feeling – in my family that it was love drove him out, and not love of the wife he married. But whether it was too successful love or whether he left in pique at an unsuccessful love, I do not know. We always preferred to think it was the former."

In New York, Samuel met and married Elizabeth Fagen, the daughter of Irish immigrants. They sailed to California and homesteaded a ranch of poor land in the Salinas Valley. "My grandfather, who had come from [Ireland] carrying the sacred name, was really a great man, a man of sweet speech and sweet courtesy. . . His little bog-trotting wife, I am told, put out milk for the leprechauns in the hills behind King City, California, and when a groundling neighbor suggested the cats drank it, she gave that neighbor a look that burned off his nose," Steinbeck wrote in *Collier's*.

Among the nine Hamilton children was Olive, who left home to become a schoolteacher, a journey regarded in that time as "an honor, a bit

like having a priest in the family in Ireland," the Steinbeck biographer Jackson Benson writes in *The True Adventures of John Steinbeck, Writer*.

Olive Hamilton would marry John Ernst Steinbeck, and they had three daughters and one son. John Steinbeck was born in 1902. He and his sisters spent summers on the Hamilton ranch, and listened by night to the tales of fairies and enchanted forests told by their Irish mother.

On his way to the pantheon, Steinbeck lived in stone-soup poverty for nearly 20 years before he enjoyed his first taste of financial security, with the publication of *Tortilla Flat* and *In Dubious Battle*, then with *Of Mice and Men* and *The Grapes of Wrath*, for which he won the Pulitzer Prize in fiction.

By the late 1940s, his work and fame were firmly staked. In 1947, his friends Burgess Meredith and Paulette Goddard suggested he write a play for Dublin's Abbey Theatre about a modern Joan of Arc persecuted for warning against atomic warfare. "The idea appealed very much to Steinbeck's pride in his Irish background and his interest in Irish mysticism," writes Benson. "He was also excited about doing a play for the Abbey Theatre, the scene of so much controversy and theatrical ferment, and an Irish audience. It was a connection he longed to make, for he still felt, as he would tell an interviewer that spring, that his gift for writing was based on his sensitivity to sound, a gift, of course, that he believed came to him through his mother's family." That project fell apart with the collapse of his second marriage.

As a correspondent in World War II, Steinbeck frequently landed in Ireland, but never quite set himself towards Derry. Married happily to his third and final wife, Elaine, they at long last visited in 1952. The trip was such a catastrophe that it became one of his best pieces of journalism, "I Go Back to Ireland," published in *Collier's*. The Steinbecks found Derry a bleak city, the hotel where they stayed uniquely short in the barest hospitality. They had arrived two

minutes late for dinner, and could not beg a morsel; they were not allowed a drink or a sandwich in their room; they could not arrange a morning newspaper. No one would take a bribe.

More to the point, when they drove out to Ballykelly and to the farmland called Mulkeraugh, the last of the Hamiltons had been dead for two years. Her name was Elizabeth, and she had grown strange, the neighbors told John, calling out to the dead brother who shared their bachelor quarters. Another strangeness, the neighbors told Steinbeck, was that she had found a "cause" in her final days. She decreed that all her property be sold at her death to fund a political party that would resist joining Ulster with Eire.

Years later, the Steinbecks would return to Ireland as guests of the director John Huston at St. Clerans, his estate in Galway. They wandered through the countryside. "The west country isn't left behind – it's rather as though it ran concurrently but in a nonparallel time," Steinbeck wrote in a letter in 1965. "I feel that I would like to go back there. It has a haunting kind of recognition."

Beyond the clear lines of genealogy, the hard facts of trips, there is the sensibility of a man who cherished the land, saw magic in places, and gazed without blinking at the brutality that closes the circle of farm life – much like Seamus Heaney, another son of Derry. Heaney writes: "Running water never disappoints."

And so it is for the young boy in *The Red Pony*, the first great story by Steinbeck, set on the dry, dusty ranch of the Hamiltons, half a world away from Derry:

"Jody traveled often to the brush line behind the house. A rusty iron pipe ran a thin stream of spring water into an old green tub. Where the water spilled over and sank into the ground there was a patch of perpetually green grass. Even when the hills were brown and baked in the summer that little patch was green. The water whined softly into the trough all the year round."

Ed Sullivan
The Talking Head
"It's gonna be a really big shoo . . ."

He had his own unique way of pronouncing the word, but every Sunday at 8 p.m., over 30 million Americans turned their TV dials to *The Ed Sullivan Show*, and watched him become part of history. From 1948 to 1971, Sullivan hand-picked the greatest names known and then unknown in music, comedy, stage and screen to perform live. Showcasing over 10,000 performers in 23 years, *The Ed Sullivan Show* became the nation's premiere television variety series, and an American institution.

Born Edward Vincent Sullivan in New York City in 1901, he was one of seven children. His parents, Peter Arthur Sullivan and Elizabeth Smith, were both of Irish descent. Sullivan grew up in Port Chester, New York, and first discovered his writing talent in high school.

Sullivan worked as a newspaper reporter after graduating from high school, starting with coverage of sporting events but eventually moving over to report on show business. His column "Little Old New York" began appearing in the New York *Daily News* in 1931. From there it was an easy rise to stardom, and Sullivan was soon appearing on TV screens.

In 1942, CBS introduced *Ed Sullivan Entertains*, and Sullivan's talent soon led to a spot hosting a weekly variety show on that network called *Toast of the Town*. That show officially became *The Ed Sullivan Show* in 1955. Sullivan also continued writing his newspaper column. In 1957 he co-founded the National Academy of Television Arts and Sciences.

The first program to break all previous viewing ratings with an appearance by a young Elvis Presley, *The Ed Sullivan Show* had all the world's biggest stars jumping at the chance to make an appearance, from Bing Crosby, Judy Garland, and Frank Sinatra, to Rudolf Nureyev and The Beatles. A typical Ed Sullivan evening could included some dancing bears, Robert Goulet, Joan Rivers, a plate spinner, a film clip, Red Skelton, then The Rolling Stones to close. Sullivan won an Emmy Award in 1971. He died in 1979, and was inducted into the Television Hall of Fame in 1984.

A Final Word

1900 and 2000

BY NIALL O'DOWD, Founding Publisher, *Irish America* Magazine

Cast your mind back to this very time in 1900 at the beginning of a new century and compare what Irish America looked and felt like to today.

In some ways there are uncanny similarities. Back then the "New Departure" of Irish America, the Fenians and Parnell had almost brought about Home Rule. Now, the combination of Irish America, President Clinton, Irish nationalism and Sinn Féin – the so-called "nationalist consensus"– is also on the verge of a historic new dispensation in Ireland through the peace process.

Back then as now, there was also a great flowering of intellectual and cultural forces. William Butler Yeats, J.M Synge, the new Abbey Theatre, the Gaelic Revival were all underway. Now we have the astonishing success of Irish writers and filmmakers, *Lord of the Dance* and *Riverdance* and the music of U2 and other leading rock bands.

Back then Irish Americans like Chicago cop Francis O'Neill, who collected all the Irish airs for posterity, and Sligo emigrant musician Michael Coleman, who saved many of the same airs for future generations when he used new-fangled American technology to record the songs, played a huge role in the cultural revival.

Likewise nowadays, the role of Michael Flatley and Jean Butler, Irish Americans both, in creating the new form of Irish dance that has now become so famous, was invaluable. It was Irish America which reinvented Irish dance and, in tandem with Irish producers and composers, created a new art form. Similarly, Oscar-winning directors such as Jim Sheridan and Pulitzer Prize writers such as Frank McCourt were able to meld their American and Irish experiences to produce their greatest art.

It is uncanny how little the fundamental questions have changed, too. Back a century ago the Irish Americans would ask, in the words of the ballad, "How is old Ireland and how does she stand?" The answer back then according to the ballad was "the most distressful nation that you have ever seen, where they're hanging men and women for the wearing of the green."

The same question would be foremost on most Irish Americans' minds today – how are things in the old country? Well, it is clearly no longer the most distressful nation. Back in 1899 the Irish Famine was only 40 years gone and still in the lifetime and memory of many who saw in the new century. Rampant emigration was a fact of life; widespread evictions were still carried on in rural areas.

Now we have the Celtic Tiger, the booming economy of the Irish Republic which economists tell us now outstrips the British one. *The Financial Times* reported in 1999 that the Gross Domestic Product of the Irish economy has finally surpassed the GDP of the United Kingdom.

Just ponder that for a moment. One hundred years ago the British Empire was still the dominant force in the world, fighting for its right to hold onto its colonies such as India and Ireland. That the sun never set on their worldwide holdings was no idle boast. Ireland, by contrast, was a country beset by the consequences of famine, emigration, and rebellion and as backward an agricultural economy as existed in Europe.

One hundred years on and that backward rural economy has become, in the words of *The Financial Times*, "Ireland's Miracle." What the Irish Republic has done is offer a stable English-speaking base mainly for American technology companies operating overseas. They have also invested heavily in the education of their workforce, making them among the most skilled in the world. Such forward thinking has paid off.

Yet the question of Northern Ireland would be as understandable to the generation from 1900 as it is to Irish Americans today. Unlike the economic situation, the political landscape is far more recognizable. There are the British, the unionists, the nationalists and the republicans, all apparently still locked in the same circular dance. There is still the Orange Card, first mooted by Lord Randolph Churchill in 1896 when the father of Winston Churchill wrote, "I decided some time ago if Gladstone [then Liberal Party leader] went for Home Rule then the Orange Card is the one to play."

One hundred years later, as the latest efforts to bring about a representative government in Northern Ireland was on the brink of failure, that same Orange Card was played by a Unionist leader, David Trimble, when he refused to agree to a solution worked out by the British and Irish governments in their "Way Forward" document

and to abide by the terms of the Good Friday Agreement voted for by 71 percent of the citizenry in the North.

The only factor in the equation that would look very different to a man or woman from 1900 would be the role of the U.S. president and his direct involvement. Back then it was unthinkable, as Irish leader Eamon de Valera and several others were later to find out, for an American president to roil the calm waters between the U.S. and Britain. The notion of a U.S. president committing his administration fully to bring about peace in Ireland as Bill Clinton did would have been an idle pipe dream for our Irish Americans a century ago. That has been the greatest change brought about by Irish Americans this century.

Of course we can idly wonder how it will all be a century from now, what yet unseen forces will control how the Irish American/ Irish relationship will be then. We can be sure of one thing, however, the astonishing progress of both Irish America and Ireland in the past century will be very hard to match.